YEARLY DEVOTIONAL

by

BOB DORNAN

ARPress
45 Dan Road Suite 5
Canton MA 02021
Hotline: 1(888) 821-0229
Fax: 1(508) 545-7580

Ordering Information:
Quantity sales. Special discounts are available on quantity purchases by corporations, associations, and others. For details, contact the publisher at the address above.

Printed in the United States of America.

ISBN-13:   Softcover   979-8-89356-734-2

Library of Congress Control Number: 2024907655

TABLE OF CONTENTS

Preface..1

New Year's...3

Appearances 11

Attitudes 19

Bible...27

Change...35

Choices 43

Christmas...52

The Church..59

Discipleship..67

Easter 75

Election Day 83

Examples..91

Faith...99

Family and Friends..107

Fathers 115

Forgiveness...123

Future 131

God...139

Grace...147

Gratitude..155

Halloween 163

Holy Spirit 171

Hope...179

Humility 187

Jesus 195

July 4th 203

Labor Day..211

Love...220

Marriage..229

Memorial Day...237

Mothers...245

Obedience..253

Peace...261

Perseverance..269

Plans..277

Prayer..285

Promises of God..293

Rewards...301

Sacrifice...309

Salvation..318

Satan...326

Sin...334

Suffering..342

Temptation..350

The 10 Commandments..358

Thanksgiving...367

Thought Life...375

Valentine's Day..383

Veteran's Day...391

Work/Works...399

PREFACE

I decided to write this devotional, which is a compilation of the sermons (in abridged form) I have preached over the length of my public ministry, not necessarily because I have any special insight or ability, but because I have been told by a number of people that I have been able to convey the Bible in an easily understandable way. Now, whether they were just being kind or patronizing, I'll leave it up to you, the reader. Nevertheless, my perspective on the word of God and its application to life has been formed by many influences- my family, my friends, growing up in the 50's and 60's in southwestern Pennsylvania, my school experiences, my work Experiences and the time I spent in the military, among other things. It is not necessarily a unique perspective nor one without some personal pain. But I tend to look at life rather optimistically and with a good sense of humor.

These factors, I hope, will help to make this book worthwhile- along with some personal reflections between each section.

REFLECTIONS

New Year's

New Year's was always too close to Christmas to ever really make much of an impact on me, personally. Yes, I've Watched many a ball drop and everyone from Guy Lombardo to Dick Clark "bring it in'. The best new year's Parties were ones Connie and I hosted in our home in Dubois. What made them special was the people who came and the good feeling having them together gave. Other memories involved having to have pork and sauerkraut so that the new year would be prosperous. Growing up, we always would watch the "Rose Parade" from Pasadena, California. It was from those broadcasts that my brother George got the idea that he'd like to live somewhere where it was warmer when he got on his own. I never was one for new year's resolutions probably because I'd seen how easily they got broken. The other thing that has gained more importance to me at New Year's as I get older is the need to make better use of the time I've been given. After all, my guess is that, at the end of my life, I won't wish I'd spent more time at work or less with family and friends.

New Year's Lessons - Part 1 of 7

Text: Genesis 39:19-23 (From larger context: Gen.37-50)

Key Verse: Gen.50:20a"…you meant it for evil, but God meant it for good…"

A doctor gave an older man a battery of tests and declared that the guy was healthy for his age. But the guy wanted to know if he would live to be 80. "Well", said the doctor, "do you smoke or drink? "No" "Do you eat a lot of red meat?" "No" "Do you spend a lot of time in the sun-golfing or sailing?" "No" "Do you drive fast cars or date beautiful women?" "No" "Then why do you care?"

We do seem to have an obsession with time, and, especially, how much more time we have. But the fact is we will have as much as the Lord allows. So, it's not so much a matter of counting the days as it is in making the days count. The problem arises, however, during those times when we seem to be "in a rut" and are making little headway. We get frustrated and wonder why God is allowing this interruption of our plans?

I think that Joseph in the book of Genesis might have asked himself that question at several places in his life. After all the dreams he had of greatness, what place did his time in slavery, his betrayal, and his being forgotten in prison have? The answers to these questions did not come to him immediately. It was only in the passage of time and in the way, God worked for his good that he came to see it. I believe that God works in our life in the same way.

A story is told of a man bringing a cocoon home to see it change into a butterfly. When he saw what a struggle the butterfly had in getting out, he decided to help by cutting away the opening so the butterfly could get out. But the result was much different than what was anticipated. Instead of a beautiful butterfly, out came a swollen lump with shriveled wings that never was able to fly. It would appear that, in our lives as well, some struggle is necessary so that we can become all that we can be.

New Year's Lessons - Part 2 of 7

Text: Genesis 3;8-13

Key Verse: proverbs 16:3 "commit to the Lord whatever you do, and your plans will succeed."

A "lame duck" president met with his successor in the oval office. Near the end of their orientation, the President presented the incoming president with 3 numbered envelopes with specific instructions to open them, in order, when difficulties arose. After the new president completed his "honeymoon" period with Congress, the nation experienced an economic downturn. So, the President opened the first envelope-which read, simply "blame me". So, he did, which gained him some time to solve the problem. For a while, things went smoothly. But suddenly, social upheaval caused another domestic crisis. So, the President opened envelope 2-which read, simply, "blame my party". This he did and this problem, too, blew over. Again, there seemed to be a period of prosperity that lasted until it was time for re-election. This time a foreign policy problem arose that threatened the President's plans to stay in office, so he opened envelope 3-which stated, simply, "prepare 3 envelopes".

As we face the new year, blaming something or someone else is one possible course of action. But it does not address a solution. We see this in Genesis 3, where God catches Adam and Eve in their sin. Adam blamed Eve and Eve blamed the serpent. But nothing was solved, and the damage was done.

Similarly, when the Japanese attacked Pearl Harbor in WW2, the newly installed radar system gave early warning. But nothing was done about that report as someone assumed that it must be friendly planes returning from the mainland. Blame was assigned but the problem was not solved, and the damage was done.

How much better it would be, then, if we would prepare ourselves prayerfully for our responsibilities, take credit for our mistakes and learn from them.

New Year's Lessons - Part 3 of 7

Text: Mark 1:16-20

Key Verse: Ecclesiastes 3:1 "To everything there is a season, and a time to every purpose under heaven"

Many years ago, a Russian man stood on a street corner in Moscow and shouted, "down with Khruschev". He was immediately arrested and put in prison for 10 years. While he was in prison, he had a change of heart and began to see Khruschev in a whole new light. However, what he didn't know was, while he was in prison, things changed for Khruschev. He was deposed, kicked out of office and publicly denounced. When the man was released, he wanted to show the world that he had changed. And so, he went to the same street corner and shouted, "hooray for Khruschev!" Once again, he was arrested and put into prison- which just goes to show that timing is everything.

The same could be said about our service to God in word and deed. In our text, Simon, Andrew, James and John make themselves immediately available to the call of Jesus on their lives. And their response is held up as a model for us to follow. Unfortunately, we often don't have that same sense of urgency regarding our call- sometimes delaying it or ignoring it.

In the movie, Castaway, Tom Hanks are portrayed as a FedEx employee who leads all aspects of his life on a tight schedule. He thinks he has things pretty well figured out-great job, great girlfriend. But a plane crash and subsequent stranding on a deserted island for 4 years changes everything. When he is finally rescued and returned home, he finds that his company and girlfriend have "moved on" without him. Now he has "all the time in the world" with nothing to do, nowhere to go and no one to share his life with.

I'm sure that, if he had to do it over again, he would have done things differently. But we get no do-overs in life. That's why we must make the best choices possible. In our own strength and wisdom, we would likely be doomed to repeat our errors. That's why a relationship with God through Jesus Christ –marked by a familiarity with the Bible and a regular prayer life- is so important. He understands our weaknesses but loves us too much to leave us there.

New Year's Lessons - Part 4 of 7
Text: John 6:1-13
Key Verse: Isaiah 11:6c "; And a little Child shall lead them."

A son who was working away called his parents to wish them a happy new year. He then asked them what their new year's resolutions were. The dad responded that his resolution was to make the son's mother as happy as he could. The mom responded that her resolution was to see that the son's dad kept his resolution.

As we approach another new year, we should all try to keep our loved ones happy as we can, but it will involve more than willpower. When I served a stint of my Army Reserve duty at the drug and alcohol ward at St. Francis Hospital in Pittsburgh, PA., I saw first-hand the today's lesson, taken from the gospel of John, Chapter 6 , talks about the power of child-like faith to make miracles happen. In this story, Andrew brings a boy with 5 loaves of bread and 2 fish to Jesus. The boy was willing to bring his little to help meet a need. Andrew, on the other hand, did not have even that much faith. He said, "but what is this among so many?" Yet Jesus rewarded that little boy's contribution by making his little feed so many-with 12 baskets left over!

It seems to me that today, Jesus is still asking us to bring our little (our little faith, our little contributions, etc.) so that he can bless it and meet the need. The question is: Do we have the child-like faith to do it? Perhaps we need to feel a tug.

A little boy was flying his kite when a low-drifting cloud came by and covered it from view. A man came by and asked the boy what he was doing with a string in his hand? The boy replied that he was flying his kite. The man said, "I don't see a kite." And the boy replied, "Neither do I, but I know it's up there because every so often I feel a tug."

New Year's Lessons - Part 5 of 7

Text: Matthew 25:1-13

Key Verse: Romans 13:11B" For now is our salvation nearer than when we believed."

An insurance agent received a phone call from an excited woman who said that she wanted to insure her home by phone. He told her that he would have to see the home, first. "Then," she said, "you'd better get over here right away because it's on fire!"

These days it would appear that time is of the essence... Our scripture verse indicates that nothing should be as high a priority as our salvation, however. Unfortunately for the world, salvation does not rate as high a priority as it should.

Our Bible story, taken from Matthew 25, shows the danger of that kind of thinking. In the parable, five of the ten bridesmaids did not plan for any delay in the coming of the bridegroom and missed out in the wedding celebration. In real life, many people have not adequately planned in getting their salvation settled while there was still time, and so will miss out when the Lord returns. This is also the theme of the popular "Left Behind" book series of several years ago.

And there is evidence of this lack of proper prioritizing throughout history-with predictable results. During General Stonewall Jackson's famous Valley campaign, he found his army was on the wrong side of the river. So, he called his engineers in with the urgent demand to get a bridge built immediately. Just after, he called in his wagon master to advise him of the problem. The wagon master immediately started gathering all the rocks, logs and fence rails he could find, built the bridge and got all the general's artillery and supplies across the river while the engineers were still planning.

When we are charged with the responsibility to share the good news of the gospel with unbelievers, time , not planning, is of the essence.

New Year's Lessons - Part 6 of 7

Text: Exodus 2:1-10

Key Verse: Hebrews 10:35-36/message

"It's still a sure thing! But you need to stick it out, staying with God's plan so you'll be there for the promised completion."

One morning there was a terrible snowstorm, yet the neighbor was surprised to see the mother of 3 small children out shoveling the driveway. So, he asked, "Why isn't your husband out doing this?" "Someone had to stay inside with the kids, so we drew straws to see who went out." "Oh", he said, "sorry about your bad luck." She replied, "Don't feel sorry for me- I won!"

Often times, bad things can be a blessing. A lot of it is in how you see it. God does specialize in bringing good out of bad- but you have to be open to it.

On one vacation to Myrtle Beach, our families went out to a zoo in the country. After taking that in, some of us were anxious to get back to the hotel, but some of the kids were dallying around. To me, this seemed a little frustrating. But when we did finally get going, we found that we had just missed a horrific traffic accident that we easily could have been a part of, had we been timelier in our exit from the zoo. This is, obviously, just a small example of what I'm talking about-but an example, nonetheless.

In our Bible story, we can see some of this "Good news- Bad news" concept. It would appear that baby Moses picked a bad time to be born as the Egyptian rulers had declared that all Israelite male babies were to be destroyed. So, after the mother could not safely hide her baby any longer, she put him a floating basket at the edge of the Nile River. Clearly, it would be just a matter of time.

Until disaster struck, right? But God intervened (as only God could do!) in the person of Pharoah's daughter, and Moses' own mother got to wean him for her.

New Year's Lessons - Part 7 of 7

Text: John 11:1,3-4,6-7,11-15,17

Key Verse: Ecclesiastes 5:4A "When you make a vow to God, do not delay in fulfilling it."

While cleaning out his desk, a man found a shoe repair ticket that was 10 years old. Figuring that he had nothing to lose, he went to the shop and gave the ticket to the repairman, who, in turn, began to search the back room for the unclaimed shoes. After several minutes, he reappeared and gave the ticket back to the man. "What's wrong?", asked the man, "couldn't you find my shoes?" "Oh, I found them alright. They just won't be ready until next Friday."

This story points to the too-human trait of procrastinating. Truly, in most cases, "The Spirit is willing, but the flesh is weak". Sometimes we feel like God procrastinates, but this notion is faulty. God acts at the best time so that his purposes can be achieved. This concept is beautifully portrayed in the raising of Lazarus.

When Jesus receives word that his friend Lazarus is seriously ill, he stays where he is for 2 more days before traveling to where Lazarus is. So, by the time Jesus arrives in Bethany, Lazarus has been dead for 4 days. Initially, this seems strange as we think Jesus perhaps could have kept his friend alive if he hadn't waited. But, perhaps, people might not have really believed that Lazarus was dead if Jesus would have raised him earlier. So, essentially, in doing it this way, the miracle was really considered a miracle.

Unfortunately, our procrastination does not usually have any forethought or benefit to it. Such is the case when King Agrippa hears Paul's faith story and then tells him that he almost persuaded him to become a Christian in Acts 26. These are sad words, indeed, as the Bible records no later confession of faith by that king.

Let us not "put off" so important a decision.

REFLECTIONS

Appearances

The old saying goes, "Appearances Can Be Deceiving". I would agree with that- particularly in making character assessments. The Dornan family of Monongahela, Pennsylvania did not look poor from all outside appearances, but we were. The thing was; however, we didn't look too different from most other people and we didn't feel poor. My mother always said that there was no shame in being poor, as long as you were clean-and she made sure of that! Later on, when I started working for the Department of Welfare, I began to see the difference that being clean in body (and Spirit) made. I saw that one's attitude toward oneself could make a world of difference in one's outlook, even in poverty. Conversely, outside appearances cannot long hide one's poorness in Spirit. That's why we're often surprised to hear of one's taking of their own life, when it would appear that they had so much to live for. Clearly, we need to take the time to get to know people better.

Lessons About Appearance - Part 1of 7

Text: 1st Samuel 16:6-7

Key Verse: 1st Samuel 16:7b "God doesn't look at things like humans do."

A middle-aged lady has a heart attack and is rushed to the hospital. While on the operating room table, she has a near-death experience and sees God. She asks him, "Lord, is this it?" "No", God answers, "you have another 40+ years." So, the lady recovers, and, since she had some money, decided to stay in the hospital a while longer to have some extensive plastic surgery done. She even changes her hairstyle and hair color. When she is leaving the hospital, she gets hit by an ambulance speeding by and is killed. When she appears before God she says, "God, I thought you said I had another 40+ years." And God says, "Dorothy, is that you?"

Now we all know that God could never lose track of us, but let's face it, we can be fooled by outside appearances. We can also be fooled by the way that someone acts towards us. But God looks on the heart and thus, cannot be fooled.

This is clearly demonstrated in today's scripture story, taken from 1st Samuel 16. In this lesson, God instructs Samuel to anoint a new king from the family of Jesse, since he has rejected Saul. So, when Jesse calls each of his sons forward, Samuel is trying to figure out which looks the most like the new king. But God clearly checks Samuel by telling him not to be impressed by outward appearances, for he looks on the heart and since God can look on the heart, he knows the attitude we bring to the service we bring him. That's why we must do all that is entrusted to us "as unto the Lord."

Lessons About Appearance - Part 2 of 7

Text: Matthew 22:15-22

Key Verse: Luke 6:27b "Love your enemies! Do good to those who hate you."

In a small country village in Sicily, there lived 2 brothers, Luigi and Joe. Both happened to be a part of the mafia and had many enemies among the townsfolk-many of which they had cheated in one way or another. When Luigi died, Joe came to the local priest to ask him to do Luigi's funeral and say something nice about him. If the priest would do this, he would contribute $100,000 to the church's building program, which was sorely needed. The priest was in a bind. How could he say something nice about Luigi when everyone knew what a rascal he was? Yet, there was so much to do in the little church and so little to do it with. So, upon thinking about it, he advised joe that he would do the service, and this is how he started: "Luigi was a cheat in his business and in his marriage, but, compared to his brother Joe, he was a saint."

Jesus had enemies too, and they constantly tried to catch him up. In today's lesson, they asked him whether it was right to pay taxes to Caesar. This was a clever question, aimed at getting Jesus to side with Rome against Jewish sentiment or vice-versa. Yet, Jesus never saw people as being his enemies. It wasn't important to him to discredit anyone. His goal, as always, was to seek and to save. And so he answered: "Render to Caesar the things that are Caesar's, and unto God the things that are God's."

It is said that Abraham Lincoln became a Christian after viewing the terrible human losses at Gettysburg. And, from his actions, it was evident that he spent much time in prayer, seeking guidance as to how he might be an instrument of peace. A former enemy, now his Secretary of War, Edwin Stanton, once asked him for advice as to how to handle a troublesome complaint. "Write a sharp letter", he was told, "Then tear it up and write a different one once you've cooled down." Good advice for us, as well.

Lessons On Appearance - part 3 of 7

Text: Mark 2:13-17

Key Verse: Mark 2:17c "I didn't come to call righteous people, but sinners."

Two men were talking. The one says to the other "Did you hear about Harry?" "No, what's happened?" "Well, the way I heard it, he embezzled quite a bit of money from his work and ran off with Tom's wife in a stolen car while drunk." "That's awful! But I wonder, who's going to teach his Sunday School class?"

The bigger question might be: What role does integrity play in a Christian's life? The answer should be obvious, yet many do not act as if it were. As many people already feel many Christians are hypocrites, such behavior only serves to substantiate their opinion.

Jesus, too, was accused of being a hypocrite when he associated with known sinners and tax collectors (even worse!). But his answer- our key verse- showed that what he did, he did knowingly. The religious leaders who questioned Jesus' motives, however, were only concerned with what looked righteous. Later on, Jesus said that their actions amounted to only keeping the outside of the cup clean and not the inside.

Clearly, we, as Christians, need to keep our behavior above reproach whenever possible. That does not mean that some people won't mistake our motives for something else. We can't worry about that-and shouldn't if we are true to ourselves and the cause of Christ. The other piece of that is just as important: speaking the truth about love.

This is a mistake that has often been made by Christians and non-Christians, alike. Henry Clay, who waited until his public life was over before professing his Christianity, once took an unpopular stand on an issue of great importance to him for which he received this counsel: "If you take this position, you will never be President of the United States." He answered, "I'd rather be right than President." We must, then, be consistent in our prayer life and open to the leading of the Holy Spirit before making such statements as Godly testimony without love can do more harm than good.

Lessons On Appearance- Part 4 of 7

Text: Acts 19:13-16

Key Verse: 2 Corinthians 5:17 "Therefore, if anyone is in Christ, he is a new creation; old things have passed away; behold, all things have become new."

A guy was stopped at a stoplight and noticed that the person in the car in front of him looked like they were going through some papers. When the light turned green, that person didn't move their car, and they missed the light. This made the guy very upset, and he began to make threatening gestures at that person and honk his horn impatiently. Before he knew it, a policeman showed up at his window, asking him to get out." Hey, you can't arrest me for getting upset in my car!" "Well, we'll see about that!", said the policeman. And so, for the next 2 hours, the guy found himself sitting in a holding cell at the jail. When the officer released him, he explained it this way: "i didn't arrest you for throwing a fit in your car. But when I saw a cross dangling from your rearview mirror, and a Jesus fish on the back of your car and the way you were acting, I thought that this couldn't have been your car."

I guess you might say that having those symbols doesn't make you any more a Christian than walking into your garage makes you a car. Yet, you have to admit that there is some expectation that you're displaying them predisposes your acting in a particular way. And, like it or not, it is true for the Christian. Our job is to draw people to Christ. Why wouldn't we want to show that we are his?

Yet, more importantly, we need to live out our faith in our actions. That way, nothing will have to be assumed. We find, as our story begins, that Paul has had amazing success in casting out evil Spirits- so much so that others try to do the same without the power of the Holy Spirit. They use the name of Jesus as sort of a magic word without allowing him the Lordship of their life. Their story ends tragically, as will ours without that commitment.

Lessons On Appearance - Part5 of 7

Text: Luke 19:37-38

Key Verse: Psalm 118:26 "Blessed is he who comes in the name of the Lord."

A woman was in the doctor's office, awaiting the findings of her husband's tests. The doctor came in with a grave look on his face and said, "I don't like the look of him." "Neither do I", said the wife, "but he's good to the children."

When Jesus made his triumphant entry into Jerusalem, the religious leaders of the day didn't like the look of him, either. He looked too much like a savior. And since Jesus did not respect their authority as much as they thought he should, they were ready to get rid of him. For the people, however, they liked the look of him- laying clothes and palms in his path and shouting: Hosanna, blessed is he who comes in the name of the Lord!

But, alas, looks are not a solid foundation for success. Jesus, himself, did not put too much stock in them- as he knew how fickle fame could be. Indeed, many of the same people who shouted "hosanna" on Sunday would be yelling "crucify him!" come Friday.

For those of us that are sports fanatics, we are familiar with how quickly players came go from "Hero" to "Goat" and back again. In 1986, a baseball catcher by the name of Bob Brenly was asked to play 3rd base because the regular 3rd baseman couldn't play. Now it had been a while since he had played there, but he felt confident in his abilities- at least until the 4th inning. In that inning alone he committed 4 errors that led his team to a 4-0 deficit. But, since the game lasted 9 innings, he was able to hit a home run in the 5th, single in 2 more runs in the 7th and hit the game-winning home run in the 9th.

And so, it can be for us; that is why it is called fate. Nevertheless, we need to remember that whether our fate be good or bad, God makes a practice of bringing something worthwhile out of it. That's where faith comes in. Faith causes even the bad to be redeemed. In Matthew 9:29 Jesus tells 2 blind men that" according to your faith it will be done for you." And that means you, as well!

Lessons On Appearance - Part6 of 7

Text: John 4:4-42

Key Verse: John 7:38 "Whoever believes in me, as the scripture said, streams of living water will flow from within him."

A man in Alabama came upon a wild dog attacking a young boy and killed it. A reporter saw the incident, congratulated the guy and told him that the story would be in the paper the next day under the headline: "Local man saves child by killing vicious animal." But when the guy advised that he was just visiting from New Jersey, the newspaper reporter said the headline would read: "Yankee kills family pet."

I guess you might say it was just a difference in perspective, but, oh, what a difference it made! In Jesus' time, people from Samaria were looked on very poorly. In fact, Jews traveling in the direction of Samaria often traveled many miles out of their way just to avoid it. But not Jesus. In this story, Jesus came to a well near a town called Sychar, while his disciples went into the village to buy some food. A woman came to the well at that time to draw water and Jesus speaks to her, asking for water. She was surprised that a Jew would even talk to a Samaritan- much less a woman. But Jesus, recognizing a lost soul, saw no reason for discrimination, and asked her to call her husband and return. When she advised that she had no husband- something that Jesus had already discerned, she thought him a prophet and brought others from the town to hear him. And they believed!

Clearly, here was a situation where people who were considered inferior in every way quickly opened their heart to a saving message-something that most "acceptable" people up north had not done. It just shows that appearances, like perceptions, can be very misleading.

Lessons On Appearance-part 7 of 7

Text: 1 Thessalonians 1:7-10

Key Verse: "Brothers, children of Abraham, and you God-fearing gentiles, it is to us that this message of salvation has been sent."

It has been said that Mark Twain loved to fish but hated to catch fish. His problem was that, when he caught a fish, it ruined his concentration because he had to do something with it. But, if people saw him fishing, they wouldn't bother him for autographs and the like. So, he came up with what, he thought, was a perfect solution: when he would go fishing, he would take a pole, line and bobber-but no hook. That way he could sit back and relax-not bothered by fish or man alike.

Some people do their personal evangelism that way, as well. They look the part, but "lay back", waiting for "fish" to bite –without any bait. It's a little like what happened when, several years ago, the city of Pittsburgh constructed a large new post office building-but forgot to include a mail slot.

The usual "culprit" for this kind of behavior is a loss of mission orientation or a lack of urgency about the mission itself. A salesman was complaining about a big sale that he lost and used that old phrase in explaining it to his boss: "You can lead a horse to water, but you can't make it drink." The boss then replied, "it's not your job to make it drink, it's your job to make it thirsty." We need, as Christians, , then, to present an environment and a message that leaves the seeker "thirsty" for more- like the church at Thessalonica.

In the absence of it, however, great opportunity is lost. Mahatma Gandhi, in his auto biography, stated that, at one time, he was strongly considering converting to Christianity. He believed that the teachings of Jesus held the key to the elimination of the caste system in India. Yet, when he went to a "Christian" church, was denied a seat and told to worship with his own kind, he decided to remain a Hindu.

REFLECTION

Attitudes

It has been said that when you change the way you look at things, the things you look at change. As I reflect on my life and the events that took place, I tend to agree. Yet, to a large extent, a Christian outlook has made me to look at things differently. During my lifetime, the following events helped shape me and my generation; the Kennedy and King assassinations, Beatlemania, the Civil Rights movement, men on the moon, Vietnam, Woodstock, Watergate, the Women's Movement, the fall of the Berlin Wall, fast food, computerization, 9-11 and cell phones. For the most part, when these things happened, I was not more than a nominal Christian. And so, I reacted to those things as I reacted to much more mundane happenings. That is, if something did not affect me personally, I didn't pay too much attention to it. My faith, however, forces me to consider these events again in terms of how they brought pain or joy or direction to other people. The things that did affect me personally (love, work, achievement and loss), I must also re-consider through the lens of faith.

Lessons On Attitude - Part 1 of 7

Text: Ecclesiastes 2

Key Verse: Ecc. 2:1b "Everything is pointless."

A story is told about a dog that loved to chase other animals. It bragged far and wide about being able to catch just about anything. One day, however, his claim was put to the test by a little rabbit, who easily outran it into a hole. The other animals who were watching laughed and laughed, to which the dog explained: "Actually, it's pretty easy to see how this happened. I was just running for fun while the rabbit was running for its life."

It does make a difference, doesn't it? Yet, there are many different motivators that can come "into play" in assessing why people do the things they do. These days, fun seems to be one of the main ones. Now, don't get me wrong, fun can be a positive motivator. But fun, like other motivations, can be taken too far.

This seems to be the essence of Solomon's thoughts in today's lesson. Solomon has been considered by many to have been the world's smartest man. And, with good reason-his wisdom was given to him by God! So, in today's lesson, he tries different pursuits to see which would yield the greatest pleasure. But his search yields only our key verse for today: "everything is pointless."

A few years ago, the singer, Peggy Lee, sang a song entitled "Is That All There Is?" about the futility and lack of satisfaction in seeking fulfillment in the wrong things. And although most of us have learned by experience that this is true, we often continue along this same path. How much better it is, then, to learn from this error and seek satisfaction from someone who offers so much more! That person is Jesus. He tells us that he has come to give us life and to give it more abundantly. Clearly, not to learn from Solomon and our own experience seems to be pointless and just not too much fun. Don't you agree?

Lessons On Attitude - Part 2 of 7

Text: Luke 10:30-37

Key Verse: Colossians 3:12: "Therefore, as God's chosen people, holy and dearly beloved, clothe yourselves with compassion..."

A woman had a pet cat that died. And since she loved the cat so much, she tried to arrange for a Christian funeral. She tried first with a Methodist pastor, but since he had no order of worship for such a service, he advised her to try some other denominations. So, she contacted the Baptist, Lutheran and Presbyterian churches, but got no positive response from any of these. She then came back to the Methodist pastor to tell him what trouble she was having and just happened to mention that it would be a shame that no church would be getting the thousand-dollar donation she had in mind for the church that performed the ceremony. The Methodist pastor then piped up and asked, "Why didn't you say your cat was Methodist? We'll do the service tomorrow."

It would appear that all denominations can at least speak the same language in one respect! Yet, it is too bad that that same language is not compassion or caring about others enough to do something about it. Of course, we not only see differences from one denomination to another, but across the spectrum of races and creeds.

In today's lesson, the parable of the good Samaritan, we see that some people don't practice what they preach, and some people aren't as bad as they are made out to be. Yet, their responses are individual rather than generalized ones. Specifically, both a priest and a Levite, very religious people, pass a man lying on the road badly beaten, without helping. Another man, who is of a group of people who are not held in high esteem, comes upon this man and goes beyond reasonable expectation to provide help. He is the one Jesus deems as neighbor.

Lessons On Attitude- part 3 of 7

Text: Luke 18:1-8

Key Verse: James 1:4 "Perseverance must finish its work so that you may be mature and complete, not lacking anything."

A guy came into the clubhouse one Sunday morning, all out of breath. "What took you so long?", asked one of his partners. "I couldn't decide whether or not to go to church or play golf, so I flipped a coin." "I still don't know what took you so long". "Well," the guy said, "I had to flip the coin 17 times." I guess one can be perseverant about the wrong thing, but examples abound of great results yielded by great perseverance.

Such was the case of Thomas Edison, who used over 2,000 different substances in 10,000 experiments in perfecting the lightbulb. He didn't see a failed experiment as a waste of time but as a means of eliminating another wrong assumption: "Opportunity is missed by most people because it is dressed in overalls and looks like work."

Today's lesson, taken from Luke 18:1-8, is about a lady who perseveres in order to get justice from an unjust judge. In essence, the judge is worn down by the woman's perseverance to get what she seeks. One could infer from this parable that God can be similarly worn down by our perseverance. But the true sense of this is, if an unjust judge can be influenced by our perseverance, how much more can God be influenced to act by our prayerful perseverance because of his great love for us? Knowing this, we should be amply motivated to keep praying.

Lessons On Attitude - Part4 of 7

Text: Luke 19:1-10

Key Verse: Romans 11:22 "Consider, therefore, the kindness and sternness of God: sternness to those who fell, but kindness to you, provided that you continue in his kindness. Otherwise, you also will be cut off."

A woman was suing her husband for divorce and was explaining to the judge that she had done all she could to get him to change his ways. Thinking of the Bible verse that advises that showing kindness would be like putting coals of fire on his head, the judge asked the woman about that tactic-to which she said she hadn't although she had tried scalding water.

Apparently, it hadn't suited her to show kindness as a means of conflict resolution. And it still doesn't suit many people today. But Jesus shows us in today's lesson that kindness can go a long way in helping them find their way to salvation. In this story, Jesus' kindness helps a tax collector re-assess his previous way of life and make a change. At that time, that would have been thought to be impossible since tax collectors were considered the "Scum of the Earth". Since we cannot know to what extent Zaccheus may have internalized what people thought of him, it is hard to explain how this turned him around so much other than to say that with God, kindness has great power.

Perhaps, if we were not in such a hurry, we could see for ourselves what kindness could do. A little lame boy was hurrying to catch a train but was slowed down by the basket of fruit and candy he was carrying. In all the bustle, the basket got knocked out of his hand, sending fruit and candy everywhere. Another traveler, however, stopped and helped the disabled boy to collect his things, smiled at him and went on his way. The little boy, not used to such kindness, called after the man: "Please, sir, are you Jesus?" "No", he replied, "Just one of his followers." How about you?

Lessons On Attitude- Part 5 of 7

Text: Genesis 18:1-14

Key Verse: Genesis 18:14a "Is anything too difficult for the Lord?"

A woman was planning a romantic evening for her and her husband as he had just returned home after a 5-day hunting trip. As she unpacked his bag, she heard him say behind her, "Oh baby, did I ever miss you!" When she turned around to give him a hug, she saw him kissing the tv remote control.

Clearly this was not the encouragement she was hoping for. Nevertheless, encouragement is one of the best things we can do for one another. A junior high teacher was upset about the amount of bickering that was going on in her class and gave them the assignment of writing the nicest thing they could say about each of their classmates. She then prepared a separate piece of paper for each student with all their positive affirmations on and passed them out. Little did she realize the impact of that piece of homework! For not only did the bickering stop, but, as she was to learn later, each of the students kept that paper for many years in their important documents.

Encouragement also went a long way with the Old Testament character, Abraham. What he longed for was a son-an heir to carry on his name. But alas, he and his wife were very old and way past the age of childbearing. In this lesson, Abraham was visited at his tent by God in disguise, who promised him a son. Sarah, who was listening inside the tent, doubted this good news-which caused God to declare our key verse: Is anything too difficult for the Lord? We would do well to learn from her mistake as it is impossible to please God without faith in what he can do.

Lessons On Attitude - Part 6 of 7

Text: Luke 2:25-35

Key Verse: John 16:13a "However, when the Spirit of Truth comes, he will guide you into all truth."

A preacher who was on a diet prayed that if it was God's will that he not have any donuts that day, that God must not allow there to be any parking places in front of the donut shop. Later, when someone asked him how that worked out, he replied that he ate 2 donuts because there was a parking place open in front on only his 8th trip around the block.

Unfortunately, too many people use this kind of logic in thinking that they are being obedient to the leadership of the Holy Spirit. Clearly, they are just doing what they want to do. Not so with the main character in today's Bible lesson, Simeon. Simeon was an old man who the Spirit said that he would not die until he saw the Messiah. So, being led by the Spirit, he came to the temple in Jerusalem at just the precise time that Mary and Joseph were bringing Jesus in for his circumcision and so got to hold him and bless him.

It is important, then, that we, too, be attentive to the Spirit's leading so that we will receive the blessing of that guidance. We just won't know the nature of it until it's revealed. Such was the case of Dawn Robinson as she followed her usual morning routine in getting ready for work on the morning of September 11, 2001. She worked in New York City at the World Trade Center. And she had just got seated at her desk that morning when the North tower got hit. A voice came over the intercom advising all employees in the South tower (where she was) that they were in no danger and to continue to stay where they were. Yet Dawn felt a compelling desire to leave, which she did. By the time she reached the 42nd floor, the South tower got hit where her office was. And she knew that if she had not been attentive to the leading of the Holy Spirit, she would have been killed.

What is the Spirit saying to you? Please listen!

Lessons On Attitude - Part 7 of 7

Text: 2 Corinthians 11:24-27

Key Verse: Romans 8:28 "All things work together for good for those who love God and are called according to his purposes."

A little girl was being punished for having to eat alone in the corner of the dining room. Her family did not pay attention to her until they heard her pray: "Thank you, Lord, for preparing a table before me in the presence of mine enemies."

To her it probably felt like she was enduring great tribulation. But, compared to Paul, most of us have no idea what tribulation is. In today's lesson, Paul is recounting the many trials he had endured for the sake of the gospel. Yet it was not said out of pride but as a means of defending himself against charges that he was a false prophet. Indeed, his suffering for the sake of the gospel proved that he was a follower of Christ, as followers are said to endure the trials of their master.

This, of course, is not a message that people like to hear. Yet, to Paul, his suffering was a necessary means of preparing him for faithful service- a sort of refining process. And that is why it is good- because the testing of our faith yields endurance. You see, there are no shortcuts to that quality.

A farmer's mule fell into a dry well. But the farmer felt that neither the mule nor the well was worth saving. And so, he gathered his neighbors- assuring them that he was only doing what was best for his mule by burying it and putting it out of its misery. Unfortunately, the mule was not consulted about this decision and decided it would do something about it. So, every time a shovelful of dirt fell on its back, it shook it off and stepped up. Finally, what was meant to bury him helped him to step out of the well.

So, it can be for us when trouble comes. What doesn't kill us makes us stronger.

REFLECTIONS

Bible

One way to look at the Bible is as a set of directions. Although it doesn't tell you that tab A is to go in slot B, it does tell you that there are some ways of constructing a life that will work better than others, and that God gave these instructions with our best interests in mind. Where he gives no specific directions, we are to use prayer and the leading of the Holy Spirit. So considered, then, the Bible is not specific enough for some and yet way too specific for others. Regardless of the way one views it, however, the beauty of the Bible is that it is a book that invites our participation. In my early life, the Bible was not a set of instructions for me as I knew little of what was in there. I kind of lived my life in accordance with the way I thought it should look. And we all know how that works out. When I began to attend an Assembly of God church and teach in the Sunday School, I did begin to study the Bible and was convicted to live more as the Bible suggested. In my later years, after reading it as a daily devotional and studying it in sermon preparation, I see it as a faithful counselor.

Lessons On the Bible - Part 1 of 7

Text: Deuteronomy 32: 44-47

Key Verse: Deut. 32:47a "This is no trivial matter for you-this is your very life."

A little girl was reading a storybook about Jonah and the whale while on an airplane. The man who was sitting next to her asked if she believed that story. "Yes," she answered, "Because it's in the Bible." "But how can you prove it?", he asked in a superior attitude. "I'll just ask Jonah when I get to heaven." "But what if he isn't in there?" "Then you can ask him."

Jesus talks of our need to have a child-like faith. I believe that kind of faith should include our perception of the Bible as the inspired word of God. Moreover, when it is in the form of a set of instructions for living, it should be doubly important. I believe that this is why Moses characterized it as important as life itself for those preparing to enter the Promised Land. Now please understand that Moses was talking to them as a father would talk to his children-not as some disinterested third party. He wanted them to be successful; he wanted them to be blessed. And so, I think it should be for those of us who love the people under our care.

Years ago, a man was hired to paint the lines on a rural highway. As his company had little money and no trucks to spare, he had to paint the lines on foot. After the first day of work, the guy's supervisor was impressed that he got 3 miles' worth of lines painted. But on the second day, he only got 2 done and on the third day, only 1. So, the supervisor called the guy in to let him know he was being fired. As the guy began to walk away, he turned back for one final complaint; "I never worked so hard. It's just that the paint bucket kept getting further and further away."

As silly as it sounds, when we only read the Bibles in the pews and not the ones in our homes, we do the same thing.

We're working too far from the bucket! Let us resolve to read our Bibles and read them more faithfully.

Lessons On the Bible - Part 2 of 7

Text: Matthew 7:13-14

Key Verse: Psalms 104:9 "You set a boundary they cannot cross"

A man had a secret that he could not, in good conscience, keep, so he went to his priest to admit he had been stealing building supplies from his place of work. The priest then asked him how much he stole. He said enough to build his house in town and the one at the lake as well as his children's homes. "That's very serious", said the priest, "Have you ever thought of doing penance?" "No, I haven't, Father", he replied, "But if you can get me the plans, I can get you the building supplies."

It sounds as if he came to a boundary but was inclined to go further, if the priest would allow him. The Bible can be characterized as "boundary-setting", yet I believe, for our own good. Indeed, we find security in defined boundaries-which starts in childhood.

In the early days of the progressive-education movement, an enthusiastic behavioral scientist took down the chain-link fence that surrounded the nursery school playground in hopes that this would allow the children more freedom of movement. What he found instead was that the children would only huddle in the middle of the playground and go no further.

Today's lesson talks about the Christian walk as being a narrow, uneasy passage. One has to constantly be on guard for influences that would seem to enlarge the boundaries of acceptable behavior when, in fact, they exceed the boundaries that God has set for us in the Bible. The Christian, however, is able to tell which is which by the "fruit" that taking such a road yields. The narrow way leads to such fruit as love, joy, patience, kindness, goodness, faithfulness, gentleness and self-control. The broader way does not.

Lessons On the Bible - Part 3 of 7

Text: Proverbs 2:2-6

Key verse: Psalms 119:105 "Thy word is a lamp unto my feet and a light unto my path."

Grandma had given her granddaughter her first Bible and now, 15 years later, was preparing to give her the old family Bible with all the births, deaths and important notes. She patiently and, to the best of her ability, answered her granddaughter's questions until she asked: "Which virgin was the mother of Jesus? The Virgin Mary or the King James Virgin?"

Maybe she wasn't ready for the family Bible, after all. But, quite honestly, the Bible is not the easiest book to understand. And one might be tempted to "give up" instead of staying with it. But there is a benefit in staying with it.

Today's lesson tells us that if we search for meaning as one would search for hidden treasure, the Lord will provide it. In essence, then, our failure in understanding may come from a lack of effort on our part more than the Bible's difficulty in expressing it. The Common English Bible's translation advises us to stretch our mind toward understanding. This, I think, gives the proper interpretation of what our efforts should look like

"An old grandpa in the heart of the Appalachians had the right idea in trying to explain this to his grandson. You see, his grandson was questioning why he had to read the Bible when he couldn't understand it or retain it. Grandpa said," take this coal basket down to the river, fill it up and bring it back." This the grandson did 3 times, but each time the water ran out. The grandson then said, "It's useless, Grandpa." "Useless, is it? Look at the coal basket. It's clean as can be. That's what the word of God does to you. You may not understand it or retain it, but it cleans your basket." It gets rid of the impurities of mind and heart, so we can see more clearly.

Lessons On the Bible - Part 4 of 7

Text: Acts 3:1-10

Key Verse: Matthew 28:19a "Go and make disciples of all nations...".

The football coach is going over possible game scenarios with his team in hopes of getting them all "on the same page'. And so, after each one he asks a different player what he would do. At last, he comes up with this scenario: the team is down by 6 points. But with seconds to go, we are on the opposing team's goalline on 4th down. "What would you do, John?", asked the coach. Now John had not played all year, so he said, "I'd slide down the bench so I could get a better view."

From John's point of view, this was an honest answer. But from the coach's viewpoint, it was all wrong since he wanted all his players to think like players, not bench warmers. By the same token, Jesus gives the great commission to all Christians with the idea that we all have roles to play in the salvation of souls. The Bible, then, becomes the playbook by which we are told what we are to do.

This fact comes into play in today's lesson, where Peter and John heal a man, crippled from birth, as they are about to enter the temple. They do this, not in their own strength, but in the name of Jesus, whom they have seen and learned from. And the people who see the man are utterly amazed because the man is leaping and praising God. It appeared to them that these men now possessed the same power to heal that Jesus had-the same power!

A man comes into a hardware store to buy a chainsaw. He tells the salesman that he's heard it can cut 10 cords of wood a day. So, he buys it and takes it home. The next day he comes back into the hardware store, all worn out, and says to the salesman," something must be wrong. I worked as hard as I could, but i could only cut 3 cords. My old-fashioned saw could do better than that." So, the salesman took the saw and the guy out back to try it out. But when he pulled the cord and the saw started up, the guy yelled, "What's that noise?" That noise, friends, is the power, available and ready to use for us all.

Lessons On the Bible - Part 5 of 7

Text: Numbers 22:22-35

Key Verse:1 Thessalonians 5:20 "Don't brush off Spirit-inspired messages..."

A severe rash prompted a man from a rural area to come into town to see a doctor. Since the man didn't drive, his neighbor brought him in. After the doctor's exam and several tests, the doctor advised that this rash was caused by the man's dog and that he needed to get rid of it. On the way home the man told the neighbor what the doctor had said and so the neighbor asked the man if he was going to sell the animal or give it away. "Neither one", explained the man. "I'm going to get one of them "second opinions" I've always heard about. It's easier the get another doctor than a good bird dog."

I guess you might say that that's a good thing about advice: you can always take it or leave it. Yet when that advice comes from the Bible, we had better reconsider. Today's key verse gives us the advice not to brush off Spirit-inspired messages. The upshot of that seems to be that we need to evaluate those messages more carefully. But how do we know a message is Spirit-inspired? That's not an easy question to answer because the Spirit, like God, operates in many ways. However, God's messages seem to be accompanied by strong pulls of conscience or circumstances.

A family from Scotland dreamed of starting a new life in America. They had scrimped and saved and finally purchased the tickets for the trip. But, a week before their departure, their son was bitten by a dog. The doctor took care of the boy but had to quarantine the family for 2 weeks as a precaution against rabies. Since the tickets were non-refundable, their plans were ruined. So, on the day that their ship was to depart, the dad stomped down to the docks to see the ship off (with them not on it), the ship's name: Titanic.

In today's Bible story, a donkey is allowed to speak to stop Balaam from going against God's will. You see, God speaks and acts in mysterious ways, so we need to pay attention.

Lessons On the Bible - Part 6 of 7

Text: Matthew 7:32a

Key Verse: 2 Timothy 3:16a "Every part of scripture is God-breathed and useful in one way or another..."

A South Sea islander proudly showed his Bible that he had received from a missionary many years before to an American G.I. during WWII. The G.I replied, "That's nice but I haven't followed that book since I was in Sunday School." "Well, it's a good thing that we still do, or you would have been my evening meal."

The Golden Rule, our lesson for today, tells us to treat people the way we would like to be treated. But one wouldn't know it unless one read and understood it. You see, the Bible is meant to be lived out and we, like it or not, are their Bible, until they begin to read it for themselves.

An army chaplain was visiting wounded soldiers in the hospital. When he came to this one soldier, he talked to him for a while and then felt led to read some Bible passages to him. "What I'd really like," he said, "Is something to make me warmer." So, the chaplain took off his field jacket and put it around him. Next the soldier asked for some water. So, the chaplain propped the soldier's head up and gave him water from his own canteen. Then, once again, the chaplain asked if he could read some Bible passages to the soldier. This time he said, "is there anything in that Bible of yours that caused you to do what you just did? Read those parts to me."

Lessons On the Bible - Part 7 of 7

Text: Hebrews 4:12-13

Key Verse: Hebrews 4:12a "...God's word is living, active and sharper than any two-edged sword."

A supply pastor had been preaching at a church in Texas for about 3 months and had gotten into a nice routine. First, he'd go to a small coffee shop in town, go over his sermon then go to the church to preach. One Sunday, while at the coffee shop, a guy came over to where he was and asked to sit down. The preacher said that it was ok. Then the guy asked him, based on the way he was dressed, if he was a preacher or something. The preacher said that he was and was preaching at the church down the street. "Wow!", said the guy, "I'm a member of that church!" "Well, I've been preaching at that church for 3 months and never saw you there." "I said I was a member, not a fanatic!"

Unfortunately, many people feel the same way about reading their Bible. Yet many of those same people think nothing of the time they spend in front of a tv, watching football, or reading a predictable romance novel or surfing the net. You might say it's a question of priorities. Regrettably, when they stand before God, they will wish that they were more of a "fanatic". You see, it is possible to know God without reading his word. But it is impossible to fall in love with him without reading the Bible. And it is impossible for us to become active Christians without his word because it is a book that transforms as well as informs.

A homeless guy asked the street preacher for his Bible because the pages seemed just right for rolling into cigarettes. The preacher said he would give it but only if the guy would promise to read the page before smoking it. Three months later, the guy appeared like a different man before that same preacher, who asked him the reason for the change. He said that he smoked Matthew, Mark and Luke but got "smoked" by John. Similarly, when we let the Bible get into us, we cannot help but be changed.

REFLECTIONS

Change

Like it or not, the one thing we all have to get used to is change. As I grow older, however, it seems harder than it should be. I have always liked things to get into a routine so I could feel more confident about handling them. But change throws us out of our routine and into new ways of acting and reacting. Growing up, the family dynamic changed each time a family member left but, most of all, when my mother died. Her death changed the type and frequency of our mutual communication- which, in a way, helped us all in dealing with the individual life changes we all would face. When I consider the changes in my life-like changes in relationships, work roles and living locations, I'd like to think that I learned something positive from each. After all, we have to adapt and "move on" to changes in our circumstances because, usually, we cannot make our new circumstance adapt to us. The other piece here is that change can be helpful to lift us out of ways of acting that are harmful for us. Clearly, routines that are dysfunctional should not be continued for routine's sake.

Lessons On the Change - Part 1 of 7

Text: Genesis 37:5-7,9/ 45:5-8

Key Verse: Genesis 50:20 "Even though you planned evil against me, God planned good to come out of it."

An old man lived alone and was rather limited as to what he could do above basic needs. But, up until this year, he had always put it in the garden with the help of his son, Vinnie. Vinnie was not able to help this year since he had gotten into trouble and was sent to prison. So, the old man sent Vinnie a letter, lamenting his inability to plant his garden. Within a day, Vinnie wrote back telling his dad that was just as well since the garden was where the bodies were buried. The next day about 4 am in the morning, the FBI and local authorities arrived at the old man's house and dug up the whole garden area- but found no bodies. They apologized to the old man and left. The next day the old man received this letter from Vinnie: Dear pop- go ahead and plant your garden now. It's the best I could do under the circumstances. -love, Vinnie.

This is a good example of making the best of things when change comes. Some people, however, use change as the reason for not acting. We should not be among them when we know that God can bring good even out of the biggest changes.

One of the best examples of this was the Old Testament character, Joseph. We know joseph because of his coat of many colors. But the most important part of joseph's story involves his resiliency in coming back from several serious personal setbacks. I mean, when one considers his being sold into slavery, being thrown into prison on false charges and being forgotten there by people who could have helped him, we realize that he was able, with God's help, to overcome enough trouble for several lifetimes.

You see, change that brings hardship can build character. It's just a question of how it's used. Take electricity, for example. When harnessed, it can bring light and heat. Unharnessed, it can bring death.

Lessons On the Change - Part 2 of 7

Text: exodus 3:1-10

Key verse: exodus 3:5b "take off your sandals, because you are standing on holy ground."

One Sunday morning, the pastor noticed 7-year-old Alex staring at the large plaque in the foyer. When Alex saw him, he asked, "Pastor, what's this?" "it's a memorial to all the young men and women who died in the service." "Which one, asked Alex, "the 9 o'clock or the 11 o'clock?"

Not what the pastor expected to hear. But then again, life is full of the unexpected. Such is the case today in our lesson on Moses, the shepherd. Probably, life was pretty routine as a shepherd- so much different than what he'd been used to in Pharoah's court. But when Moses sees a burning bush that does not get consumed, he decides to check it out and comes face-to-face with God! He expected to see a freak of nature and ends up with a commission to lead the Israelites out of Egyptian slavery.

Clearly, this is not God's usual way of interacting with us. But God is not predictable, especially when he has an important assignment to give. Nevertheless, God does continue to work in mysterious ways. Yet, since we know that God is good and desires to bless, we should not fear the unexpected or what can come of it.

Mavis Jackson lived in Anaheim, California and often walked by Robert Schuller's crystal cathedral. She always thought she'd like to go there someday and finally decided that next Sunday she would. So, when the day came, she joined some 3,000 other worshipers and thoroughly enjoyed the music and the sermon. On the way out, she struck up a conversation with a young woman who had sat next to her- only to find out that that woman was actually the baby girl she had been forced to give up many years before. Friends, that's God in the unexpected!

Lessons On the Change - Part 3 of 7

Text: Exodus 13:21

Key Verse: Psalms 61:2b "Lead me to the rock that is higher than I."

A mom took her 9-year-old daughter out for a mother-daughter breakfast. During breakfast, the mom took a breath then asked her daughter how she could be a better mom. The daughter replied," you still do yell a lot. I know you've been praying about it but it hasn't helped much so far."

I'm not sure that's a question we really want to ask. Nevertheless, it is important that we try to make progress in all the roles in which we find ourselves. John Wesley, the founder of the methodist movement, always asked prospective pastors if they were "moving on to perfection." I don't know about that but if I let more and more of the example of Jesus into my heart, I'm sure I'll be happy with the outcome.

In today's scripture lesson, we learn that God led the Israelites through the wilderness by a pillar of cloud by day and a pillar of fire by night. And I think to myself, what a blessing to be so clear about the leading of God in our life! But, in reading the book of exodus, I find that this was not the mindset of the people-generally speaking. They bickered and complained to Moses almost daily, in spite of the wonders they regularly experienced. And, generally speaking, there is little or no evidence in the narrative to suggest that they learned anything at all. The question that seemed to be continually on their lips was, "Where is God in this?"

This question seems to be on a lot of modern-day lips, as well. Some have suggested that perhaps it is a loss of signal, where the guidance that God gives is somehow lost in transmission-like the loss of signal that we sometimes get with our cell phones that is caused by changes in geography or distance from a transmitter. The same could be proposed for a storm that temporarily interrupts our communication. But, in reality, no such problem exists on God's part. It is, instead, our distancing from him. If we but draw near to him, he will help us both here and improve.

Lessons On the Change - Part 4 of 7

Text: Judges 6:13-16

Key Verse: 1 Thessalonians 5:11a "Therefore, encourage one another and build each other up…"

A woman who was called to jury duty told the presiding judge that she should be disqualified because she was opposed to capital punishment. The judge explained to her that this was a civil case and not a criminal one and that it involves a man who took $5,000 of his wife's money to spend on gambling and other women. "Well, in that case, I'll be glad to serve, she said," and re-consider my stance on capital punishment."

Isn't it amazing what a little guidance can do for a person's point of view? The same can be said of encouragement. The Old Testament character, Gideon, is an excellent example of this. In today's scripture lesson, an angel's encouragement makes a timid coward ready to lead an army. Of course, this doesn't happen without some testing of God's support along the way. But it was a necessary first step.

Sometimes, however, people take a little more convincing. In the case of Edwin Stanton, Abraham Lincoln's secretary of war, it took quite a bit more convincing. Prior to being selected as secretary of war, Stanton was on record of calling Lincoln "a low, cunning clown, a gorilla and a fool." Yet Lincoln felt him to be the best choice for the job. Because of Lincoln's patient, forgiving attitude, however, Stanton was finally able to say at the time of Lincoln's death, "There lies the greatest ruler of men the world has ever seen."

Leaders, in order to be effective, must be able to get the most of those who serve under them. Being forgiving, open-minded and encouraging are all traits that will help make their organization more than the sum of its parts and thus be truly successful.

Lessons On the Change - Part 5 of 7

Text: Matthew 2: 9-12

Key Verse: Matthew 18:3b…, "Unless you change and become like little children, you will never enter the kingdom of heaven."

Two construction workers on lunch break opened their lunch pails to see what they had to eat. One says, "Not baloney again. This is the third time this week I've gotten baloney!" The other worker looks at him and says, "Why don't you ask your wife to make you something different?" "I'm not married", the complainer said," I made these myself."

Resisting change for the sake of resisting does not seem to be an effective decision. Yet it seems to happen fairly often, anyway. The fact that the three wise men were open to change, however, reveals that they didn't fall into that trap. In today's lesson, we find that, after visiting the Christ-child, they went home differently than when they came because they were advised to in a dream. Some commentaries like to point out, however, that their change was more than a direction. They suggest that seeing the Christ-child changed their hearts, as well.

When Diane Hanny decided, at the age of 43, to get a college degree, there was only one class she feared: math. And she had felt that way since the 8th grade because her math teacher at that time, Mrs. Jamison, convinced her that she was no good at it. But because she was committed to her goal of graduating, she knew that, somehow, she must pass it. At first, she did have some problems with it but her teacher, Mrs. Nash, was so helpful and encouraging that she soon caught on and passed the course with flying colors. The unusual aspect of this happening, however, did not involve Diane as much as it did her teacher. You see, Mrs. Jamison and Mrs. Nash were actually the same person. When she was Mrs. Jamison, she was unhappy and going through a divorce. When she became Mrs. Nash, she changed to a much more happy, encouraging person. Clearly, people, as well as attitudes can change -with God's help.

Lessons On the Change - Part 6 of 7

Text: Matthew 17:1-7

Key Verse: romans 12:2b "…be transformed by the renewing of your mind"

A man went to see his doctor and said," doctor, I've been misbehaving lately, and my conscience is really bothering me." "And you want me to give you something that will strengthen your will power?", the doctor asked. "not exactly," explained the man," I was hoping you'd give me something to weaken my conscience."

Clearly, he didn't want to change. In today's lesson, Jesus' disciples didn't seem to want to change, either. But Jesus realized that his time with them would be limited so they needed to change to be able to carry on his work without him and they needed something big to give them the incentive in doing so. Thus, we have transfiguration. Not only did this get their attention, but Jesus also used this teachable moment to connect them to the learning they needed. It didn't hurt that this transfiguration only involved Jesus' closest disciples (peter, James and john) because they were more ready for that teaching. And I'm sure, it was hoped that they would help bring the rest of the disciples "up to speed" later on.

Similarly, teachable moments are extremely helpful in getting us ready for learning. In our central Pennsylvania area, the penalties incurred when a college football program becomes too big to care for more important things gave us all the occasion to reflect on how such things could happen. And, as difficult and painful as these penalties were, they did lead to many positive developments and the beginning of the healing process.

Lessons On the Change - Part 7 of 7

Text: Acts 9:1-20

Key Verse: acts 9:4 "Saul, Saul, why do you persecute me?"

Two caterpillars were crawling across the grass one day when a butterfly flew over them. One looked at the other and said," You'll never get me up in one of those things!"

Oh yeah? It's kind of the same idea that occurs to us before God enters the equation. You see, God rarely does things that get in the way of our free choice. But that doesn't mean that he can't! He's God, after all. And nothing illustrates this better than the Damascus Road conversion of the apostle Paul. Paul, who was known previously as Saul, was a zealous opponent of the early Christian movement. Yet, opponent is probably too kind of a description for what he did to Christians. Indeed, he acted as judge and jury of them as he hunted them down, had them arrested and officiated at their stoning. And it was while he was going to Damascus to do more of the same when Jesus got his attention.

There are several ideas here, however, that we need to take away from this lesson. Not only does God act in direct ways to change the course of people's lives when he so desires, but he does so in order that more people will be able to make an informed choice about the importance of having God in their lives or just so he can bless them. It also shows that God can use former enemies to lead his cause and that his love can change anyone for good. And it isn't in just the big things!

A woman had been wanting new kitchen cabinets for a long time. But her husband had "shot down" her hopes by saying they were a luxury they couldn't afford. But, after spending two weeks at her mother's, she was overjoyed to come home and find that new kitchen cabinets had been installed. A few days later, a neighbor came over to visit and admire the new cabinets and commented, "All of us were so glad that the fire your husband had while you were away confined to the kitchen." Isn't God good?

REFLECTIONS

Choices

Choices have consequences. But, in large measure, I believe that God can bring positive outcomes- even when those choices have not been done with much forethought. When I think of my life before college, most of my decisions were in accordance with my parents' desires. The first choice of any consequence I made was what College to attend. For the most part, this decision was not Made with a whole lot of forethought. I thought I might Like to be a librarian and clarion state college was supposedly a good school for that. In retrospect, it was a good choice - but not because of any special consideration on my part. My choice as to life's work was equally unplanned. I had a diploma, but little else. I knew what I didn't want to do and took civil service exams for things that seemed service related. That, also, worked out pretty well. Until connie came along, I had less than favorable results with choices for life mate, however, using my usual decision- making method. It was only in retrospect that I realized that, to ensure better results, all decisions should be made in consultation with God.

Lessons on Choices- Part 1 of 7

Text: Joshua 24:13-15

Key Verse: Joshua 24:15c " ...;but as for me and my house, we will serve the Lord."

After the baptism of her baby brother at church, the older sister cried all the way home. "What's the matter, honey?" The dad asked. "That preacher said that he wanted us to be brought up in a Christian family, but I want to stay with you guys."

Obviously, she didn't know she was in a Christian family! Now that might not matter to some, but the choice to become a Christian family can make a big difference in a lot of ways.

Clearly, this must have been on Joshua's mind as he prepared to lead the Israelites into the promised land. He had seen their many disobediences to God and the punishments that resulted and didn't want those to continue. But regardless of what they decided, Joshua proclaimed that he and his family would continue to follow God. Would that the Spiritual head of each family could speak so confidently about their own household!

It may seem like a small choice, but few decisions can so last a result. A small courthouse in Ohio stands in a unique location. Raindrops that fall on the north side of the roof go into Lake Ontario and the St. Lawrence seaway. Raindrops that fall on the south side of the roof go into the Mississippi river and into the Gulf of Mexico. This represents a difference in final destination of about 2,000 miles. And just a gentle puff of wind at the peak of the roof makes all the difference.

The Spiritual application seems pretty clear: by the smallest choice of the source of guidance in one's life, one sets in motion forces that not only change life in the here and now, but for all eternity.

Lessons on Choices- Part 2 of 7

Text: Esther

Key verse: Esther 4:14b "Yet who knows whether you have come to the kingdom for such a time as this?"

Little Billy was allowed to sit in his father's place at the dinner table when his dad was absent. So, on this particular night when his dad was not there, Billy took his father's place- which his older sister resented. So she said, "If you are the head of the family tonight, tell us what 2 x 14 is?" Without a second's hesitation, Billy responded, "I'm busy. Go ask your mother."

Apparently, this was the model of responsibility Billy picked up from his father. While this is understandable by a child, it can leave something to be desired by an adult. Of all the models of responsibility we have observed, it will be our choice as to which is most appropriate for the situation that we are in. As Christians, however, it will not only be which model is most appropriate, but which one is most God-honoring.

The name of God is not mentioned in the book of Esther, but God's influence can be perceived throughout. Moreover, we see in this short book different models of responsibility- not all of which are God-honoring. We see that the king shows poor judgment in dismissing his queen and in taking Haman's advice without considering its implications. We see Haman's poor judgment in allowing his anger to dictate the official policy of the land. We see Mordecai's prudent actions in seeking Esther's help and her bravery in deciding to risk her life for that of her people.

When I was a national guard company commander, I had about 100 people under my command. When i assigned responsibility, i gave responsibility to check whether or not something was done to another officer or NCO. But I checked that checker, myself. I took the time to know my fellow officers and my NCO's well enough to know which gave the wisest and most prudent advice.

Regardless of what position we are in, however, we all have a higher power to which we will answer for the choices that we make.

Lessons on Choices- Part 2 of 7

Text: Matthew 25:14-30

Key verse: Romans 14:12 "So then, each of us will give an account of himself to God."

The Sunday school teacher had just finished telling his students about the story of the rich man and Lazarus. He then asked his young boys which of the two characters they would like to be. One boy put up his hand, then said;" the rich man while I'm living but Lazarus when I die."

Good choice, but the real problem comes up when the answer must be one or the other. Each choice carries consequences, and we don't get to pick what they are. That's just human nature- the desire to sew our wild oats then pray for crop failure.

In the parable of the talents, three servants are given a money amount in proportion to each's abilities with the understanding that an account of their actions will be required at some later time. Two of the servants are industrious and earn a profit from what they've been given. The other just buries his money. When the master returns, he demands an accounting from each- with the servant who buried the money being cast out for the lack of effort he demonstrated.

This story has been played out in many places throughout human history with similar results. An elderly carpenter was ready to retire and told his employer-contractor of his intentions. But the contractor asked him to do one last job to which he reluctantly agreed. But as the work progressed, it was clear that his heart was not in the effort. He took shortcuts in workmanship that he had never done before and in the materials that he used. Finally, the contractor did the final inspection and then-surprise of surprises- gave the keys to the carpenter, saying" it's all yours for the faithful service you have given."

By the same token, we are sending up building materials for the home our heavenly father is preparing for us. If we send up inferior materials, we have no one to blame but ourselves.

Lessons on Choices- Part 3 of 7

Text: 1 Kings 5

Key verse: Proverbs 16:18a "Pride goes before destruction,…"

A man who had a high opinion of himself got on a scale that gave your weight and your fortune. After reading the wording on the card that came out, he gave it to his wife with a smug look. The card read:" you are dynamic, a born leader, handsome and much admired by women for your personality." Giving it a second look, she said," it looks like it got your weight wrong, too."

Some people approach life as if they have all the answers. Obviously, they don't, so having such a high opinion of oneself can be a difficult position to maintain-even a harmful one, at times. In our Bible lesson today, Naaman almost makes the mistake of his life by thinking he knew it all. He was upset that Elisha didn't make a big deal of his request to be healed and was about to go away without following Elisha's advice. It was only when his servant requested, he re-consider that he forsook his pride and bathed in the Jordan river.

The attitude with which we approach life is a choice we make. If we can admit , each day, that there is something to learn , we will be surprised at how meaningful our life can be. Pride can stand in the way of that, if we let it. There was once a frog who desired to go south for the winter and had an idea as to how to do it. He asked 2 geese who were making their annual migration to hold a stick in their beaks while he hung on by his mouth in the middle. This worked so well that as they flew above the heads of 2 men walking below, they wondered aloud as to whose idea it was. When the boastful frog claimed, "It was my idea!", he lost his hold and was killed in the fall.

Lessons on Choices – Part 4 of 7

Text: 2 Kings 6:1-7

Key verse: Hebrews 11:6 "But without faith it is impossible to please him;…"

A monk joined a monastery and took a vow of silence. Even so, once every 10 years, he was allowed to express any concerns he had to the head monk. After the first 10 years, he said, "food bad." At the end of the second 10 years, he said, "bed hard." After the third 10 years, he reported, "I quit." To which the head monk replied, "it doesn't surprise me. All you've done since you've been here is complain."

Having a negative view toward life is a choice we can make. From a scriptural point of view, negativity is similar to doubt. And doubt gets us nowhere with God. But please understand having faith (the opposite of doubt) in God is not believing that nothing bad will happen to you. Matthew 5;45 tells us just the opposite-that God makes rain to fall on the just and unjust. Having faith means that we believe God can bring good out of bad.

Such is the case with Elisha in today's lesson. Elisha goes on a mission trip with some other prophets. While they are in the midst of a building project, one of the other prophets loses the head off the ax they were using. The problem was, however, that it was borrowed. But having faith that God would help, Elisha throws a piece of wood into the river where the ax head went in, and up floats the ax head-ready to be retrieved.

That doesn't mean that God will do a miracle each time you need something. But faith is the mindset that tells us he can. It is a mindset that reverses the idea that seeing is believing. It took faith for eric Weihenmayer to become the first blind person to successfully climb mt. Everest. When asked what he looks for in teammates, he said that he looks for people that have an unrealistic optimism toward life-people that believe "believing is seeing." He said, "You've got to believe first in what you're doing and be sure you have a reason to believe it."

Lessons on Choices – Part 5 of 7

Text: Luke 10: 38-42

Luke 10:41a "One thing is necessary."

A woman went to the pet store to buy a parrot but returned the next day to say it hadn't said a word, yet. The store owner suggested that she get it a mirror. So, she bought one and still no talking parrot. On successive days, then, the store owner suggested a ladder, then a swing, but nothing seemed to work. Finally, the lady came back to advise the store owner that the parrot had died. The store owner asked if the parrot had said anything before it died. And the woman said, "yes", it said, "don't they have any food down there?"

One of the most important decisions that we make is regarding priorities. Without prioritizing, everything becomes important, and we end up not getting much of anything done. In today's lesson, we find that, when Jesus comes to visit, sister Martha is flustered that she had to make all the dinner preparations herself. Jesus, however, told her that her priorities were mixed up and that she should follow her sister's lead in listening to his teaching.

Unquestionably, we get our priorities mixed up when we put other less important things ahead of our service and worship of God. We see this clearly on Sundays where most people tend to do everything else but church. Someday those choices may come back and bite them. So, it is crucial that we do the things we can look back on –without guilt.

A survey done of a number of people over age 95 asked them just one question: if you could live your life over again, what would you do differently? There were many different answers to this question, but 3 answers kept repeating: I would reflect more; I would risk more, and I would do more things that would live on after I died. Where do you stand on these things?

For many, their children represent their greatest legacy. But sadly, many do not realize the importance of even the smallest investment of time. Witness the diary entries of a man and his son for the same day: father- went fishing with my son-a day wasted; son- went fishing with my dad-the most wonderful day of my life.

Lessons on Choices – Part 6 of 7

Text: John 20:24-29

Key verse: Luke 6:45a "A good person produces good from the good treasury of the inner self, but an evil person produces evil from the evil treasury of the inner self."

The boss came by and saw Calvin staring out the window and asked Calvin why he wasn't working. Calvin answered, "I didn't see you coming."

Apparently, this was Calvin's mindset- that one didn't have to work unless the boss was looking. His mindset directed his actions- or lack of them. The old saying for this was" garbage in; garbage out." So, if we are to act like Christians, it is important that we put Christian thoughts in first.

For the disciple Thomas, his mindset was one of seeing is believing. That's why, when the other disciples told him they had seen the risen savior, he said that unless he saw for himself, he wouldn't believe. This is very counter-productive to the concept of faith- which bases its power in the unforeseen. Indeed, Jesus says in john 20: 29b that" blessed are they who have not seen yet believe."

Some years ago, the letters "WWJD" were popular because they referred to the "what would Jesus do?" Movement. This concept forced one to re-evaluate possible courses of action in terms of the words and example of Jesus Christ. Yet, without proper grounding of our thought life in that which is good and pure, such reflection only serves to reveal our true natures: a man seeing a display of hats with "WWJD" on them asked the clerk what those letters meant. When she gave him the answer, he thought for a moment and said, "I'm sure Jesus wouldn't spend $17.95 for a hat like that."

Lessons on Choices – Par 7 of 7

Text: Mark 2:1-12

Key verse: proverbs 18:24 "One who has unreliable friends soon comes to ruin, but there is a friend who sticks closer than a brother."

The lone ranger and tonto were riding on a train when the lone ranger got thirsty and asked tonto to get him a drink. So tonto got up and returned in a couple of minutes with a glass of water. "Thank you, friend", the lone ranger said, then drank the water. A while later, the lone ranger got thirsty again and asked tonto to get him another glass of water. So tonto got up and left the train car. This time, however, it took tonto a half-hour to return. "What took you so long, my old friend?", the lone ranger asked. "Paleface sitting on well."

I guess you might say that the lone ranger didn't specify as to where tonto should get the water or you might say the two of them weren't such good friends, after all. In today's Bible lesson, the friendship of the crippled man's friends could not be questioned. For when they saw that it was impossible to get their friend in the door, they opened the roof to let him in. That's the kind of friends I want. How about you? Remember, your choice of friends is one of the most critical decisions you will ever make.

During times of war, friendships can become some of the strongest ties that a person will ever know. Such was the case of two guys who enlisted together, trained together and were shipped out to WW1 together. However, in one attack, the two friends became separated, and one of them was so badly wounded that he couldn't crawl back to safety. When the other friend found out he started to crawl out of his foxhole to rescue him but was pulled back by his sergeant, who explained, "it's too late for him. You'll only get yourself killed if you try it." But when the sergeant turned his back, out he went. A few minutes later he staggered back with his dead friend on his shoulder although he, too, was mortally wounded. "he's dead and you will soon be. What a waste!" "Not so, sarge," explained the dying soldier, "his last words were "I knew you'd come!"-a sacrifice that Jesus understood only too well.

REFLECTIONS

Christmas

Christmas has always been the highlight of my year. The presents were a part of this but Christmas for us was the whole experience-the smell of the tree, the presence of extended family and the Christmas music. Later it became the pervasive goodwill of the season. My faith, I'm sure, had something to do with this change in attitude - as well as my maturity. But the desire to give and make others happy represented a real change from a life that had previously been so focused on personal happiness.

Yet the fact that so many other people are so similarly affected cannot be easily dismissed. It seems to me that the old hymn "There's a Song in the Air" represents something of what we feel. Though some would call this magic, I feel it is more of a Spiritual reality. It is a reflection of the atmosphere that existed at that first Christmas so long ago. And that atmosphere can still be felt today in those who have outgrown those selfish inclinations. It is but another of the manifestations of the Love of God.

Lessons on Christmas - Part 1 of 7

Text:2 Timothy 3:1-5

Key verse: 2 Timothy 3:1-2b "There will be terrible times in the last days. People will be...,lovers of money,..."

A man driving a Yugo pulled up to a man driving a Rolls-Royce, rolled down his window and asked a couple of questions: Do you have a tv in there like my Yugo? Do you have a refrigerator like my Yugo? To which the man replied of course, my car is one of the most luxurious cars in the world, Of course I have those things. "Well, do you have a bed in there like my Yugo?" To that the Rolls –Royce driver sped away-not wanting to admit that he didn't have a bed aboard. But that question really bothered the Rolls-Royce driver so much that he did get a bed installed and then went looking for that Yugo He finally located it in the parking lot of the local Wal-Mart and knocked at the door. The windows were all steamed up so he knew someone was in there, so he knocked again. This time the Yugo driver stuck his head out of the window with his head covered in soap and asked what the guy wanted. The Rolls-Royce driver said, "I got a bed installed in my car now." And the Yugo driver replied, "You got me out of the shower to tell me that?"

Of course, this story is a little far-fetched, but it does have some relevance during the Christmas season. It would appear that the fastest-growing religion in the world is not Islam or Christianity but consumerism, which tends to rob us of the joy we should be having at this time of year from our celebration of the gift of the Christ-child. You see, at the heart of consumerism is dissatisfaction and discontent with what we have for something new or newer. And it has as its basic tenet is that love equals money.

That is, I will buy you that which is commensurate with my love for you.

This is not by any standard a new phenomenon, as today's scripture verse and text talk about it over 2,000 years ago. However, the cure for this ailment is found in emulating the life of the one who gave Christmas its original meaning. As we give more and more of our life to him, we will find the things of this world will lose their luster.

Lessons on Christmas - Part 2 of 7

Text and key verse: Luke 2:34 "…this child shall be rejected by many, and this to their undoing. But he will be the greatest joy of many others."

As one child was explaining to another, "Santa watches for naughty stuff in December, but God takes over the rest of the year." No wonder kids get confused. And they're not the only ones.

In today's lesson, Simeon has just blessed Mary and Joseph as they brought Jesus to the temple for dedication. They know that this child is special but have no idea how this will play out. As with all newborns, they imagined a normal childhood, a trade, and perhaps a family. But Simeon's words seemed to portend something quite different, and they were confused.

Christmas does come across rather confusingly to many. For example, a Pennsylvania court ruled some time ago that there could be no public display of the nativity scene unless there were secular displays with it.

Yet when the true Spirit of Christmas comes through, there is no confusion whatsoever. The love of God reflected in the Christ child becoming one of us is unmistakable. Two girls were walking down the street discussing what they hoped to get for Christmas, when they saw an old man on his hands and knees, pulling weeds from around an old oak tree. When they asked what he was doing, he explained that his mother had always loved her trees and her yard, and so, as a present to her memory, he did this every Christmas. He must have been quite a sight to these young girls, in his shabby clothes and garden gloves with the fingers out. So, they decided to earn some money doing chores and such so they would have enough money to buy the old guy a Christmas present. Two days before Christmas, then, they bought him some new gloves and a card, came to his house and sang some carols and presented his present to him, along with a pumpkin pie that one of their moms baked. When he saw what they had done, he cried tears of gratitude. He had been remembered at Christmas after all.

Lessons on Christmas - Part 3 of 7

Text: Matthew 2:1-12

Key verse: Matthew 2:2 "Where is he born king of the Jews?"

A reporter was interviewing an African safari guide and asked him, "Is it true that jungle animals won't harm you if you are carrying a torch?" He replied, "It depends on how fast you carry it."

In today's lesson, we discuss the three wise men and their trip in following not a torch but a star. There are not a lot of facts known about these men. History portrays them as kings or as astrologers from the east-perhaps from what would be known as Persia. Nevertheless, their focus on following this star was extraordinary as it took them a long time over unfamiliar terrain with much hardship and not a little expense to finally reach the object of their search. The question, then, for them would be this: was it worth it?

I guess that would depend on what was important to them. Was it their work? Was it the expectation of riches or fame? That we do not know. But a review of the literature of that day revealed a hopelessness for the future. Could it be the search for something of meaning that they hoped to find? Or could it be that God had heard their prayer and was leading them to the answer to that question?

Their quest, in that respect, then does not essentially differ from ours. We, too, search for meaning. The problem arises, though, when we focus on the wrong things.

In the spring of 1608, the settlers at Jamestown, Virginia thought they had found gold. So they forsook their efforts to plant crops, build buildings and do all the things that would prepare them for winter. By the time they sent the results of their "find" back to England, they found it was nothing other than iron pyrite, or "fools' gold". As a result, they would not have survived if the Indians had not kept them fed.

In retrospect, we know the 3 wise men had their focus on the right thing. We can too if we allow the Holy Spirit to lead us.

Lessons on Christmas - Part 4 of 7

Text and key verse: Luke 21:36a " Keep a constant watch."

A mother brought her 16-year-old daughter to the doctor with symptoms of morning sickness and weird food cravings. After examining the girl, the doctor advised that the woman's daughter was 4 months pregnant. "That's impossible!", claimed the mother. "She's never even been with a boy-have you, Jane?" No, mother, I've never even kissed a boy!" The doctor got up and went over to the window and stood there looking out for some time, not saying a word. "Is there something happening outside, doctor?" "No. It's just that the last time this happened, there was a star in the east and three wise men on camelback and I don't want to miss it this time."

The doctor, acted as if he was going to watch for the signs of another blessed event. From the end of the Old Testament, there was a 400-year period where many people were looking for signs of the Messiah's birth. Obviously, that was a long time to watch. And no doubt many gave up waiting. They failed to realize that God would be true to his word.

As we approach another holiday season, we are reminded that Jesus promised to come again. Yet since it's been over 2,000 years, many have given up the wait and act like he won't be coming. But we who know better know that we should be ready and watch for the signs of his return.

The apostle Paul wrote in 2 Timothy 3:1-7 about some of these signs. And we see many if not all of them in evidence-even at Christmas. What we must do as Christians, then, is to demonstrate that we have not given in to the Spirit of this world which says he's not coming but to display the fruits of the Spirit that says he is. After all, if we are to be a light and salt influence in the world, we have no choice but to reflect the Spirit of that first Christmas- that Spirit of quiet faithful watchfulness for the God who keeps his promises.

Lessons on Christmas - Part 5 of 7

Text and key verse: Luke 2:10 'Don't be afraid! I bring you the most joyful news ever announced, and it's for everyone!"

After an evening out on Christmas eve, the parents came home and were pleasantly surprised to find all their kids asleep. As the babysitter was leaving, however, she relayed one piece of incidental information-she had promised their son Sammy that he would get a pony in the morning if he went to sleep with the rest of the kids.

So much for their pleasant surprise! And so much for any Christmas Spirit that they might have had! Yet we know that Christmas joy is not dependent on external circumstances. This joy is the result of the gift of God that keeps on giving-the gift that cancels out our sin and gives us the hope of heaven.

Surely the angel that announced the birth of our redeemer had no idea what the celebration of Christmas would come to represent this far in the future but I believe the angel knew what that gift would represent to sinful mankind-which includes even the lowliest.

In Jesus' time, the lowliest would probably be considered the shepherds, who had the thankless task of watching sheep. It was a dirty job and one that kept them ceremonially unclean as well as physically unclean. Yet the good news expressed to them was received joyously. It didn't change their physical status, but it certainly improved their Spiritual one. And so, their joy was more in keeping with the real reason for the season.

More importantly, the shepherds realized that this was news too good to keep to themselves and began to spread these good tidings to all who would hear. This is now our faithful portion- we who know that the joy of Christmas is not to be found under a Christmas tree surrounded by gifts. Let us then be faithful to the task set before us so that all can have this same joy.

Lessons on Christmas - Part 7 of 7

Text and key verse: Luke 6:38 "Give and it shall be given unto you."

A wife of an army colonel had just landed after an all-night flight with her 9 children all under the age of 11at the base where her husband was now stationed in Germany. Collecting their luggage they now entered the customs area where a young customs official stood amazed. "Do all these children and luggage belong to you?", he asked. "Yes, they're all mine", she replied. So, the customs official began his interrogation: "Ma'am, do you have any weapons, contraband or illegal drugs in your possession?" "Sir," she replied, "if I had any of those things, I would have used them before now."

Most parents have at one time or another, probably felt that way. But that does not mean they loved their children any less. Indeed, they no doubt would have given their own lives up for them if that was what was required. This was learned behavior picked up from the love and care first shown to them- a love first demonstrated at Christmas by our Heavenly Father.

How we seem to lose sight of that is a mystery. But every once in a while, we get reminded: a young guy noticed an older woman pulled off the road looking at her flat tire and pulled over to help. He had her wait in her car while he changed her tire. She was greatly appreciative and offered to pay. But, in spite of how much he and his wife needed the money he turned her down, advising her to put it forward. Later on, the lady pulled into a diner for lunch. She was waited on by a very pregnant young waitress, who was very kind and attentive to her older customer. When the lady was ready to leave, she thought of the young man's admonition to pass it forward and gave the waitress a $100-dollar bill and quietly left before the waitress could return. Not only that, but when the waitress returned with the change, she found a note with 4-$100-dollar bills inside. The note read: you don't owe me anything. I've been where you are, too. I'm just passing along something nice that someone did for me." That night, when the waitress went home, she told her husband of the windfall, which eased his mind considerably. He just didn't know that it was his good deed that started it.

REFLECTIONS

The Church

As I've stated before, church was not an option for The Dornan family of Monongahela, Pennsylvania. Church for us was a beautiful brick edifice located just a few Blocks down the main street. It was a Presbyterian church and worship was quite often a very solemn affair. We would have been shocked to hear someone exclaim "Praise God!" Or "amen!". One just did not do that kind of thing there. Now, not all the Dornan's stayed Presbyterian, but the ones who left definitely had an adjustment to make. I know, because I was the one who left. I needed to learn that church was not a Building but a people, that church did not just involve one's head, but one's heart and feet and hands. I needed to learn that church was not a duty but an opportunity to fellowship with friends, share mutual joys and concerns and be cheerful givers of our time, talent and resources. Over the years, I attended catholic, Baptist, and Pentecostal churches and found that each had important contributions to make to my understanding and Christian growth. And, as long as the worship of God and the example of Christ is lifted up, the church can take many acceptable forms.

Lessons on the Church – Part 1 of 7

Text: John 4:4-42

Key verse: 1 Thessalonians 5:11a "Therefore, encourage one another and build each other up,"

Many years ago, a fire broke out in a small church in the Midwest and almost everybody from the town came out to watch. Included in that group was the church's pastor and a member of the church that had not attended services in some time. Thinking that he might embarrass the absent parishioner into coming back, the pastor called out to him and said, "Haven't seen you in a while!" Not to be outdone, the absent member retorted, "It's been a while since I've seen our church on fire."

You might say if your intent is to embarrass, be ready to receive some embarrassment, yourself. Similarly, if your intent is to encourage (and I believe this should be one of the church's main goals!), then be prepared to receive some encouragement yourself.

In today's Bible lesson, the woman at the well, Jesus encounters a Samaritan woman whose lifestyle left something to be desired. But instead of criticizing her, Jesus encourages her with news too good to keep to herself. Often times today, Christians feel overwhelmed with the enormity of the task of making a difference. Yet Jesus demonstrates that we can make a difference- one person at a time.

When Cheryl Prewitt was just 4 years old, she hung around her father's small country grocery store. And, each day when the milkman came, he would address her as "My little Miss America." Cheryl would giggle at that comment but eventually came to dream of that possibility. In time, then, that dream became a goal and finally a reality in 1980, when she became "Miss America."

Clearly, not all such goals are attainable, but encouragement makes them possible. More importantly, for the person who feels the Christian walk is just as difficult, our encouragement just might make the difference.

Lessons on the Church – Part 2 of 7

Text: Matthew 25:31-46

Key verse: 1 peter 3:8 "Finally, all of you, live in harmony with one another; be sympathetic, love as brothers, be compassionate and humble."

A little church needed a pastor but had little money. So, they hired a retired pastor and moved him into the church's tiny parsonage. The first Sunday there, the old pastor preached a good 30-minute sermon, for which the elders of the church were most grateful. Some of them even came by the next day to see how things were in the parsonage, the old pastor said that everything was fine except for the upstairs bathroom-which was too small for he and his wife to get ready at the same time. The elders said they'd look into it but didn't. The next week the old pastor preached another good 30-minute sermon-which the elders liked. And again, they sent a small delegation to check how the pastor was making out at the parsonage. Once again, the pastor advised of the bathroom and once again the elders failed to follow through. The next Sunday, the old pastor preached for 2 hours and a half. This time the elders were very upset and confronted the old pastor after the service about it. The pastor was very apologetic about it but explained that because the bathroom was so small he had inadvertently put in his wife's dentures instead of his own. And once his wife got talking, she didn't know when to quit. The next week contractors came in to start the bathroom renovations.

Clearly, it was unfortunate that the pastor had to make his point that way, but the church should have been more attentive to the pastor's need. It shouldn't have come to that. On the other hand, when a church acts with love and compassion, not only is the pastor pleased, but the church and the community is blessed. According to today's Bible lesson, the compassion of the church will someday be revealed for all to see and will be based on its service to the least of these.

Lessons on the Church- Part 3 of 7

Text: Luke 10: 25-37

Key verse: john 13:35 "By this everyone will know that you are my disciples, if you love one another."

A couple was going out for the evening. Toward that end, they had made all the arrangements so that there would be no distractions. But when the taxi pulled up to take them and they opened the door, the cat shot back into the house. Since they didn't want the cat in all night, the husband went back in to put it back out. The wife, on the other hand, didn't want the taxi driver to think the house would be unoccupied all night, explained to him that her husband was just going back in to say good night to her mother. A few minutes later, the husband gets into the cab and says, "Sorry I'm late. The old thing was hiding under the bed and I had to poke her with a coat hanger to get her out."

"What nice people!", the taxi driver must have thought. Not! Not telling the truth can get one in that kind of situation. Yet, it's even worse when the church is perceived that way. So, we must be prepared to "go the extra mile" to make sure they don't.

Such is the case with our Bible story today, the Good Samaritan. In this story, a man provides help to a complete stranger and then provides resources for whatever additional help is needed. As a result, his kindness is forever remembered in God's word and given as an example of what being a neighbor really is.

This is not Rocket Science, friends, it's just the natural outcome of having compassion for one another. A woman who was hard of hearing called who she thought was her daughter. When a lady answered the phone, the woman assumed it was her daughter and asked how she was. "Terrible", she said, "My head's splitting and the kids are driving me up the wall." So, the woman says, "Go lie down. I'll be right over to make lunch for you, help clean the house and take the kids for a walk. But, by the way, how's Harold?" "Who's Harold?" "Harold, your husband." "My husband's not Harold!" "Oh, I must have dialed the wrong number!" "Does that mean you're not coming over?"

Lessons on the Church- Part 4 of 7

Text:1 Corinthians 3:1-9

Key verse: 1 Corinthians 12:20 "As it is, there are many parts, but one body."

A famous organist was giving a recital on a pump organ- the power of which being supplied by a young boy. All was going well until the young boy stuck his head out from behind the organ to say," I guess we're doing pretty good, aren't we?" "What do you mean "we"?" retorted the famous organist. A few minutes later, in the middle of a beautiful part of the recital, the organ suddenly stopped playing- at which time the young boy's face again popped out from behind the organ. With a big smile on his face, he asked, "Now do you see what I meant by "we"?"

In the church, there are many duties- but no unimportant ones. This seemed to escape the attention of many in the church at Corinth at the time of Paul's ministry there. People there tended to argue about many things and that arguing almost split the church into many factions. Thus, Paul came up with his famous body part analogy- to show how the different parts of the church depended on each other. This teaching is also critical for the modern-day church. We all still need to work together.

During the Nazi occupation of Paris in WW2, a husky stormtrooper stepped into a subway car and tripped headlong over the umbrella of a little old lady that sat by the door. After picking himself up, he launched into a tirade of abuse against the old woman and then bolted from the car at the next station. When he was gone, the passengers burst into spontaneous applause for her. "I know it isn't much", she replied to the crowd," but he's the 6th one I brought down today!"

Lessons on the Church- Part 5 of 7

Text: 1 Corinthians 12:1-11

Key verse: 1 Corinthians 12:7 "The Spirit's presence is shown in some way in each person for the good of all."

When the little boy saw his uncle at Thanksgiving, he thanked him profusely for the harmonica he received from him last Christmas. "Well, thank you!", said the uncle, "do you play it pretty well by now?" "Not really", said the little boy, "My mom pays me a dollar a day not to play it during the day and my dad pays me a dollar a day not to play it at night."

Apparently, the little boy did not have a gift for playing the harmonica. And, as with the other Spiritual gifts, when someone has it, you know it. To make use of one's Spiritual gifts in church, then, is crucial to the church's effectiveness. Of course, such gifts can be used outside of church, but the original intent for their use was for worship purposes. This is clearly expressed in today's Bible lesson. However, much too commonly, a person tries to serve God without the appropriate gifts. When that happens, the church is not blessed and the person experiences "burnout".

A story is told of a man from a remote 3rd-world country coming to the big city for the 1st time. He was amazed at many things but most of all by the electric lights he saw there. So, not having much money but desiring to take something of his experience home, he bought some bulbs, switches and sockets. When he returned home, he immediately started to string the lights all over his house. When the villagers asked what he was doing, he just smiled and said to wait until dark. When darkness fell, he turned on the switches, but nothing happened. You see, he didn't know you needed electricity for the lights to work.

Similarly, without the Holy Spirit, little happens in worship that is truly meaningful. That's why we must help others to find their gift and use it in church so we can all be illuminated by the blessing of God.

Lessons on the Church- Part 6 of 7

Text: Colossians 3: 12-17

Key verse: Colossians 3:14 "And over all these virtues, put on love, which binds them all together in perfect unity."

A burglar broke into a house that he thought was empty. But when he walked into the bedroom, he saw a man and his wife, sitting up in bed, holding on to one another for dear life. Surprised, the burglar got out his gun and pointed it at them. "What's your name?" Demanded the burglar of the woman. "Elizabeth", she said. "You're lucky, "said the burglar, "My mother's name was Elizabeth, so I'd never shoot anyone by that name. "Then he asked the man his name." Harry", he said. "But everybody calls me Elizabeth."

My guess is that he hoped to be associated with that name so he wouldn't be shot. There is not so much pressure on us to be associated with the word "church", but it would be wonderful if we wanted to be as much as that man. Yet before one makes that decision, it is important that they know what attributes are included in the description of church. It is found in our Bible lesson today. These attributes are tolerance, peace, songfulness, forgiveness, thankfulness, Bible proficiency and, especially, love. Of course, a person may be stronger in some of these than others, but they are perceived as trying to grow in all these areas.

American frontiersman tried to spread as much of these attributes as he could in addition to planting apple trees. As he had no home, he would stay with kindly settlers along the way. And he would pay close attention to that family's needs. Then, when he'd leave, he'd tear out a page of his Bible that dealt with that need and give it to them. In the same way, in our travels, we should leave the people we touch our love demonstrated by our actions.

Lessons on the Church- Part 7 of 7

Text: Hebrews 10:22-25

Key verse: 1 Timothy 5:20 "Those who sin is to be rebuked publicly, so that the others will take warning."

Mrs., Smith, the Sunday School teacher, saw one of her students making ugly faces at another student and decided to take him aside privately to correct that behavior. She said, "Now, Johnny, my mother used to tell me not to make faces at other people because my face would stay that way." "Well, Mrs. Smith," said Johnny," you can't say you weren't warned."

You might say little Johnny didn't get the message. And, as the church, some people might not get the message of our attempts at correction. But that doesn't relieve the church of its duty to provide a warning.

In the Old Testament, prophets had the duty of warning God's people about sinful practices. And, clearly, they were often despised for this practice. Nevertheless, these prophets were more afraid of God's wrath than they were of people's indignation. Such was the case with the prophet, Nathan. When David, the king, seduced Bathsheba and arranged for her husband's death, Nathan was given the responsibility to confront David about it. Please understand, however, that as despicable an act as this was, the king had absolute authority to do as he pleased and could have Nathan killed as well. But Nathan was faithful to his calling, confronted David with his sin, which caused remorse and confession on David's part.

Perhaps we would do well to learn from the example that geese give in sounding the alarm to the flock under their care. If you've ever watched them, there are always 2 or more geese that act as guards while the other geese are feeding. Should someone get too close, they will honk at the perceived intruder until they leave, or they will sound the alarm to take off. Their failure to do so will result in a severe penalty as the other geese will attack and kill the erstwhile guarding geese. In the final analysis, our guarding function as church is no less crucial.

REFLECTIONS

Discipleship

The word "disciple" was not in a working part of my vocabulary, early on. I knew that Jesus' closest followers were called disciples, but I did not think that word could apply to me. Indeed, until I heard the word defined to mean "Being the hands and feet of Christ", I didn't think the term could apply to any person living today. Yet, if we use this definition, many could be called disciples. Actually, it is even rather easy to be one when under the influence of the Holy Spirit. It is merely allowing Christ's love for others to flow through us. To the extent we can do this, we can all be disciples!

Lessons on Discipleship – Part 1 of 7

Text: Exodus 17:8-13

Key verse: 1 Corinthians 3:6 "I have planted, Apollos watered, but God gave the increase."

A young man shopping at the grocery store noticed a little old lady who seemed to be following him closely. He didn't think much about it, however, until she moved in just ahead of him at the check-out and turned around to speak to him. She said," I hope I didn't make you uncomfortable by staring at you so much, but it's just because you look so much like my late son." "That's ok," said the young man. "Now, I know this may sound silly, but I wonder if you could call out "Good-bye, Mom" as I leave the store? It would make me feel so good." Thinking that it wasn't too much to ask, he agreed. So, after she checked out, he called out "Good-Bye, Mom", and she waved and smiled and continued on her way. When he went to check-out, the clerk said, "That'll be $121." "No way, "the young man said," I only got 5 items." "That's true," said the clerk, "but your mother said you'd be paying for hers, too."

She had tricked him into taking responsibility for her bill. But there's no escaping our responsibility in terms of our discipleship. That we must do ourselves. And that starts with our understanding that, without our help, people could be "going out into eternity without Jesus as their Lord and Savior. "Yet, we don't have to do it all ourselves. We just have to do our part. In today's lesson, the defeat of the Amalekites, 4 people had distinct responsibilities. And, if any slacked off, the tide of battle quickly turned. Implicit in this, however, is the assumption that everyone knows their part. That isn't always the case.

A hospital patient accidentally knocked over a glass of water, making a spill on the floor. Not wanting to fall, the patient asked for help to clean it up. But, neither housekeeping or nurses' aid thought it was their responsibility. The matter could not be settled until the patient, then, spilled the whole pitcher on the floor. How much easier it would be, in all things, to simply do what needs doing.

Lessons on Discipleship – Part 2 of 7

Text: Luke 5:1-11

Key verse: Luke 5:10 "Don't be afraid. From now on you will be fishing for people."

The barnyard animals were discussing how committed they were to the farmer's success. The cow said, "without my milk, the farmer would be sunk. Now that's commitment. The chicken then said, "you're not more committed than I am. Without my eggs, the farmer couldn't make it, either. "That's nothing!" exclaimed the pig. "I give bacon and ham. You can't get more committed than that!"

During Jesus's first year of ministry, the call he made to follow was only for a short term of duty. But now in his second year, he was looking for those who would follow all the way. And so he put Peter, Andrew, James and John to the test- asking them to go fishing again after they just put in from an unsuccessful night's work. This time, however, they could hardly bring all the fish in. This showed them all they needed to know. So, when they brought their boats to shore, they dropped everything to follow him.

They were sure. But not all people have that kind of certainty. And, as a result, they often go through dry periods that test their devotion. Such was the case with a guy who had gone into sales. After some initial success, his sales started to go down while his anxiety went up. Finally, he decided to tell his boss he was quitting. When he said that to his boss, the boss said No, you're not." And why not? "asked the salesman. "Because you can't get out of a business you never got into!" The salesman realized his boss was right-he had not fully committed to doing the job in the first place.

In our service to God, the same is true. If we play at discipleship, the results will soon frustrate and discourage us. You see, who the Spirit calls, he also empowers. And with that power, we cannot fail.

Lessons on Discipleship – Part 3 of 7

Text: Acts 2:42-47

Key verse: 1 Thess. 5:11a "So continue encouraging each other and building each other up."

After reading a book on marital relations, the wife sighed and said, "Sometimes women don't want their men to solve their problems. Sometimes it's better if he just puts his arms around her and tells her everything will be ok." The next morning the wife's car had a flat tire. Her husband checked it out and assured her that everything would be ok, gave her a big hug, then went off to work. She left out the need to agree as to when those times were.

When we look at the church in the early days after the infilling of the Holy Spirit (our lesson for today), we see a sort of "honeymoon" period. It was a wonderful time of growth- for many reasons. First, there were the miracles to attract people's attention. Second, there was the widespread practice of sharing goods and services, so that no one was in need. And third, most importantly, there was the love expressed toward others in many tangible ways. Now, whether it was all these things or some special dispensation of the Holy Spirit, there was also a Spirit of agreement among the believers as to what needed to be done, who was to do it and in what priority that the church has not seen since. It was a "climate" of building up hope, reaching out to the least and last, of patience and attention to needs and a climate that looked out for and encouraged the best in others.

That Spirit can be found today but not in large supply or concentration. That's why we are touched when we encounter it. A young lady walked into a fabric shop and asked for some noisy, rustling, white material. The shop clerk found 2 bolts of that kind of material but had to ask why she asked for it in that way. She replied, "I'm making a wedding gown that my fiancé' will hear-because he's blind. When I walk down the aisle, I want him to know I've arrived at the altar, so he won't be embarrassed.

Lessons on Discipleship – Part 4 of 7

Text: Acts 9:26-27

Key verse: Acts 11:24a "Barnabas responded in this way because he was a good man, whom the Holy Spirit had endowed with exceptional faith."

As the passengers settled in for their flight, the flight attendant announced, "We'd like you folks to help us welcome our new co-pilot, who'll be performing his first commercial landing for us today. Be sure to give him a round of applause when we come to a stop." The plane made an extremely bumpy landing, bouncing hard 2 or 3 times before taxiing into the gate. Even so, the passengers all applauded. Once again, the flight attendant came on the intercom," Thank you for flying with us. And don't forget to let our co-pilot know which landing you liked best."

Regardless of our station in life, we all need encouragement. This certainly was the apostle Paul's need after his conversion. As today's Bible lesson indicates, the disciples were all afraid of him- doubting his true conversion. But Barnabas helped the disciples accept Paul as a brother in faith and helped Paul get started on his life of Godly service.

When the great painter, Benjamin West, was a young boy, he tried to paint a picture of his sister while his mother was away and made a terrible mess. When his mother got home and saw the mess, she remarked about the quality of the picture itself, and then kissed him. That kiss made a great difference in his life as he was reported to have said later in life, "With that kiss, I became a painter."

Let us then be encouragers of people's gifts and graces whenever we can. For who knows? If we are more like Barnabas, maybe we can find more Paul's.

Lessons on Discipleship- Part 5 of 7

Text: Philippians 4:1-9

Key verse: Philippians 4:9a "Practice these things: whatever you learned, received, heard or saw in us."

A little league baseball coach was talking to one of his players, "Do you know what co-operation is? Do you know what the word "team" means? Do you understand that we lose or win as a team? That means that when you are called out on strikes that you don't argue or cuss out the umpire. Do you understand, son?" The little boy nodded. "Good", said the coach, "Now go explain that to your mother."

At one time or another, our lives have been influenced by a coach. That may or may not have been a good thing, depending on the attitude and example of the coach. Nevertheless, we, as disciple-making Christians, need to be the best coaches we can be.

The apostle Paul realized this and so advised the churches that he planted to learn from his example. His example, then, exemplified the following: to make people do things they don't want in order to achieve the things they do want, to believe in a person even when they don't believe in themselves.

Probably one of the greatest coaches this country has ever seen was a man by the name of Knute Rockne. He, as much as one person ever could, made Notre Dame football synonymous with excellence. But his means to greatness was not always understood. For example, there was a writer for the local newspaper who consistently made negative comments about the team that made the players angry. But when they came to the coach about him, he would just say that the best way to get back at that writer was to go out and prove him wrong. What he didn't say was that he, himself, was that writer.

Now you might say that that is all well and good but that you are not a coach. And that would be where you would be wrong. Whenever you have been in a situation where you influenced another person, you were a coach. And, friend, your coaching can make all the difference-even to one!

Lessons on Discipleship- Part 6 of 7

Text: Romans 10:14

Key verse: Romans 10:9 "If you confess with your mouth that Jesus is Lord and believe with your heart that God hath raised him from the dead, thou shalt be saved."

Billy Graham, the famous evangelist, wanted to send a letter but did not know where the post office was in the town in which he was preaching. So, he asked a little boy who was walking by, and the boy gave him directions. Billy thanked the boy and invited him to his crusade that night in that city. He said he'd tell him how to get to heaven. When someone asked him what the great evangelist said, he replied, "He said he'd tell me how to get to heaven, but I doubt that he knows since he didn't know where the post office was."

The fact that someone might not think that I have anything of value to share with them must not stop me from sharing the good news of the gospel. This is our obligation, but it is their life. I mean we would want to do what we could if we had the medical ability to save a dying person, so why do we shy away from giving them the words of Spiritual life? Our scripture lesson for the day asks the crucial question here: How can they hear without a preacher? We cannot assume people will hear it from someone else.

When Henry Ford purchased a rather large life insurance policy, it became big news in the local newspaper. A friend of Ford's, who was an insurance broker, heard the news and visited Ford to ask if it were true. When Ford said it was, the old friend asked him why he didn't buy the policy from him. And ford replied, "Because you never asked me."

We cannot afford to make the same mistake with people's eternal destiny at stake. After all, friends don't let friends go to hell.

Lessons on Discipleship- part 7 of 7

Text: 1 Corinthians 15:3-4

Key verse: Acts 1:8 "You will receive power when the Holy Spirit has come upon you, and you will be my witnesses in Jerusalem, in all Judea and Samaria, and to the end of the world."

A young lawyer representing a railroad company who was being sued by a farmer for taking his prized cow was able to get the farmer to settle out of court for half of what he originally wanted. And so, after the farmer signed the check, he decided to "rub in" the farmer's naivete by telling him he really had no case and couldn't have possibly won the case in court. The farmer then responded, "Well, I'll tell you, young fella, I was worried about winning the case myself when my cow showed up this morning."

The lawyer thought he had news too good to keep to himself-until he heard the farmer's news. But, for us, we need not worry about better news-there isn't any! It's a little like the situation that a pastor experienced walking down the hospital wing where he planned to visit a sick parishioner. A man came up to him that he did not know with tears streaming down his face, saying, "She's going to make it-she's going to be ok!" That's the kind of good news I'm talking about.

And that's the Spirit in which the apostle Paul shared the gospel with the church in Corinth. But please understand, because Paul could not stay with that church after getting them started, they allowed other teachers to influence and dilute his original preaching-making it something very different. That church also let other, less important issues divide them. That's why he wrote to them as he did- trying to reiterate his original message.

You see, although we do our part, we cannot believe it and live it for them. We must depend on other people in the church giving them the same message. If they don't, how can we expect it to "stick"?

REFLECTIONS

Easter

Growing up, Easter was all about chocolate bunnies, jellybeans and coloring eggs. Usually, we also got something new to wear to go to church on Easter Sunday. But as far as any religious connotation, it never seemed to get much mention. For me, the religious part got lost in the candy- almost like Christmas got lost in the presents. Maybe my parents did not want to put in the effort or were of the opinion that we were too young to "get it." Nevertheless, I did start to "get it" when I started to get serious about my faith. I began to see Easter as the highlight of the Christian year- the defining moment of Christianity. As I taught Sunday School when my kids were young, I emphasized the religious part of Easter. But I also made sure they got their Easter candy and their Easter egg hunt.

Today, I'm not sure what happens in most homes at Easter, Christian or otherwise. My guess is that religious education is practically non-existent regarding Easter or any part of the Christian year. This must change!

Lessons on Easter - Part 1 of 7

Text: Matthew 20:25-28

Key verse: Philippians 2:3 "Do nothing out of selfish ambition or vain conceit, but in humility consider others as better than yourselves."

The small plane was carrying 3 passengers: a Boy Scout, a pastor and a man who considered himself a brilliant statesman. The pilot came back and warned of an impending crash and added, "We only have 3 parachutes. I must take one so I can report the accident to the proper authorities". And, taking one of the parachutes, he jumped out. Next the brilliant statesman stood up and said that he had to take one of the parachutes as he had a great more to contribute to society. And he took a parachute and jumped out. Next the pastor stood up and said to the Boy Scout," I've lived a long, good life and yours is just at its beginning, so you take the last parachute and God bless you." "There's still 2 parachutes, pastor. The brilliant statesman took my knapsack instead of a parachute". No doubt the brilliant statesman would make an impact-just not the kind he envisioned.

There are many references in the Bible to our need for humility. Even so, even the people who spent the most time with Jesus-his disciples- needed to be reminded of it often. In today's lesson, the mother of James and John came to Jesus, requesting the honor of their sitting on Jesus' left and right hands when he came into his kingdom. This made the rest of the disciples very angry-either because they didn't think of it first or because they were offended at their ambition. In response, Jesus teaches them all about the need for having a servant's mind and heart- as was his example-particularly at Easter.

In the story behind the sculpture "The Praying Hands", Albrecht Durer and a friend drew straws to determine which of them would support the other while going to art school. When Durer finished his studies, his friend could not go for his hands were too damaged from working. Yet the friend was not angry but happy for him.

Lessons on Easter - Part 2 of 7

Text: Matthew 21:1-11

Key verse: Matthew 21:9c "Blessed is he who comes in the name of the Lord."

After the Sunday service, a woman came up to the pastor to tell him what a nice sermon he gave. The pastor responded, "Don't thank me, thank God." The woman thought a moment, then said, "I thought of that. But it wasn't that good." She was just doing what was expected. Thus, it was not real praise but the praise of conformity.

In today's lesson, Jesus makes his triumphant return into Jerusalem to loud shouts of hosanna from the people. But Jesus, knowing the difference between true praise and the praise of conformity, took it all in with "a grain of salt." He knew how quickly things could change.

In our world today, the darkness of sin appears to be the rule rather than the exception. The fear for us, then, is that Godly people get used to the darkness. It is a lot like going into a dark movie theatre when we are not acquainted with the lack of light. We allow ourselves to get accustomed to the darkness. However, the dim moral and Spiritual insight of this world is not the standard by which we should walk. We should dare to make a difference-to let our light shine. This is true praise and not the praise of conformity.

Lessons on Easter - Part 3 of 7

Text: Matthew 28:1-10

Key verse: Matthew 28:6 "He is not here, he has risen,..."

A man was driving down the road when, unexpectedly, a bunny carrying a basket full of eggs and candy, jumped out in front of him. The man tried to swerve to avoid an accident, but too late. He knocked the rabbit to the side of the road, with eggs and candy smashed up everywhere. The man pulled his car over off the road and got out and began to cry. A woman, who was traveling the same road, saw the man crying off the side of the road, pulled up and asked him the trouble. "I killed the Easter bunny and now there won't be Easter! What will I do?" "I know," said the woman, who pulled over, opened her trunk, got out a can of something, and sprayed it all over the rabbit. Miraculously, the rabbit got up, gathered what was left of the eggs and candy, waved and hopped off. Obviously relieved and in shock, the man asked the woman what she sprayed on the rabbit. She gave him the can, which said "Hair Spray; restores life to dead hair."

The man thought this was the end of the Easter bunny. Similarly, Jesus' disciples thought that his crucifixion was the end of him. So did the religious leaders, who precipitated his demise. No one could come back from the dead, could they? Yet, if Jesus could, then this must mean that he must be who he said he was. And if they caused his death, it certainly could not go well for them, could it? This type of thinking is typical for us humans because our thinking tends to be limited and finite. But, for God, this was just the beginning.

What do we expect of God? How large can we think? In 1947, a professor at the university of Chicago offered to teach an advanced seminar in astrophysics. When only 2 students signed up, everyone thought he'd cancel. But he didn't. He taught the class; the students learned so well that, 10 years later, they won the Nobel prize in physics. Not what anyone expected. And so, it is with God. Who would think that God would care enough to send his only son to die for us while we were yet sinners? But he did, praise God!

Lessons on Easter- part 4 of 7

Text: Luke 23:44-24:6

Key verse: Luke 24:5b "Why do ye seek the living among the dead?"

A police dog responds to an ad for an opening for work at the FBI. He is told that he must be able to type 60 words a minute. He immediately sits down at a computer screen and types 80 words a minute. He is then told that he must pass a physical examination and complete an obstacle course, which he does with flying colors. Finally, he is told that he must be bi-lingual, to which he says, "Meow!"

Obviously, this story does not meet our expectations on many levels. Yet the news of Jesus' resurrection is greeted similarly by many who experienced it. We, who are called to have faith, seem to be seriously lacking in it. But we are not alone. The women who came to Jesus' tomb, expected to find a dead man-in spite of his teachings. So they are scolded by the angels there; "Why do you seek the living among the dead?" Clearly, this reprimand is also leveled at us. How often do we react defeated when we have every reason to hope.

On a busy street with people hurrying to get to work, Set a familiar sight-an old lady selling flowers and boutonnieres to any who would stop. One day, a man decided to stop to talk to her, imagining that her job would not put her in a pleasant mood. Yet she was very cheerful, so the man asked her why. "Why shouldn't I be?", she replied." Well, I'm guessing that you've had a lot of people ignore you or be rude to you over the years", he said. "You can't reach my age and not have some of those things. But it's just like Jesus and Good Friday." "What do you mean?" "When Jesus was crucified on Good Friday, everyone thought that was it. But then, 3 days later, Easter came and his resurrection. So, when I have troubles, I wait 3 days and things usually get straightened out."

Lessons on Easter - Part 5 of 7

Text: John 12: 12-19

Key verse: John 12: 18 "Many people, because they had heard that he had given this miraculous sign (raising of Lazarus), went out to meet him."

A man went into a restaurant and asked the manager if he could have a free meal if he showed the manager something truly amazing. "We'll see," said the manager, "I've seen some amazing things in my life." So, the man gets out a hamster and a small piano and the hamster starts singing "Amazing Grace". "Not bad," said the manager, "but I'll have to see some more." "No problem," said the man. Then he got out a frog who starts singing "The Old Rugged Cross". When one of the other diners at the restaurant hears the frog, he offers the man $1,000 for it, - which he readily accepts. "Ok", said the manager, "you can have the free meal, but I think you've made a big mistake in selling the frog." "Not really," said the man," the hamster is also a ventriloquist."

People are naturally drawn to the unusual. And, to a certain extent, people were drawn to Jesus for the same reason. Yet there is a difference between coming to Jesus out of curiosity and coming to him out of need. As is related in the key verse, Jesus had raised Lazarus from the dead prior to Palm Sunday and so many people came to see the one who had done this great thing. Jesus knew the difference and was not impressed. His hope, however, was to give them another reason to pay attention to what he said and did. Perhaps, then, Jesus did not really care why the people came, as long as they came. Maybe we can use a similar approach.

A young lady was going to meet her boyfriend's parents for the first time and was anxious to make a good impression. So, when she looked at herself, she noticed that her black pumps were a tad dingy, so she wiped them off with the same paper towel she used to blot her breakfast bacon. She turned out to be a big hit with the parents and also their dog, who hung around her all night. When she left, they noted the dog's attention as evidence of her acceptability.

Lessons on easter- part 6 of 7

Text: Hebrews 12:1-3

Key verse: Hebrews 12:1c "…and let us run with perseverance the race marked out for us."

A truck driver was sitting at a booth of a diner, eating his lunch when 3 mean guys from a motorcycle gang came into the diner-looking for trouble. They sat down at his booth. One took the driver's hamburger and ate it. Another took the driver's pie and ate it. While another took the driver's coffee and drank it. The truck driver said nothing, got up from the booth and went out the door while the motorcycle guys laughed and laughed. When the waitress came over to their booth, one of the motorcycle guys remarked, "Not much of a man, was he?" The waitress replied, "And not much of a driver, either, as he ran over your 3 bikes."

I'm guessing that if the truck driver had been in the business long enough, he would have encountered a few roughnecks along the way. You might say that it comes with the territory. Nevertheless, for most of us travelers, we keep our eyes on the final destination. And, although that's not a bad thing, we miss something important if we don't also enjoy the journey.

Today's lesson, taken from Hebrews, advises us to run our race-to travel our life journey- with perseverance as we have many heavenly people watching us. If that is indeed the case, we should want to do our best all the way through-and not just at the finish line. And, more importantly, we have many people we can help to run their race, as well. Figuratively, there are people who have stopped running or who have fallen and can't get back up that need some help- our help. So, as Christians, it is about the journey as well as the destination.

Jesus, our example, touched many people along the way. But he did so with an eye not to just his finish line, but also to ours. Likewise, there are many that could use our help to get back on track. Friend, Easter may not be your finish line, but it might be for some. Will you help them to get there?

Lessons on Easter- Part 7 of 7

Text: John 13 and 14

Key verse: John 13:7 "You do not realize now what I am doing, but later you will understand."

A Sunday School teacher asked her class of young children what happened at Easter to make it so special. One little boy suggested that it was the holiday when the family got together and ate turkey and watched football. Then another little boy suggested it was the holiday when the family put up a tree and people gave each other gifts. Finally, a little girl in the class suggested that it was the holiday where we talk about Jesus' death on a cross and then his being put in a tomb. "Finally, someone knows!", thought the teacher, who then asked, "What happened next?" "Well", said the little girl, "then everyone gathers by the tomb and waits for Jesus to come out. If he sees his shadow, though, there will be 6 more weeks of winter."

If that's the best our kids could do with Easter, I wonder what they'd say about Maundy Thursday? Jesus was aware that his time on earth was drawing to a close and he was anxious to make these last moments count with his disciples. He knew they were too self-centered to be effective and so he washed their feet, just as a servant would do. He introduces the Holy Spirit to help them know they won't be doing his work on their own-that the Holy Spirit will empower them. You might call these remarks Jesus' famous last words. But in living with these men for so long, he knew what they needed, and he loved them too much to leave them ignorant.

Similarly, our lack of humility and failure to use the Holy Spirit's power are our worst problems as well. Failure to learn these two points can be dangerous to our future Christian witness. This concept is illustrated by a story that is told about how Di Vinci's "Last Supper" was painted. Di Vinci actually used the same model for both Jesus and judas Iscariot but didn't realize it because of the model's fall from grace. Without humility and the Holy Spirit's empowerment, we would fare no better.

REFLECTIONS

Election Day

In a free country such as ours, people can freely complain about how they are governed, among other things. But if they don't exercise their right to vote, it seems to me that they have nothing to complain about. And oftentimes Christians complain about government but have similarly abstained from doing anything to make it better, including running for office or working on behalf of a candidate who they support. As Christians increasingly find themselves in a minority position, this inaction cannot long continue. We have a voice that must be heard. If it is not, we cannot be surprised when Christian candidates get mocked and discredited because of their faith. And we cannot be surprised that issues contrary to our faith are proposed and passed. Yet one other issue is even more critical. We are charged in various places in the Bible to set a good example for our children. If we are apathetic about our voting or about participating in government, what does that say to our kids? For their sake we must do better.

Lessons on Election Day - Part 1 of 7

Text and key verse: Proverbs 16:33 "Make your motions and cast your votes, but God has the final say."

Two young engineers were applying for a position at a computer company. And since they had similar qualifications, the HR director had them take a quiz. When the results were tabulated, it was found that they had each missed only one question-the same question. The HR director called the first engineer in and told him that the company was going to hire the other applicant, even though they had both missed just one question. "How can you do that if we both missed the same question?" "Actually, it was quite easy: he put down I don't know, and you put down neither do I."

Integrity is still important, apparently. Yet today we see little of it-which makes it hard to know who to vote for. Although today's key verse tells us God is in control, it is still important for us to make an informed choice rather than a "shot in the dark. To that end, then, it is important for us to ask ourselves two questions: "Which candidate is most likely to do the most good for issues I think are important? And which candidate is most likely to do the most good on issues that God considers most important?

The person we pick will have considerable say in which priority will be addressed. And although God does have the final say, there will surely be more pain than necessary if our candidate does not pick God's priority. A mere human cannot hope to fake his way around with God.

Many years ago, a man conned his way onto the Chinese emperor's orchestra. Although he could not play a note, he pretended to play and got away with it for a while. Then one day, the emperor decided he wanted to hear a solo from each musician. The fake musician had to "face the music". When our priorities don't match up with God's, we will have to do the same.

Lessons on Election Day - Part 2 of 7

Text: Nehemiah 1:11; 2:1-5,16-18

Key verse: John 15:16 "You didn't choose me; but I chose you…"

A guy was just learning to play golf and was so excited about getting out on a real golf course that he forgot his tees. So, on the first hole, he put his ball on top of an anthill and swung mightily, completely obliterating the anthill, but leaving the golf ball intact. 2 ants who narrowly missed getting killed turned to each other and said: "We'd better get on the ball."

This was the message of Nehemiah, cupbearer to the king, to the exiles who had returned to Jerusalem about rebuilding the walls. And that same message is particularly relevant to those Christians who routinely forsake their duty to vote. We as Christians are not called to take a passive role in our nation-building, but an active one if we are to have the kind of freedom that we say we want. The first exiles who returned to Jerusalem had lost their vision and purpose-the visual reminder being the sad state of affairs with the walls surrounding the city.

This is not a new story or an unfamiliar one. The people of God are not to simply mark time waiting for God to step in and make things right. He has chosen us!

There was once a church in Dallas, Texas that was established with a lot of energy and passion. The building itself was made to accommodate some 700 people. The sign outside proclaimed their vision: Jesus only. But over time the people of that church lost their vision and purpose-the visual reminder being the ivy that grew up over that sign, leaving just this much: us only.

Neither the kingdom of God nor our duty as citizens can be left to those who do not actively pursue it. If we are chosen, then we must work and we must vote.

Lessons on Election Day - Part 3 of 7

Text and key verse: Colossians 4:6 "Let your conversation always be full of grace, seasoned with salt, so that you may know how to answer everyone."

Two kids were coming out of Sunday School where they had been discussing Lot's wife turning into a pillar of salt. The one, then, asked the other if he thought that was possible. The other said, "Yeah. My mother was backing her car out of a parking spot and looking back, turned into a telephone pole."

Although we are not talking today about pillars of salt, we are going to talk about salty communication as it describes in today's Bible verse. Perhaps a better way to put this is found in Ephesians 4:15 where it talks about speaking the truth in love. Truth and salt in this context are comparable to grace and love. The problem today, however, is that too few Christians are willing to state the truth for fear that it might alienate or suppress the freedom of someone else. And in neglecting to do so, have lost the ability to bring a salty influence to bear. Thus, when we as Christians have lost our salty or truthful influence, we aren't of much good.

Clearly, there is also a danger of putting on too much salt. In that case we are in danger of gaining a reputation for being brutally honest and uncaring. Thus, we must strive for more middle ground by means of grace.

This is particularly true in the political arena. Today, charges fly across both sides of the aisle of our state and federal legislatures that one party, or the other is deliberately lying and being impossible to work with- Whereas the truth of the matter is in their being unwilling to speak the truth in love. One side wants to hurt and discredit the other. When people decide to get along, the results can be amazing.

Abraham Lincoln was able to get along with his Secretary of War (who hated Lincoln) because he made his mind up that Edwin Stanton was the best man for the job. There needs to be more of this.

Lessons on Election Day - Part 4 of 7

Text and Key verse: Exodus 18:21 "But select capable men from all the people-men who fear God and trustworthy men who hate dishonest gain-and appoint them as officials over thousands, hundreds, fifties and tens."

Two opposing political candidates happened to be having breakfast in the local diner when one said to the other; "You know why I'm going to win this election? It's my personal touch. For example, i tip the waitresses here very well and ask them to vote for me." "Oh, is that so?", replied the other. "I always tip them a nickel and ask them to vote for you."

We have to be careful during election season to base our votes on more than that. We need to familiarize ourselves with the issues and where each candidate stands on them so we can make an informed choice. Otherwise, we have no excuse for complaining.

This is not exactly the context under which God gave his advice to Moses, however. Moses had been having everyone come to him with their issues to settle and was clearly getting worn out. He was God's representative and settled these matters through the Spirit of God that was in him. The advice of God, then, was that God's Spirit be put in each of these representatives so that the people would receive the same fair judgment.

I think to myself that it would be wonderful today if our elected representatives would agree to work under the same arrangement. What a wonderful world this would be!

One must remember, however, that Israel's government at the time of Moses was a theocracy-a rule of God. Today this is not the case. People by and large don't want to be responsible to or governed by God. Nevertheless, God's Holy Spirit is available to all or any who seek it. Let us then pray that our leaders will become humble enough to ask.

Lessons on Election Day- Part 5 of 7

Text: Isaiah 11:2-5

Key verse: Isaiah 11:2 "The Spirit of the Lord will rest on him..."

The overweight office worker decided to lose some weight and stayed with his program for a while. But one day he showed up at the office with an enormous coffee cake. When asked about this departure from his previous regimen, he explained it this way: he had driven to work that day by his favorite bakery and noticed the wide variety of baked goods so attractively displayed and prayed "Lord, if you want me to get something from this bakery, please provide me a parking place right in front. And, lo and behold, on my 8th trip around the block, there it was."

When we really want to do something, we can usually justify it to ourselves. By the same token, when we really don't want to do something, we can usually justify that, too. This is a dangerous course of action, however, when it comes to election day. It is hard work to do the background on our elected candidates so we can make an informed choice- so hard as a matter of fact that we would greatly prefer someone else to do it or to just not do it at all. If we give in to this lazy mindset, then, we should not be surprised when the candidates that are picked don't work out so well.

Such was the case in the mayoral New York City election of 1870. A group of committed citizens tired of the greed and corruption going on in city government, ran a candidate of their choosing against the incumbent- "Boss" Tweed. And they did quite well for a while until Tweed's men started to play rough and many of the concerned citizens started to drop out. No one was surprised, then, when Tweed easily won re-election. The way the New York Times put it was that "the good people stopped being good before the bad people stopped being bad."

This should be a lesson for us as well. We need to do our own evaluation of who we decide to vote for and not take the media's word for it. We will never have the perfect candidate until Jesus reigns, but we can do better with a little work.

Lessons on Election Day- Part 6 of 7

Text and Key verse: Psalm 5:9a "Not a word from their mouth can be trusted;"

A politician went out to the reservation to try and gain support from the native Americans. And he addressed them in their council hall: I promise better education for native Americans! And the crowd shouted: "hoya, hoya!" I promise more social reforms and job opportunities for native Americans! And again, the crowd shouted: "hoya! hoya!" The politician came away feeling he had done pretty well and asked the chief if he could see the large herd of cattle grazing on the reservation. The chief assured him that he could, but to be careful not to step in the hoya.

Campaign promises are a staple of electioneering. So, we must be careful not to put much stock in them. Instead, we should study a candidate's past history to see if his or her actions match up with their promises. We must determine whether or not the source can be trusted.

Many years ago, Indian youths would go away in solitude to prepare for manhood. And so, it was a particular young brave decided that he would test himself against a tall, rugged mountain peak, capped with snow. Upon making it to the top he encountered a rattlesnake, which said this to him: "I am about to die. It is too cold for me here. Put me under your shirt and take me down to the valley." "No!", the youth replied. "i know your kind. If i pick you up, you will bite, and your bite will kill me." "Not so!", said the rattlesnake. "I will treat you differently. I will not harm you." The brave resisted for a while but changed his mind and took the rattler down to the valley and set it down. Then the snake bit him on the leg. "You promised!", said the brave. "You knew what i was when you picked me up", replied to the snake as it slivered away.

Lessons on Election Day- Part 7 of 7

Text and key verse: Romans 5:19 "One man said no to God and put many in the wrong; one man said yes to God and put many in the right."

The friendly usher helped the elderly woman up the steps into the sanctuary and then asked her where she wanted to sit. "In the first pew, please", she said. "You don't want to sit there", the usher said. "Why not?", the woman asked. "The pastor is really boring." "Do you know who I am?", she asked. "I'm the pastor's mother." "Do you know who I am?", asked the usher. "No". "Good, "he replied.

One person can make a difference. And today's scripture backs that up. Though, the Bible is full of many solitary persons who made a difference. The difference we can make may not be as sensational as these, but it might be enough to change a life, and there's no more important change as that.

Unfortunately, we are often told on election day that our votes don't make a difference. And when the media pollsters pick the winner of a particular contest before all the votes are counted, it does seem that way. The point is we don't know who or what we may be influencing by our vote. So for that sake alone, it is worth it.

Many years ago, a Federalist farmer set out to vote late one afternoon when he heard the squealing of a pig whose head had got caught in a wire fence. Because he took the time to rescue the pig, he was too late to vote. As a result, the opposing party won the Rhode Island legislature by one vote. As the state legislature also picked the senator of the state to the federal congress, that one vote also went to the opposing party. With that one vote, furthermore, the Federal Congress decided to go to war against England in the American Revolution.

REFLECTIONS

Examples

As I was growing up, my family members provided me with good examples to follow, if I wanted to follow them. My dad was a Christian businessman, who took his role of breadwinner, seriously. He attended church regularly and expected no less from his children. My mother was a very kind woman who always looked for the best in people. She worked very hard but did so out of love for her family. My sister just enjoyed life and made even mundane things seem more exciting than they were. My oldest brother, Charles, seemed to always have a smile and a kind word for everyone. My next older brother, John, was a very no- nonsense, hard–working kind of guy who could be depended on to do his part especially if it was in helping out my parents when they were older or serving in the fire department or ambulance service. My brother George was the athlete of the family but also the one who would do anything for a person in need –if he had it to give. Paul, my next older brother, was the family's intellectual and political activist. He, too, was a stalwart supporter and tireless worker for his church. I was blessed to have such examples.

Lessons on Examples- Part 1 of 7

Text: Psalms 73:1-17

Key verse: Psalms 73:27a "Look! Those far from you die;"

Jack's mother ran into the bedroom when she heard him scream. It was because Jack's 2-year-old sister was pulling his hair. She gently released the little girl's grip and consoled Jack, saying, "There, there, now. She didn't mean it. She didn't know it hurt." But she barely made it out of the room when she heard her daughter scream. "What happened?" She asked." "She knows now," said Jack.

Kids have a fairly strong grasp on fairness, especially as it is stated in the Bible: "an eye for an eye". Yet, as we know, the example of Christ superseded this when he advised us to "turn the other cheek". This is not an easy matter for kids to get but a necessary one for us Christian parents- a lesson best taught by our example.

And, of course, we parents are not immune to childish behavior at times. The 3-year-old grandson was delighted when he received a water pistol as a birthday present from his grandma. The child's father was not so delighted:" Mom, I'm surprised at you!" The child's father said. "Don't you remember the trouble we caused you with those water guns when we were little?" "I do remember" smiled the grandma.

In today's lesson, the Psalmist is initially angry at God for letting the wicked get away with so much. He went so far as to even question why he had tried so hard to be good. But the Psalmist had a change of heart when he went into the sanctuary and considered the final destiny of the wicked. Their apparent good fortune would eventually come to an end and then it would be all over for them.

Now that may have been good for the Psalmist, but it cannot be for us. Knowing the final end for the sinner should give us the incentive to pray for them and/or help them to "see the light" before it's too late. That's how the example of Jesus should change us. And that example, hopefully, will "rub off" on our kids.

Lessons on Examples- Part 2 of 7

Text: Matthew 5-7

Key verse: Matthew 5:16a "Let your light shine before people…"

A boy came home from school with a note from his teacher, explaining to his parents that he had been punished for swearing. When his dad asked him about it, he said that he did it and deserved it- but that he had stuck up for his dad in the process. "How so? " asked the dad. "When they asked me where I heard that kind of talk, i said the parrot".

The teacher's question is a good one for us, as well: "whose example are we following?" "In today's lesson, taken from the Sermon on the Mount, Jesus says that the things he suggests are for himself as well as others. He knew that he must set the example.

In modern society, the movie star and the sports hero are looked to as examples- whether they want to be or not. Charles Barkley, a perennial NBA all-star, once said that he didn't want to be anyone's role model- that he didn't want that responsibility. But we, as Christians, do not have that luxury. For the sake of the young ones, we hope to influence for Christ, we must all be all that we can be.

If that is the case, we can reasonably ask how can we, as sinful humans, serve in that way? The answer is found in the Gospel of John, chapter 1, verse 12: "But as many as received him, to them gave the power to become the sons of God…". And this power is specially made manifest in our weakness. So, we have no excuse.

Just understand that the major difference that Jesus introduced was in terms of following the Spirit of the Law as well as the letter. This, we cannot do by ourselves. But, with the Holy Spirit's help, we can and will keep all aspects of the law simply by loving God with all our heart, soul and mind-the example that Jesus kept to the very end.

Lessons on Examples- Part 3 of 7

Text: Matthew 6:9-13

Key verse: 6:11 "Give us this day our daily bread."

A marketing research firm was interviewing people coming out of the grocery store about how they made their bread choices. A guy who had purchased a loaf of Wonder Bread was asked if he was influenced in his choice by tv commercials. He said, "No way! I'm not influenced by those things." "Fine," said the interviewer, "but could you tell me why you chose Wonder Bread?" "Sure, "said the guy. "It builds strong bodies 8 ways."

In today's lesson, Jesus is telling his disciples how to pray. They had seen the power Jesus derived from his prayer life and knew they needed that kind of power, too. In other words, they were influenced by his example. This is an important concept for us Christians, as well. Although we know God has given everyone freedom of choice, we know that there is one decision they must get right, and the influence of our example may be crucial to it.

The person who exemplifies the traits they consider the most desirable has the best chance of influencing them. Often it is the sports or movie stars. But these folks don't necessarily care about the people they influence or the type of influence they have. The exceptions are rare, but they do exist. Mickey Mantle, one of the greatest baseball players who ever lived, advised young aspiring ball players to not be like him because he had wasted the God-given ability he had been given. The large number of people (usually young people!) who show up for reality show try-outs says a lot about the influence of fame. But, once again, famous singers and entertainers usually don't care about what influence they have, as long as the money keeps flowing in.

Quite clearly, we need to be the most important example people have. And they won't care about our example unless they know we care about them.

Lessons on Examples - Part 4 of 7
Text: Luke 10:25-37
Key verse: Luke 10:37b "Go and do thou likewise."

Just to show how things have changed: in the 1950's, the school's biggest troubles were cigarette smoking and skipping class. Today, the major problems are deadly weapons, arson, drugs, vandalism and drunkenness. In any event, a teacher saw some boys huddled in a corner of the gym and went to investigate. "What are you boys doing?" They said that they were shooting dice. "Thank goodness," she replied, "I thought you were praying."

Indeed, the expectation these days of students is negative. It's what people see from the kids on tv, in the news and on the movie screen. In Jesus' day, the expectations of those people called Samaritans was equally bad. But in this story that Jesus tells, the good example is not the person people expected, but the hated Samaritan. It was his way of telling people not to categorize people in any particular way- because people, as individuals, are each capable of goodness- of being a good example.

And the help that is given should be given regardless of whether or not we feel they are worthy of it. During the great flu epidemic of 1918, some 430,000 people died- many more than died from the bullets of WW1. In any event, Herb Gilbey of Wallace, South Dakota was approached by the town druggist to make an emergency trip to Minneapolis to get medicine for the druggist's 7-year-old son. The druggist was himself too ill to make the 250-mile trip, but Gilbey, without complaint climbed into his unheated Model-t Ford in a driving snowstorm and made the trip. Twenty-four hours later, he returned with the needed medicine, the boy survived and went on to become a future vice-president of the United States-Hubert Humphrey. Of course, Gilbey did not know what would become of the little boy- just that he was near death and needed the medicine. Similarly, we need to be open to any chance we get to do good.

Lessons on Examples - Part 5 of 7

Text: Mark 10:13-16

Key verse: Mark 10:14b "Allow the children to come to me."

A little boy was afraid of going to the dentist, so his dad went along with him. When it came time for the boy to get into the dental chair, he began to cry. So, to show him that there was no need to cry, the dad went into the dental chair, where the dentist did a quick check-up. "It looks like there's a tooth that needs to be pulled", said the dentist. "How much will it cost?" asked the dad. "About $50", said the dentist. Now the dad felt like crying, but he asked, "How long will it take?" "About a minute", said the dentist. "Wow", said the dad, "I get paid by the hour for a fairly important job, but $50 for a minute's work seems excessive." "I can pull it a lot more slowly", the dentist said.

Sometimes our best intentions go awry. And sometimes that happens when we are trying to be a good example. In today's lesson, however, Jesus clearly leaves a good example for his disciples in terms of caring for children. Jesus declared that the kingdom of heaven is for those whose faith is like theirs and he hugged and blessed them.

In 1952, a probation officer in New York City tried to find an organization to assist in the adoption of a 12-year-old boy. Since the boy's religious affiliation was not protestant, Jewish or Catholic, no organization would help and the probation officer was not able, then, to do anything constructive. Yet, if he could have found a helping hand in this, one wonders how things might have been different for the young boy- Lee Harvey Oswald.

Lessons on Examples - Part 6 of 7

Text: Philippians 3:17-4:1

Key verse: Philippians 3:17a "Brothers and sisters, be imitators of me…"

A young boy went to the movies with his little brother. After they had seated themselves, the older brother asked the younger if he could see. When the younger responded that he couldn't, the older said, "Just laugh when I laugh."

In today's Bible lesson, Paul asked the church at Philippi to imitate his service for Christ. And, as far as we know, they had been obedient to that in their sacrificial giving to the persecuted church in Jerusalem.

As Christians, we hope that our example is one worth following. But that is not likely to occur in our own strength.

A man was driving through the black hills of South Dakota when he ran into a snowstorm and lost all sense of direction. But when he spotted a snowplow, he felt relieved and followed behind him as close as he could. After a while, the snowplow stopped, and the operator got out and walked over to the car. "Where you headed, mister? said the snowplow operator. "to Montana," the driver said. "Not as long as you're following me, "said the operator, "I'm plowing out a parking lot."

Thankfully, we have a sure guide in Jesus Christ. Not only does he know the way, but he is also the way!

Lessons on Examples - Part 7 of 7

Text: 1 Peter 5:1-7

Key verse: 1 Peter 5:2a "Like shepherds, tend the flock among you."

Two shepherds lean on their crooks at the end of a long day and the first asks the second, "So, how's it going?" The second one sighed and shook his head, "Not good, I can't pay my bills, my health isn't good, my kids don't respect me, and my wife is leaving me." The first replied, "Well, don't lose any sheep over it."

Unless you have done the job, you don't likely know what is required. That is why it can be confusing to follow a shepherd's example. Shepherds in Jesus' day were not held in the highest esteem. They were religious outcasts, borderline social outcasts with very little contact with other people. Most of the time, they were 'living out in the fields'. This was not a 40-hour a week job. They didn't come home at night. They were with the sheep 24 hours a day, 7 days a week. So what was it that we are called to follow?

We were called to shepherd people instead of sheep- to be there for them, to watch out for them and to lead them by example. There is no down-time in this job as Satan takes no time off in causing problems. Even though people are not as dumb or helpless as sheep, they need a constant good example of how to live so they will not fall victim to the "dark side" of sin. This is a difficult job for us as human beings want to be good, but not too good, and not quite all the time.

Peter, as he writes this epistle, is clearly thinking of the example of Jesus and of his own failures in following Him. That's why he tells the churches in Asia Minor to look at Jesus and not at him. You see, Peter remembered Jesus' attitude in shepherding- out of love and not of duty. With that attitude and the help of the Holy Spirit, we will not "lose sheep".

REFLECTIONS

Faith

Faith has always been a part of my vocabulary as long as I've had a vocabulary. But I always have considered it as something I never had enough of. I mean, if I did, then this good thing would have happened or that bad thing would have been avoided. It was only relatively lately that I have begun to see faith differently- as something we all have in varying degrees but that, regardless of the amount, we all have as much as we need. And I've also come to that place where I realize that my faith doesn't obligate God to act in any particular way. It just helps me to know that God is always good and that he loves me- which gives me peace. Thus, faith does predispose that I may act in a way that may not make sense to others. But the actions I take are with the belief that God will help me- whether it appears that he will or won't. I just have to realize that God's help may not come in the form I want or expect.

Lessons on Faith - Part 1 of 7

Text: Genesis 12:1-4

Key verse: genesis 12:1 "The Lord said to Abram," leave ... for the land that I will show you."

An atheist was spending a quiet day fishing when suddenly the Loch Ness monster appeared and attacked his boat. With one easy flip, the beast threw the man and his boat high in the air and opened its great mouth to swallow them both. As the man sailed high overhead, he cried out, "Oh God, please help me!" At that point, everything froze and a voice out of heaven boomed out:" I thought you didn't believe in me!" "Come on, God. Two minutes ago, I didn't believe in the Loch Ness monster, either."

It is said that there are no atheists in foxholes. But the kind of faith that pleases God is not of the "fire extinguisher-type". It is, instead, the kind of hope and assurance that sustains us day-by-day and hour by hour.

Clearly, Abram or Abraham had the kind that pleases God. How else could he leave all that was familiar to him and travel many miles to go to a place he had never been before? With faith, we are not privy to the big picture, but only motivated to get moving. We have to put the final destination in God's hands.

In a manner of speaking, faith is what a trapeze artist displays when he swings out on a bar, lets loose of it and grabs for the next one. As we've seen on tv or at a circus, there is a breathless moment of mid-air placelessness. This is the moment of faith. Yet it can never be achieved until the trapeze artist has the courage to let go.

By the same token, we, as Christians, experience that same kind of breath-taking transition between when we pray and God answers. We just know that God loves us too much to leave us there.

Lessons on Faith - Part 2 of 7

Text: Genesis 24

Key verse: Genesis 24:50 "This is all the Lord's doing."

For the umpteenth time, Mrs. Young was in to see the pastor about the same problem: her husband, Joe. "Pastor, Joe says he'll kill me if I continue to come to your church." "There, there, Mrs. Young," said the pastor, "That's just his way of manipulating you to do what he says. Besides, I've been praying for you and God has kept you safe so far. You just have to have a little faith." "You're right, pastor, but…" "But what, my dear?" "Well, this time Joe said he would also kill you!" "Well, then," said the pastor, "Maybe it's time we find you a church a little closer to home."

Truly, there are times when it is easier to tell someone to have faith than to have it yourself- even safer. Nevertheless, it is impossible to please God without it, so we must keep trying.

Today's lesson is all about having faith. Abraham asks his trusted servant to find a wife for his son, Isaac from among his family and homeland. This the servant sets out to do- trusting God to help him in this quest. And God delivers in such a way that no one can deny his involvement. Not only that, but when Isaac sees her for the first time, he falls in love with her- as if he had picked her out, himself.

The journey of the Mayflower to the "new world" was a similar faith story. By that I mean that, even after one ship sprung leaks and its passengers had to be put on the now over-crowded Mayflower and after the Mayflower's main beam had cracked and after most everybody got sick on board, the people still felt that God would get them through. It was clearly not a voyage for the superstitious for their faith was sorely tested- as will ours-at times. You can count on it!

Lessons on Faith - Part 3 of 7

Text: Ruth

Key verse: Ruth 1:16b "Wherever you go, I will go; and wherever you stay, I will stay."

A woman was walking along the beach when she found an old lamp-which turned out to be a genie's lamp. She rubbed it and out came a genie, who said he'd grant her 1 wish. She said, "If I can have only 1 wish, I wish for peace in the Mideast." "Wow, lady," said the genie, "those people have been fighting for thousands of years! I'm good, but not that good. You'll have to make another wish." "Ok," said the woman, "I'd like to find a husband who likes to cook and clean, gets along with my family and doesn't have to watch sports all the time." "Do you have a map of the Mideast?", asked the genie.

After all that Ruth and Naomi had been through, the hope they had that things would work out for them seemed quite far-fetched. Indeed, Naomi was very pessimistic. But, as they had to eat, Ruth went out into the field to glean the crops that had been overlooked. That could have worked out very badly for her, had not God been watching over her.

I believe that this provides an important point in our understanding of how faith can work. Ruth, as a foreigner, was not familiar with God's provision for the Jew. As such, her going into the fields was not a step of faith, as some might believe-but simply an act of self-preservation. So, I believe, that faith can come out of non-faith (as with non-believers)- especially if there is one who can explain its occurrence when things happen that are more than co-incidence-as Naomi could.

This point is also dramatically represented in Mark 9:14-29, where Jesus asks an unbeliever if he believes and he says, "I believe but help my unbelief." I think that that sentiment is an example of our lack of faith, as well. God can and does overcome our unbelief, especially when we grow from the experience.

Lessons on Faith - Part 4 of 7

Text: Genesis 22;1-19

Key verse: Genesis 22:8b "God will see to it, my son."

A pastor saw a little kitten up one of his young trees but couldn't reach him. So, he tied some rope from his car to the sapling, reasoning that he could pull the top of the tree down far enough that he could reach it. All seemed to be going well until the rope broke-sending the little kitten out of sight. The pastor searched around his neighborhood but could find no trace of it. So, he prayed to God that the kitten would be ok, then forgot about the incident-all until he saw one of his parishioners (who hated cats) buying cat food at the grocery store. Confused, he asked her about it. "Pastor," she said, "You'll never believe what happened! My daughter has been begging me to get a kitten for longer than I can remember, but I have always been able to change the subject. But a couple of days ago, I could not get her mind off of it, so I told her to go out in the backyard and pray for one. Well, I wouldn't have believed it unless I saw it with my own eyes, but after she finished praying, a kitten came flying out of the air and landed not 2 feet from her. After that, how could I say no?"

I'm not sure how far Abraham had come in his faith journey when God asked him to sacrifice his son, but, to his credit, he did not hesitate to do it. In fact, the Bible says he had to be restrained by an angel of God from carrying out God's request. I'm also not sure how much of this event that Isaac remembered, but I feel quite certain that it provided a definitive answer to the need for faith in his young life.

From all accounts, Abraham Lincoln was not much of a man of faith until his son, Willy, died. The terrible losses of the Civil War brought him even closer to God. Yet, he believed that the union's cause was just, and that God would someday bring an end to the conflict. Of course, he did not see the end of war. But, then again, isn't this what faith is about- trusting that right will prevail? Should it not be so for us?

Lessons on Faith - Part 5 of 7

Text: Daniel 6

Key verse: Daniel 6:22 "God has sent his angel, and he shut the lions' mouths."

A young American engineer was being sent to Ireland for a 2-year assignment. Although he was engaged to be married, he took the job because this assignment, if done satisfactorily, would guarantee the couple enough money to get married and set up housekeeping. They kept in regular contact, but the long absence was wearing on both of them. The girl was particularly concerned because of the availability of young Irish girls. So, she sent him a harmonica to practice keeping his mind off temptation. When he'd call, he'd say it was working and that he was getting to be a better player every day. Finally, the 2 years came to an end, and she met him at the airport. But when he went to embrace her, she held up her hand, saying "Before there's any kissing or hugging, let's hear you play that harmonica."

She wanted to see how committed he was. In our story today, we learn that Daniel certainly was. He did not forsake his prayer and worship of God-no matter what. And so, he found himself in a den of hungry lions. But he had faith that God would deliver him.

Today, we often face conflicting commitments. Thus, we find ourselves with the need to prioritize. For the Christian, God should be first- but he sometimes isn't. That's when we know that we have work to do. You see, without whole-hearted commitment, we cannot hope to have the victory like Daniel did.

Yet not everybody sees or feels the victory. That's where faith comes in. We have to believe that God is with us even when it feels as if he's not. Probably the person in my lifetime that best reflected a faithful life was Mother Theresa. Even so, she did not feel the presence of God in her work with the poor and oppressed in India. That did not show, however, in her demeanor or in her actions. She carried on without it, as perhaps some of us may.

Lessons On Faith - Part 6 of 7

Text: Matthew 14:22-33

Key verse: Matthew 14:31c "Why did you begin to have doubts?"

A blind man came into a grocery store with his seeing eye dog on a leash. Suddenly, he began to swing the dog in circles over his head. "What are you doing?" cried the store manager. "Just looking around", said the blind man.

In our lesson for today, Peter gets in trouble for looking around when he should have kept his eyes on Jesus. As the story goes, the disciples were frightened when they see Jesus' walking on the water towards them. But when Peter recognizes it is Jesus, he asks Jesus if he can come out on the water to join him. Jesus says yes and Peter starts walking on the water. But Peter takes his eyes off Jesus and begins to sink. Jesus then takes Peter's hand and helps him back into the boat the disciples were on. Quite simply, Peter lost his faith.

This can be and often is the case in our own lives, as well. This point is illustrated when a child's stuffed animal is taken from him to be washed or repaired. In other words, he does not want to let that animal out of his sight. It takes faith on his part that the animal will be returned in the same or better condition than when he let it go. The most crucial part, however, is letting go. If he can't, the animal cannot be fixed.

Today, a common Christian encouragement is let go and let God. This is the essence of faith. Yet, letting go flies in the face of all we've been taught and have been conditioned to believe. Nobody said faith was easy!

Lessons On Faith - Part 7 of 7

Text: Mark 9:17-27

Key verse: Mark 9:24 "I have faith; help my lack of faith."

A little boy was afraid to go to bed, so he asked his mother to stay up in his room with him for a while. But after a while had gone by and the boy was not sleeping, the mom prepared to leave. The little boy began to whimper, so the mom said, "Don't worry, honey. Jesus is with you." "I know, mom," the boy replied, "but I want someone with skin on."

Faith is not just a young person's problem. We see that in today's lesson, where a man pleads with Jesus to heal his son of an epileptic-type problem. Jesus tells the dad, who is beside himself with worry, that all things are possible for all who believe. But the dad feels he doesn't have enough faith to accomplish the goal.

This is also a common misconception held by many: that they don't have enough faith. The reality is, however, that we all have been given a measure of faith and that amount of faith will be sufficient. You see, faith is not just something we have but something we live. Someone may seem to have faith, but appearances can be deceiving. It's one thing to pray for rain and quite another to carry an umbrella while doing so.

When I was growing up, we used to put up our train set and village at Christmas. This village was called "Plasticville". The houses in Plasticville were never in a state of disrepair and the little people all had smiles on their faces. Of course, this was an imaginary place where all was good, and no one had any problems. Yet even though no such place exists, we seem to want to believe it does and so we believe people's smiles and words that all is well- when the reality can be much different. But it could be much better if we use the faith we have and live out that faith.

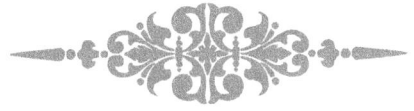

REFLECTIONS

Family and Friends

Family took on a different meaning when I had a family of my own. Now I was primarily responsible for the financial and moral support of more than myself. Although I was not the primary caretaker, I had a great amount of responsibility- especially when the twins came along. I did take those responsibilities seriously and devoted myself to them. It was, without question, the best investment that I ever made. Later on, after the separation and subsequent divorce, my responsibilities came only on weekends- where I became, in addition to being dad, the activities director. Later still, when I remarried, I learned (many times the hard way) about having a "blended" family and how to better prioritize my time and attention. Most of my earliest, best friends came from the neighborhood and not from school. Generally, we were pretty good kids and concentrated our efforts towards Sports and not mischief. In college, I began to blossom, Socially, and had friends throughout small college Clarion. After graduation altered my social contacts, I made friends at work and through sports. Today, most of my friends come from church.

Lessons on Family and Friends - Part 1

Text: 1 Samuel 2:12-36

Key verse: Deuteronomy 6:7a "Recite them (God's laws) to your children."

A Sunday school teacher asked her class: "Where does God live?" One little boy responded, "in our bathroom." The teacher asked him how he knew that. And he responded," Because every morning when my dad goes to the bathroom, he asks, "God, are you still in there?"

My guess is that dad had no idea of how his speech was being processed by his son, or the rest of his family, for that matter. This is a dangerous situation as parents are in a unique situation to "mold" their children- for at least their early years.

Eli, the priest, should have known better in the raising of his sons. But, because of his inattention, they became very sinful men. And that turn of events became even worse because Eli's sons were to become priests, just like their dad. Then, since Eli could not get them to change their ways, God punished them-certainly a regrettable situation because it was preventable and because there were probably ample warning signals.

Years ago, coal miners used canaries as their early warning system in detecting the presence of dangerous levels of toxic gases. Today, our children serve in a similar capacity. When they begin to exhibit the violence and insensitivity to sex that exist in our toxic cultural atmosphere, we know that something is radically wrong. Clearly, they need parental guidance over what they see on tv, the internet or at the movies. They need parental guidance over the video games they play. When kids are left too long on their own, who or what will give them the guidance that they need?

Lessons on Family and Friends - Part 2 of 7

Text:1 Samuel 20

Key verse: Proverbs 18:24b "…a true friend sticks by you like family."

Two redneck friends, Billy Joe and Bubba, are out hunting when Billy Joe suddenly grabs his chest and falls to the ground. He doesn't seem to be breathing so Bubba gets out his cell phone and calls 911. "Help me! Help me! I think my friend is dead. What do I do?" "Now, now there. Calm down. I can help. First of all, let's make sure that he's dead." There is silence, then a gunshot, then Bubba comes back on the line. "Ok, now what?"

The old saying goes: "With friends like that…, right?" Seriously, friends can be lifesavers. It certainly was true for David and Jonathan. We see in today's lesson that Jonathan's dad, King Saul, planned to kill David but, initially, Jonathan didn't believe it. So, they came up with a plan to find out the king's true intentions. And when Jonathan learned that David's suspicions were true, Jonathan helped him get away. We, too, should try to be that kind of friend- but we must be open to the Holy Spirit in order to be the timely help that Jonathan was.

As he walked home from school one day, Mark noticed that the boy ahead of him had dropped a big armload of stuff. So, Mark helped him pick it up. The boy, named Bill, who dropped the armload was quite grateful and invited Mark to his house for a Coke and to play some video games. They became friends that day and kept track of each other all through school. Just before graduation when both boys would be going on to different colleges, Bill took Mark aside to tell him goodbye and to tell him something else. "Mark, do you remember that day when you helped me pick up my stuff?" "Yeah, what about it?" "Didn't you think that I had a lot to carry?" "I do remember thinking that, yes." "Well, I had cleaned out my locker that day and planned to take a bottle of sleeping pills that night. No one seemed to care, so I decided to end it all. But then you helped me, and I changed my mind. You see, Mark, when you helped me pick up my stuff, you saved my life."

Lessons on Family and Friends - Part 3

Text: Ecclesiastes 4:9-12

Key verse: Ecclesiastes 4:12c "A three-ply cord doesn't easily snap"

The dictator of a small Latin American country was bitterly disappointed that no one seemed to be using the newly minted stamp with his picture on it. When he questioned his postmaster about it, the postmaster explained it was because the stamps were not sticking. Not satisfied with this explanation, the dictator licked one of the stamps and put it on a blank envelope. "See, it sticks!" "Yes, your excellency, but the people have been spitting on the wrong side."

Clearly, the dictator had few friends among the people of his country. Unfortunately, there are also too many "Lone Rangers" among us Christians-people who think they have to make it on their own.

Today's lesson talks about the benefit of having friends. And when I say friends, I mean more than mere acquaintances. The type of friend talked about in this scripture is the type that is there for you, regardless. This type of friend gives you a reason to "hang on" when things are at their worst.

Former hostage, Thomas Sutherland, tried to kill himself on three separate occasions during his six years of captivity in Lebanon-each time by putting a plastic bag over his head to suffocate himself. But each time he tried, a vision of his wife and family came to him and the pain of never seeing them again was enough to stop him. We need to have relationships like that. But also, we need to be special enough to others that they hold on, too, when times get tough.

Lessons on Family and Friends - Part 4 of 7

Text: Mark 2:1-12

Key verse: Mark 2:11 "Get up, take your mat, and go home."

A group of guys were discussing how they might be able to help a mutual friend, who was having some financial problems. They knew he would not accept charity so they pretended that they were all in a cash drawing and had tickets drawn up and agreed that the winner would be the one who drew the number 4 out of the hat. What their friend didn't know was that all the tickets had the same number on it. When the time of the drawing was at hand, they each reached into the hat to draw numbers and then would act disgusted that they had drawn a losing number. So finally, it was their friend's turn and they all waited for him to draw out the winning number. But instead of the winning ticket he drew out the tag of the hat. When they asked him what he got, he replied, "6 and 7/8".

That's what you call bad luck. Nevertheless, in today's lesson, a group of friends sought healing for a paralyzed friend. They knew Jesus was in town and had heard of the healings he had done and were optimistic that their friend could be helped. But, when they drew near to the house where Jesus was, it was packed, and they couldn't get in. Certainly no one could blame their friends for giving up, but they weren't done yet. They hauled their friend up to the thatched roof, made an opening and lowered him with ropes down to where Jesus was. In seeing their faith, Jesus healed the man both Spiritually and physically and bid him "take up (his) mat and walk"- which he did!

The mark of a true friend, then, is one who will be there for us when there's every reason for him not to be. Such is our reality with Jesus. Even though our sins have alienated us from God, he, who was perfect, gave up his life as a sacrifice for us, to reconcile us with the Father and give us a hope that we would never have, otherwise.

Lessons on Family and Friends - Part 5 of 7

Text: Luke 10:30-37

Key verse: Luke 10:37b "Go and do thou likewise."

A woman was accompanied by her friend when the woman went to the police to report her husband was missing. "What did he look like?" Asked the policeman. "He's about 6 ft. 2 inches, with blue eyes, dark, wavy hair, an athletic build, well-groomed and soft-spoken". When the officer left the room, the friend said, "That's not what your husband is like. He's short, bald, fat and sloppy. And besides, he's a loudmouth." "I know," said the woman, "but who wants him back?"

Looks might matter in terms of attractiveness, but actions speak louder than words when it comes to friends. We know this from experience, and we see it substantiated in today's Bible lesson. This is a parable, or teaching story of Jesus and in its Jesus features a person or type of person that many people despised sight unseen. Jesus also features 2 people that everyone assumed to be of the highest caliber. Yet, each of them acts in ways that no one expected- causing us to re-think our prejudices.

A man received a brand-new car from his brother for Christmas and drove it to work. When he came out of his office to go home an obviously poor little boy was "checking out" the car. "Do you like it? said the man. "Oh boy, do I!", said the boy. "I got it from my brother for Christmas." "Wow, I wish..." the man felt sure that the boy would finish the sentence by saying that he had a brother like that. But instead, the little boy said that he wished he could be a brother like that. So, the guy asked the boy if he would like a ride home. "Yes, very much!" While they were riding, the boy asked the man if he could just wait a minute when they got there. The man smiled and said he could- imagining that the boy wanted to brag it up that he knew somebody with a new car. But instead, the boy ran into the house then came out carrying his crippled little brother. "See, there it is, buddy. Someday I'll get one just like it for you." Friends display the Spirit of love even when they aren't related.

Lessons on Family and Friends - Part 6 of 7

Text: Acts 6:1-4

Key verse: I Peter 2:17b "Love the brotherhood of believers."

A loaded minivan pulled up to the one remaining campsite. Four kids jumped from the vehicle and began unloading it and setting up the tent. Then the boys rushed off to gather firewood while the girls helped the mom set up the camp stove and cooking utensils. A nearby camper watched this with a sense of amazement and shared that with the family's dad. "that's one of the best examples of teamwork I've ever seen. How did you get them to be so disciplined?" "Well, it's all based on one simple rule: no one goes to the bathroom until the camp is set up."

A family should have similarity to a team- just like a church should have some similarity to a family. There should be mutual sharing and caring and a division of tasks based on different gifts and graces. This is quite evident in today's Bible story from Acts. Some widows were being overlooked in the daily food service. But those who were most involved and gifted in matters of prayer and preaching knew that others could do that ministry better so they could concentrate on that which they did best. So, with prayer and discernment, people were chosen to do that ministry. This worked out great and the church grew.

Yet the church should also have similarity to a team. The reasons parallel that of the church-family analogy. But there's more to it than that. Vince Lombardi, the famous, Hall-of–Fame football coach, said that the difference between a mediocre team and a great one is the difference in feeling that each team member has for each other. They realize that each one must do his job well so that their teammate can do theirs. The clear consequence of that is that when each player-church member does not have to worry about someone else's job, they can do theirs better.

Lessons on Family and Friends - Part 7 of 7

Text: Genesis 4:1-16

Key verse: Genesis 4:9c "Am I my brother's keeper?"

A few days before Christmas, a postal employee found an unstamped, hand-written, messy envelope addressed to God. Knowing that it was undeliverable, he opened it to find that an elderly woman was asking God for help since all her money had been stolen and that she would have nothing to eat at Christmas. So, the postal worker took up a collection from his fellow employees and put it into a plain envelope and had it delivered by courier the next day. A few days later, the same postal employee saw a similar-looking envelope addressed to God and opened it. It was a letter of thanks, but it referenced the fact that it was $20 short of what she had lost-which she put to the charge of the "thieving" workers at the post office.

Clearly, even doing the right thing may still lead to criticism. Yet, this is no excuse for us to act in any other way. In today's Bible lesson, Cain has brought an unacceptable offering unto God and is jealous that his brother's was accepted. Instead of making it right, he decides to kill his brother and faces the condemnation of God as a result. Our actions toward others should parallel the actions we express toward God. It is not the way we are "wired", but it is the way we must seek.

Sometimes we can learn from the animal kingdom the way we humans should act. Somewhere in our United States there is a farm where 2 horses roam. One of the horses is blind, but the owner has not put it down but provided it for its protection and care. That protector is the other horse. It has a bell around its neck, which the blind horse listens for the horse with the bell does not let the blind horse get too far from earshot and so is able to lead it to food, water and shelter. Like it or not, we are to be the horse with the bell to those around us who cannot see where to go. We are our brother's keeper.

REFLECTIONS

Fathers

Most people relate to fathers in terms of how they relate to their own father. I am no exception. However, I am also aware that many people did not have the positive relationship that I had, and, as a result, have had at least some difficulty relating to a heavenly father who loves them. Or perhaps they never knew their father or what a father is supposed to do or be. This clearly has put them at a disadvantage. Yet, we maintain the ability to choose how we will react to those or any difficulty. As such, I believe, then, that past negative experiences or the absence of any experiences with a father can be overcome.

Having said that, I believe that fatherhood changes with the times and culture. For me as I was growing up, fathers were the breadwinners but not necessarily the buddies of their children. My dad was 53 when I was born and so not only were we separated in terms of interests but the ability to pursue them. My mother handled the discipline, checkbook and the running of the household, but that arrangement worked for them. Dad never wanted much, nor did he insist on having his way-except in matters that might cause shame or disrespect on the family.

Lessons on Fathers - Part 1 of 7

Text: Luke 18:18-23

Key verse: Luke 18:18 "…,what shall I do to get to heaven?"

A family who moved into a new neighborhood was running late one morning, which resulted in their 6-year-old daughter missing her bus. The dad volunteered to take her to school even though it would make him a little late. But he needed directions from his daughter- which she agreed to provide. After 20 minutes of turns and twists, however, they arrived at school- which turned out to be just a short distance from their home. The dad, realizing this, asked his daughter why she had him take this overly long way. And she answered, "this is the way the bus goes. It's the only way I know."

For many fathers, the only way they know is to stay away from any religious instruction for their kids. Yet the Bible places the kids' religious education squarely on the fathers' shoulders. Then dads wonder why the secular media plays so large a role in children's lives- the secular media that promotes materialism.

In today's scripture lesson, the rich, young ruler cannot blame the secular media for his stance on the importance of wealth. But my guess is that his father could have but didn't give him sufficient guidance in that area, as children tend to follow the example given them. The problem is, then, if children are not taught that God is most important in their life and the one who should "call the shots", then they probably will come to the conclusion that they can set the parameters of that relationship. Thus, it's not surprising that when God requests something of importance of us, that we say "no".

Many years ago, when I was growing up, my mother would often send me to the local "mom-and-pop" grocery store for $.50 worth of chipped ham, a loaf of bread and a quart of milk with just a dollar. It seems to me that, in essence, this is what many people are looking for from God. If, on the other hand, our dads would have taken their religious education responsibilities more seriously, they could have let their kids expect more from God, and thus give him what's right instead of what's left.

Lessons on Fathers - Part 2 of 7

Text and key verse: Exodus 20:12 "Honor thy father and thy mother; that thy days may be long upon the land that the Lord thy God giveth thee."

The pastor was conducting a community-wide healing service, and so he thought that, if it were successful, there would be people coming with all levels of religious backgrounds and concerns. So, he was not surprised when a man came up to him at the service concerned about his hearing. The pastor laid hands on him, anointed him with oil and called upon God to give the man perfect hearing. After he finished praying, he asked the man how his hearing was now. And the man replied, "I don't know; the hearing isn't until next Tuesday."

A pastor is often looked to as being closer to God-whether that be the case or not. And, as such, people think he could "put in a good word" for them. Yet, I think that a dad, like a pastor, must first be the kind of person that someone would want to honor. Part of this, then, I believe, is getting the following people into their lives: An older man who serves as an example and guide; A man his own age who likes him but is not impressed by him to the point where he is unlikely to tell him the truth; and a younger man to mentor. The rationale for this advice is that other people can often see us as we are not able to see ourselves and can thus serve as a filter for our less desirable traits. The age differential can also benefit us as the old man has the life experience we don't, and the younger man still has the youthful exuberance we may lack.

A man was teaching his nervous son how to drive and thought to himself about how things come back around. You see, his son had given him this same advice when his son had asked him, many years before, to help him color a picture and he had hesitated. And so now the words came back: "I'm right beside you and you're gonna do fine. All you've got to do is stay between the lines."

Lessons on Fathers - Part 3 of 7

Text: Luke 2:1-5

Key verse: Luke 2:5 "He went there to register with Mary…"

While on a car trip, the elderly couple stopped at a roadside restaurant for lunch. After finishing her meal, the wife took off her glasses to read the bill and forgot to pick them up again. Unfortunately, she didn't miss them until they were well on their way down the road. When she told her husband what had happened, he fussed and complained all the way back, making her feel bad. Well, when they pulled into the restaurant and she got out to retrieve her glasses, he yelled to her, "As long as you're in there, you might as well pick up my hat, too."

That makes me laugh because it reminds me of my dad, who wasn't good at taking credit for failure, either. Yet, there was never any doubt in my mind, or my mother's, that he loved her. And, when one looks closely at the background of the Christmas story, I believe that there can be no doubt that Joseph loved Mary. This, for me, has great relevance for Father's Day, as I believe that it is crucially important for children to know that they have a mom and dad that love each other.

The Christmas story in Luke 2 begins with the Roman decree that people had to register for a census in their hometown. For Joseph, this amounted to making a round-trip of 160 miles from where they lived in Nazareth to Bethlehem and back. On top of this, Joseph's wife, Mary, was very close to having a baby, so such a trip would have been very hard for her. In consideration of this, it would have made more sense for Mary to stay home, as the Romans never registered women in their census-taking. So, it would appear that Joseph's taking of Mary must have been the result of poor family relations at home for Mary-possibly as a result of her pregnancy so soon after her marriage to Joseph. That is, it would appear that Joseph was protecting her in taking her along. This fits with his reaction to her announcement of pregnancy, when he didn't want her to be embarrassed.

Lessons on Fathers - Part 4 of 7

Text: Psalms 103:13-18

Key verse: Psalm 103:17b "…the Lord's love is with those who fear him,…"

A little boy was misbehaving in church. And although the parents were doing their best to maintain order, it was a losing battle. So, the father took the boy and began to walk rather sternly back the aisle to the foyer, the boy yelled out to the congregation, "Pray for me! Pray for me!"

This could well have been the request of the father, too. None of us have been required to take a training course in parenting and so we do the best that we can. Today's scripture shows that God knows this, but it is implied that we try to remember that God is merciful to our mistakes in hopes that we remember that in light of our discipline with our children.

Of course, it is easy to find mistakes in our parenting. We all have them. And many have come about rather innocently. A story is told of a dad that had an older son and a younger son who both played soccer yet one several years before the other. With the older boy, who was much more athletic, the father rewarded him with a milkshake for every goal he made. But when the younger son started to play, the same incentive didn't work, because the younger son never could get a goal. As an unintended consequence, then, the younger son felt inferior even though he had given it his best effort.

Clearly, we cannot always be aware of the future implications of our actions, but we can always pray to God (who does) for help. And so, just like the previous example, we can also do the right thing unintentionally. In another story, a dad had promised his kids that he would take them to the circus on a particular day. But just as they were about to go out the door, a telephone call came in for the dad about some business that had to be taken care of. Hearing that, the kids waited for the bad news, only to be surprised by the dad who told the caller that someone else would have to take the required action because he had promised the kids the circus. I suspect that God had something to do with that.

Lessons on Fathers - Part 5 of 7

Text: Matthew 9:35-38

Key verse: Matthew 9:38 "Ask the Lord of the harvest, therefore, to send workers in to his harvest field."

The young boy's father kept bringing work home from the office night after night. And so, he asked him why- to which the dad said, "Buddy, I just can't get it all done." "Well, dad, why don't you ask them to put you in the slower group?"

Seems pretty obvious, right? Actually, it isn't. Unquestionably, dads as well as moms are stretched very thin in trying to meet their responsibilities. The kids, though, often see it as a question of priorities-priorities where they often get the rotten side of the bargain.

Thus, those dads that make the best use of available time to spend with their kids find that this investment pays the highest and best dividend. But this time must be full of the following attributes: takes time, listens, plays with, invites to go places, lets help, treats mom well, allows comments, nice to kid's friends, only punishes when it's deserved and not afraid to admit mistakes.

A dad that scores high in these traits may not have any more time than the average father, it's just that the time he does have is better spent. A famous writer often referred to a special day in his childhood when his dad took him fishing as a day when his dad had taught him many important things. Yet, dad saw this day much differently. In his journal for that day, he wrote, "Gone fishing today with my son. A day wasted."

In today's scripture lesson, Jesus is lamenting that so many people seemed lost-like sheep without a shepherd. And so, he advised that people ask God for re-enforcements. By the same token, dads today need help in many areas. The church can and should be one of them. By taking some of the load off or providing opportunities for family-friendly activities, it can help dads find the time they need to "be all that they can be."

Lessons on Fathers - Part 6 of 7

Text: 2 Kings 5:1-15

Key verse: 2 Kings 5:13b "…My father, if the prophet would have told you to do some great thing, would you not have done it?"

A man went to his doctor to see if he could find out why he was having headaches and frequent ringing in his ears. The doctor thought that it had something to do with his teeth and so the guy went and got all his teeth pulled. When that didn't solve it, he went to another doctor who thought it was high blood pressure and put him on a strict diet. When that didn't work, he went to a third doctor who said he had a terminal disease and only had months to live. After getting over the shock of that, the guy decided to spend his savings and live it up a little. He bought a fancy sports car then went to the tailor to be fitted for an expensive suit. When the tailor called out his neck size of 16and ½, the guy said that couldn't be right as he had always worn a size 15. "That can't be right," said the tailor, "If you tried to wear a size 15, you'd be having headaches and ringing in your ears."

Too bad the man didn't see his tailor first. And it's too bad when dads aren't better people of influence. The problem is that there is a "window of opportunity" that can be missed and if it is, someone else who does not have their best interests in mind will influence them. The same is true of Christians, as well. All people have "teachable moments" when they can be influenced for good. But when those moments are missed, they may never occur again. Yet, God is merciful and is not willing that any should perish. So, he brings events to bear that would not have occurred otherwise, giving a chance at redemption when there was none before.

In today's lesson, there are at least 2 people who became "persons of influence" to Naaman- his servant girl and his servant boy. Their positions should not have put them there but their willingness to speak their heart did. In the same way, fathers must speak and care as they get the chance for a better time might not announce itself.

Lessons on Fathers - Part 7 of 7

Text and Key verse: Ephesians 6:4 "Fathers, don't exasperate your children by coming down hard on them. Take them by the hand and lead them in the way of the Master."

On his 16th birthday, the son approached his father about driving the family car. The dad replied, "Son, driving a car takes maturity and so far, you haven't showed that." "Well, what do I have to do?", the son asked. "Bring your grades up, read your Bible daily and get your hair cut, and we'll talk about it." The son knew that his dad was good for his word, but he really didn't want to cut his hair. So, he decided that he would do the first 2 things and then see what his dad would say. So, he worked hard, brought his grades up and discussed his daily Bible reading each day with his dad so he'd see he was doing it. Finally, he went to his dad and asked if he had done enough. "All except your hair," Dad said. "I just don't see why I have to do that, Dad. After all, Jesus never cut his hair." "That's right, son, and he walked everywhere he went."

Now I can't say if that dad was being too hard on his son. Everybody's different. But we do need to be sensitive to our children's unique circumstances so we can make the necessary adjustments, when necessary. I do know from personal experience that my sister, to her dying day, thought my dad was too hard on her and, as a result, did not like him.

It has been suggested that there are 4 tests that can be applied when fathers are evaluating a course of action for themselves or their children. The first test is common sense, which speaks for itself: does what I want to do or make my child do likely to give a good result?

The second test is publicity. In other words, would I or my child do this and so if everybody were to find out in the newspapers? This again speaks for itself.

The final 2 tests require some serious reflection: can they or I still do this and still be true to our best self? And can they or I still do this and be in the Spirit of Christ? If all these tests can be passed, then we and they can move ahead with some degree of certainty and assurance.

REFLECTIONS

Forgiveness

Forgiveness is the essence of the gospel and the instruction manual for how we are to interact with one another. In my life, however, I have seen the effects of what a lack of forgiveness can do. It is a poison that people take in the hope that it kills someone else- but it doesn't. We call those disagreements grudges, and they are often held for years- even past the time when the antagonists remember what the original cause had been. This is in stark contrast to what God calls for in his word and to what Jesus calls us to in the Lord's Prayer. But it is not impossible for us. Jesus modeled it in his behavior during the time of his crucifixion: "Father, forgive them, for they know not what they do." For us it starts when we ask Jesus to forgive us for the way we feel toward someone and to love them through us. We may not want to forgive but we find, in time-miraculously- that our hearts do grow "softer" toward them through Jesus' influence. Friend- don't wait another day to begin this process. It is a matter of Spiritual life-or-death.

Lessons on Forgiveness - Part 1 of 7

Text: Isaiah 1:10-20

Key verse: Isaiah 1:18 b "Though your sins are like scarlet, they shall be white as snow."

A father and his little daughter were riding an elevator when, suddenly, the lady who was standing in front of them turned around and slapped the father's face. When the elevator stopped, she stormed out, looking back with looks that could kill. The father was hurt and confused as he wondered aloud what has bothering her. The little daughter replied, "I don't know, Daddy. I think she's just a mean lady. While we were on the elevator, she stepped on my toes, so I pinched her bottom as hard as I could. That's when she started to pick on you."

This was the human response, but it is not one that displays the love and forgiveness of God. Indeed, to love in return for hurt is a response that requires much prayer and discipline. The Old Testament model for this comes to us from God the Father in many places. Today's example comes to us from the prophet, Isaiah. In our lesson for today, God is telling the Israelites that he is tired of their empty ceremonial displays of piety when their actions towards others are full of evil. In other words, they are just "going through the motions" in serving him. But God wants to forgive them and not remind them of past sins.

This is one of Satan's worst tricks-to remind of things that have been forgiven in the past in order to make us feel guilty. A young boy who had received a slingshot for a birthday present, was not a good shot-which just made him try all the harder. So, while visiting his grandma, he took a shot at her favorite duck- and hit it and killed it. He immediately hid the duck in a woodpile-Hopping that no one had seen. But alas, his sister has seen everything and promised to tell if he didn't do just as she said. For the next 2 days, the boy did both his sister's chores and his own until he couldn't take it anymore and confessed his sin to his grandma. "Johnny", she said," I saw the whole thing but forgave you because I love you. I was just wondering how long you would let your sister hold you accountable."

Lessons on Forgiveness - Part 2 of 7

Text: Luke 7:36-50

Key verse: Luke 7:47b "The one who is forgiven little loves little."

Years ago, in mining communities, it was common for people to owe quite a bit of money to the company store, as it was the only place that one could buy with credit. So, one wintry-cold evening, Sam, a miner, came in, hung up his heavy winter jacket, and proceeded to get a load of groceries. "Hey, Sam," said the store clerk, "Your bill is getting pretty high." "Sorry," said Sam, "I'm broke this week." "That's ok," said the clerk, "I'll just write what you owe right here on the wall." "But I don't want my friends to see what i owe", said Sam. "They won't", said the clerk, "I'll just cover it up with your coat 'til the bill's paid."

Indeed, forgiveness for many is a heavy burden. In today's lesson, a notorious sinner shows her remorse by anointing Jesus' feet with an expensive oil, then wipes them with her hair. To Jesus it is an act of great love, and he tells her that her sins are forgiven. But to Jesus' host, Jesus points out his lack of remorse because he apparently feels that he has done little that would require forgiveness. He is saying that one's awareness of their sin is a crucial component in recognizing their need for a savior.

In my work experience on a drug and alcohol ward, i found that people would often deny to themselves the extent of their addiction and the amount of help they really needed. They would always look for someone who was worse off than themselves and say they would stop drinking or doing drugs when they got as bad as that person. But inevitably, when they got there, they would look for someone even worse.

Clearly, then, it would appear that forgiving sooner rather than later reduces the burden just as recognizing one's addiction sooner rather than later makes the process less painful. We, as Christians, must help people think they have "hit bottom" so that they can get ready to get better. Otherwise, they will not be inclined to change.

Lessons on Forgiveness - Part 3 of 7

Text: Luke 15: 11-32

Key verse: Luke 15:24b "He was lost and now is found!"

A guy received his paycheck and found that he had been given $100 too much. The next week the company found their mistake and corrected it, giving the guy $100 less. The guy went in to complain and was reminded that he had not complained the previous week. "Yes", he said. "I can forgive one mistake but now it's getting to be a habit."

Indeed, we can certainly forgive an error in our favor much easier than the other way around. In today's lesson, the elder brother finds it very hard to forgive his brother who had wasted his part of his father's inheritance. Yet, it cost him nothing to do so. We must be on guard for this type of thinking for it is the essence of a sin that will ultimately destroy us.

The parable of the Prodigal Son is one of the best-known stories of the Bible. The forgiveness of the father reminds us of the love and forgiveness available to all sinners who repent. The remorse of the younger son after he is confronted with the error of his ways reminds us of the sin nature we all carry and the results of it when it is left unchecked. Finally, we are comforted by the healing power of forgiveness.

Even so, the lesson from the story is only made sure by the personal experience of forgiveness in our own real life. A story is told of a fraternity hazing incident in which a "brother" accidentally killed a pledge. Although it was ruled an accident, the brother carried the guilt of his actions for many years- which resulted in loss of wife and family, firing from work and alcoholism. However, when he was confronted by the victim's mother and forgiven by her, he was able to change his life for the better. We, too, in like manner have been forgiven through the undeserved gift of Christ's sacrificial death. So, we must not withhold that forgiveness from others.

Lessons on Forgiveness-part 4 of 7

Text: 2 Corinthians 5:16-21

Key verse: 2 Corinthians 5;17a "If anyone is in Christ, he becomes a new creation."

A seminary professor, who was now retired but had previously trained new pastors about love and forgiveness, was having a new concrete driveway poured. After it was done, he went inside to have some iced tea. When he came back out, he saw some neighborhood kids putting their handprints in the wet cement. Angry, he yelled at them and began to chase them down the street until he remembered his age. When he got back to his front porch, his wife was waiting for him with a stern rebuke. "I hope you're proud of yourself. You've spent your whole life talking about the importance of love and forgiveness but could not show any yourself." He realized she was right but tried to explain". "I do love those kids in the abstract –just not in the concrete."

The apostle Paul often thought back to the role he played in the early persecution of the church and, no doubt, the memories of it were painful. Yet, he was assured that his sins and past were forgiven in Christ and shared that with the Corinthian church and us. It is the essence of grace-the undeserved gift of forgiveness.

Another seminary professor hoped to teach his students about this grace. So, he made up a final exam that was extremely difficult and gave these instructions to them as he passed it out; read the test through first then see the final statement before beginning. The final statement gave the students the option of taking the test as is or just signing their name without answering any questions and receiving an A. As the students reviewed the test questions, they saw that none of them had adequately prepared for it. In taking the A, they would experience grace.

For us, we have a similar choice. Either we try to earn our way into the kingdom of heaven or just accept the gift of Christ's redeeming sacrifice. As God's standard is perfection, I hope that the choice is clear.

Lessons on Forgiveness - Part 5 of 7

Text: Ephesians 4:4-6, 15-18, 20,32

Key verse: Ephesians 4:4a "You are one body and one Spirit..."

A woman was bitten by a dog with rabies and was advised by her doctor to put everything in order. So, then she got out a piece of paper and began to write feverishly. "that's some will you're making, "remarked her doctor. "Will, nothing," replied the woman. "I'm making a list of the people that I'm going to bite!"

Certainly, not a Christian attitude, is it? When we consider today's scripture, it is in stark contrast. We should display oneness within the church. This is not possible without the example of Christ nor the help of the Holy Spirit. We take our lead from him and he, in turn, keeps us in step.

We cannot afford to let down our guard, particularly in a public place. A waitress was bringing out a gallon of thousand island dressing to replenish the salad bar but paused at the swinging kitchen doors to let another worker through. That's when both doors caught her unexpectedly, causing her to drop her open container of dressing- all over a customer's head, shirt, and suit. He went crazy calling her an idiot and threatening to sue. She quickly got the manager who apologized profusely and offered to get his suit cleaned. That was not good enough for him and he demanded $300 for a new suit- which, to avoid further trouble, the manager complied with. This was a true story, but more details must be considered. He had a suit on for a Sunday buffet-which must have meant that he had come from church. And, if this was the case, was he paying attention to the sermon or anything else that was said or done there? Granted, it was an embarrassing moment. But friends, people often accuse us of hypocrisy. When we act this way, how could that perception ever change?

Lessons on Forgiveness - Part 6 of 7

Text: Philippians 3:13-14

Key verse: Philippians 3:13b "I forget about the things behind me and reach out for the things ahead of me."

A blind man was telling some folks about how much he enjoyed the sport of parachuting. Yet some folks were a little skeptical. So, he assured them that there were people on board who would check his rigging, tell him when to jump and put his hand on the ripcord. "But how do you know when you're getting close to the ground?" they asked. "My guide dog's leash goes slack."

A blind person must remember where everything is. To forget could easily be fatal-and not just in parachuting. But to forget one's sinful past can be a good thing for Christians. In today's scripture lesson, the apostle Paul says that in forgetting the past, he can focus on the future. And, in Paul's case, he had a lot to forget. He was, at one time, the most avid persecutor of Christians in the world. Similarly, there are many people in the world today who cannot imagine being able to be forgiven for what they have done. We need to help them to see the truth about this- that there is no condemnation for those in Christ.

It's a little like coming to a baseball game expecting to be entertained and have a good time- perhaps even visiting the concession stand before taking one's seat-in hopes that the food will somehow heighten the enjoyment. But by the time they take their seat, their team is down by 10 runs- with little hope of winning. They think it's too late.

But the fact of the matter is that it's never too late as long as we have life and breath. The Bible says it clearly: if we confess our sins, he is faithful and just to forgive us our sins and cleanse us from all unrighteousness.

Lessons on Forgiveness - Part 7 of 7

Text: Hebrews 12:14-17

Key verse: Hebrews 12:15b "Make sure that no root of bitterness grows up that might cause trouble and pollute many people."

Once upon a time there was a very small, but brave knight. He was so small, in fact, that he rode on a great Dane instead of a horse. One night, the knight ran into an unexpected storm and sought lodging for himself and his animal. The innkeeper, who did not like knights, was about to turn him down when he noticed the poor dog, all dripping wet and miserable, and he relented. After all, he reasoned, how could he turn a dog out on a knight like this?

I suppose the innkeeper had his reasons for not liking knights, but to generalize like this is not good, nor Christian. Today's scripture lesson warns against this as does the Lord's Prayer- that demands that we forgive as we want to be forgiven by God. Such forgiveness, then, is a choice that we must make.

Fanny Crosby, the great hymn writer was rendered blind by the mistake of a physician who gave an incorrect treatment for a minor eye inflammation. She could have been angry for his error but instead decided to make the best of what she had left. Later in life she was quoted as being thankful for her blindness as she felt it kept her focused on her hymn writing.

Obviously, this is easier said than done. Yet we know that holding onto bitterness is not good for us. It is a little like drinking poison and hoping that someone else will die from it. This is not the example of Christ.

REFLECTIONS

Future

As I get older, my thoughts of the future seem to be much more frequent than they used to be. I find myself checking out the obituaries in the newspaper not only to see if there is someone I know, but to see if I've lived longer than they. Although that may sound morbid, I don't think it's meant to be. I'm just more aware of my own mortality. When I was younger, I often thought about the near-term future, such as in the next week or month. And I was fascinated with the latest technological breakthroughs (sort of a "Jetsons" mindset). But now those breakthroughs are happening so fast that I can't keep up with them-nor do I care to. What concerns me the most, however, is the increasing negativity associated with the Christian way of life. I see how Christian politicians are singled out for particular scrutiny by the media and by the late-night talk shows. I mean this country was founded on Christian principles, but it is as if the majority of people are ashamed of that or, at least, concertedly forgetful. So, I worry about what that will mean for my children and grandchildren. As for me, however, I know who holds tomorrow.

Lessons on the Future - Part 1 of 7

Text: Numbers 13

Key verse: numbers 13:31b "We can't go up against the people for they are stronger than we."

A blind man flew down for his first visit to Texas. When he got off the plane, he asked what gate he was at and was told "gate 50". He responded that where he was from, there were only 10 gates. "Everything is bigger in Texas", he was told. When he was taken to his hotel, he was assigned to room# 500. "Wow", he exclaimed,"500 rooms! This must be some hotel!" "Everything is bigger in Texas", he was told. While he was eating his dinner in the hotel restaurant, he asked where the restrooms were and was told that it was the 2nd door in the hallway on the right. But as he was going there, he got distracted and took the 3rd door to the right-which was the entrance to the hotel swimming pool. When he fell in the pool, he was afraid of what might happen next and yelled, "Don't flush! Don't flush!"

Just as people are led to believe that everything in Texas is bigger, God expects us to believe that his vision is better. In today's lesson, God advises Moses to send 12 spies into the Promised Land to check it out. 10 of the spies come back with a negative report and only 2 with a positive one. They saw the same things but interpreted them differently. The difference was perception. 10 spies saw things from man's perception and 2 from Gods.

Vince Lombardi, one of the best football coaches of all time, explained what makes a coach good. Good coaches know what the end result should look like.so, in effect, success is no surprise to them. They already have a mental picture of what the future could look like. But that's the closest that human beings can get.

God, on the other hand, knows the future. His problem is getting us to see it and/or getting a coach to inspire it. Regardless, the future for those deciding which perception to follow depends on our effort.

Lessons on the Future - Part 2 of 7

Text: Joshua 1:1-7

Key verse: Joshua 1:5b "I will be with you in the same way I was with Moses."

A little girl made a particularly lifelike clay model of an angel with wings then held it up in art class for everyone to see. The whole class seemed to like her model, which pleased the little girl greatly. Then she balled up her creation and held it up and asked the class what they saw. The only answer she got was that it looked like a ball. But she said, "No, it's a hiding angel."

When we look at the future, we must similarly use our imagination. What lies ahead can be an exciting possibility-or not. For Joshua, after the death of Moses and on the brink of the Promised Land, the future was full of exciting possibilities- but especially so because God would be with him. It was helpful, too, that Joshua had been there before- when he was one of 12 spies that had looked over the land.

We are often not that fortunate. We cannot often see the finish line. Such was the case for young Florence Chadwick, the famous long-distance swimmer in July of 1952, when she tried to swim the 21-mile distance between Catalina Island and the shores of California. She swam 15 hours in cold, shark-infested waters only to give up-just a mile from shore. You see, it wasn't the cold water or the sharks, it was the fog that kept the finish line out of sight.

Similarly, we are tempted to give up when we don't see how things can end up positively. But, as Christians, we know that God is with us and will see us through. That's what makes all the difference.

Lessons on the Future - Part 3 of 7

Text: Nehemiah 1-6

Key verse: Nehemiah 2:18c "Let's start rebuilding! "they said," and they eagerly began the work."

The little 5-year-old daughter announced to her mother one day that she was going to become a nurse. Her mother, though, was not sure she had given the matter adequate thought. "Honey, "she began," you can be anything you want- even President of the United States! Not that it's bad to be a nurse, if that's what you want to be." "Well," the little girl responded, "if I can be anything, I'd rather be a horse."

In today's lesson, Nehemiah, the cupbearer to the king, had what most people thought was just as impossible of a dream- to rebuild the walls and gates of Jerusalem. There were the skilled volunteers, the materials, the travel allowances to be arranged for- not to mention getting the permission of the king to go. Yet, a vision that is strong enough will only see these things as "bumps in the road".

In our nation's history, $100,000 had to be raised to erect the base upon which the Statue of Tiberty would rest. At that time, that was an impossible sum of money. But Joseph Pulitzer, the editor of the New York World newspaper, had a vision that if enough people would send in what they could, the money could be raised. Although many other newspapers mocked his idea, Pulitzer made a public appeal in his newspaper, and the money was raised.

To make a vision a reality today-especially one that glorifies God and has the potential for building up the kingdom of God- it must be "bathed" in prayer. Nehemiah's vision was. Nevertheless, his vision had considerable opposition and hardship to be overcome-despite its Godly intent. We must be willing to face the same.

Lessons on the Future - Part 4 of 7

Text: 2 Samuel 7

Key verse: 2 Samuel 7:16 "Your dynasty and your kingdom will be secured forever before me.'

The Smith's were proud of their ancestors –with one exception, Uncle George, who was sent to the electric chair. Yet, other than him, they had ancestors who came to America on the Mayflower as well as other prominent historical figures. So, in deciding to have their family history written up, they wanted to know how their hired writer would handle Uncle George. This is what he wrote:" George Smith occupied a chair of applied electronics at a prominent government institution, was attached to his position with the strongest of ties so that his death came as a great shock."

People are rightly concerned about the legacy that they leave behind. Such was the case of King David in today's lesson. Since God had given his nation peace from its enemies, David wanted to build the Lord a house. But the Lord had other plans. Nevertheless, God was pleased by David's Godly intentions and the quality of his leadership and rewarded David with the knowledge that God would secure his dynasty and kingdom forever.

We are, perhaps, perplexed that God would promise a mere human such an honor. Indeed, David, himself, was amazed at God's generosity. We, who read about this even now, wonder if God would do the same for us and under what circumstances. This is not a subject worthy of our consideration as it is the sovereignty of God. God will honor who he wants to honor. Our job is to honor Him. When we do this to the best of our ability and desire, our legacy, though perhaps different from David's, will similarly be assured.

My guess is that our legacy will best be attained, then, by keeping it on track in the short term. Former professional football placekicker, Ray Wershing, puts it best. When he got ready to kick a field goal, he never looked at the goalposts, but instead aligned himself with the field's hash-marks as they were the same width and appeared larger.

Lessons on the Future - Part 5 of 7

Text: Jeremiah 29:4-14

Key verse: Jeremiah 29:11 "I know the plans I have for you; plans to prosper you and not to harm you; plans to give you a hope and a future."

A woman went into the tent of a fortune teller at a county fair to find out her future. As the fortune teller looked into her crystal ball, she frowned. "What's the matter? asked the woman. "The next 15 years of your life will be filled with disappointment, unhappiness and poverty," the fortune teller said. Ok," the woman replied, "but what happens next?" "You'll get used to it", came the reply.

Not a hopeful outlook, is it? Well, the Israelites in exile did not have much to be hopeful for, either, from all outward appearances. But the prophet Jeremiah shared good news with them in today's lesson. It may not have been what they wanted to hear, but it was enough to show them that God still cared for them and that he had the current situation well under control. They would be staying for a while, but God would help them to prosper until the time came for their return.

When things don't turn out the way we planned, we have a choice, as well. We can complain and feel sorry for ourselves, or we can make the best of things while trusting that God cares and has our situation well under control. It's when we put our hope in anything but God that we really court problems.

A man contracted cancer, and by the time he sought medical care, it had spread to various places in his body. But he had great faith in medical science and new treatment options. So, when he heard about a new drug called Krebiozen, he had his doctor prescribe it for him. After taking it for 2 months, most of his cancer had disappeared. But when the American medical association finally said that the drug was not a valid treatment option, his cancer returned, and he died shortly thereafter. Hope for a better tomorrow is crucial, so we must be careful of its source. God, alone, can be trusted.

Lessons on the Future-Part 6 of 7

Text: Matthew 7: 24-27

Key verse: Isaiah 33:6 "He will be the sure foundation for your times,.."

Taxiing down the runway, the jetliner abruptly stopped then headed back to the gate. After an hour or more, the plane was cleared to take off again. When a concerned traveler asked what had caused the delay, he was told that the pilot was bothered by a noise he heard from the engine and that it had taken this amount of time to find a different pilot.

Not a firm foundation for trust, is it? When it comes to air travel, passenger safety should be the top priority. But when it comes to leading the best moral life, we can, God is the only sure foundation. In today's lesson, a parable is told of 2 builders who built on entirely different foundations. When the rain came, however, the choices they made for foundations were tested and one was found wanting. But, as is often the case, Jesus was not really talking about building in the literal sense, but in the Spiritual. That is, He must be our foundation.

What that means to us is several things: a familiarity with and willingness to follow God's word, as it is found in the Bible, a balance of fear of and love for God, the discernment for companions who help rather than hinder our relationship to God and a firm reliance on prayer. This is the Spirit of discipline and not compromise with the standards of this world.

After hurricane Andrew, a tv crew was filming the devastation of one Florida community. In this one neighborhood, only 1 house was left standing on its foundation. So, the crew interviewed the owner and asked him why his house was still standing. He replied that he built the house to code and did not deviate. He was told at the time that if he built according to code, his house would withstand a hurricane. He did and it did. So, it must be for us, Spiritually.

Lessons on the Future- Part 7 of 7

Text: Revelation 21

Key verse: 1 Corinthians 2:9 "Eye hath not seen, nor ear heard, the things that God hath prepared for them that love him."

A college student went into a photography studio to have a picture of his girlfriend copied. But the photographer couldn't help but smile when he saw the inscription on the back. It said, "Dearest Tom, I love you forever-but if we ever break up, I want this picture back. -love, Diane"

Sure doesn't sound like a sure thing, does it? Not so with the promises of God-including the incredible beauty and happiness that await us in heaven. Indeed, because we know it is a "sure thing" (in Jesus), we can have confidence in facing the future.

When the Golden Gate Bridge was being constructed in San Francisco, 23 men fell to their deaths. Construction was halted for a period of time because of the danger involved. But when a safety net was constructed underneath, the work proceeded 25% faster because the net provided assurance of the worker's safety.

By the same token, we, as Christians, can continue to serve the Lord even in the most difficult of situations because we have heaven to look forward to. There we will have no more pain, death or tears.

REFLECTIONS

God

What can a mere human say about God? The psalmist asks, "What is man that thou art mindful of him?" What I can say, though, is that for many years I had a mistaken concept. I saw God as a sort of grandfatherly figure that I could go to if i was in a tight spot or to ask for something that I could not hope to get on my own. I did not see him as an indifferent or vengeful power that just waited for me to make a mistake so that he could crush me. Yet I did not see him as a being who wanted to have communication with me- or a relationship. I thought him too holy for that or myself as too insignificant for him to bother with. I could not reconcile Old Testament accounts of whole peoples being obliterated with Jesus' accounts of his being a God of love. in effect I'm not sure if i ever can or to say with any certainty that I understand his ways. Nevertheless, I know in my heart that he indeed loves me. He thought enough about me to provide the means by which my sins are forgiven and for me to have a home in heaven. In my mind, though, I will never see myself as being worthy of such love- which makes me eternally grateful and desirous of being of greater service to him.

Lessons on God - Part 1 of 7

Text: Genesis 1

Key verse: Genesis 1:1 "In the beginning, God created the heavens and the earth."

Grandpa and his granddaughter were having a little talk in front of the mirror in the hallway. "Did God make you, Grandpa?" "Yes, he did," said grandpa. "Did God make me?" "Yes, he made you, too." The granddaughter thought for a while, then said, "I think God's doing better work these days."

Of course, this talk was based on their acceptance of the concept called "creationism", as it is explained in the Bible. Not everyone thinks this way. Even so, no explanation is foolproof. Each one asks you to accept some things by faith. Not everyone is "on board" with that, either though. Our third President, Thomas Jefferson, was a scientific- minded person not given to accepting anything that could not be proved, scientifically. And so, his Bible would remind you a little of Swiss cheese, as there are so many holes in it.

Friend, there is no way around it: either you accept God's explanation, or you don't. Just be aware that without faith, it is impossible to please God. Ironically, more and more scientists are coming around to accepting creationism. They do so at great personal risk to their professional career. It's just that the other so-called theories leave so much to be desired.

If we do accept creationism, however, we must also accept our responsibility for the stewardship of it. This, we have failed to do. You see, when God looked everything over, he pronounced it as very good-hardly, our assessment today. We must, then, take greater interest and greater responsibility for all things that are within our control.

Lessons on God - Part 2 of 7

Text: Psalms 23

Key verse: Psalm 23 :4b "...I will fear no evil for thou art with me;"

3 men went on a fishing trip. But when a storm came up and wrecked their boat, they ended up on a deserted island. After a week, 2 of the 3 became very sad over missing their former way of life. One, a cattle rancher, missed his ranch and ranching. Another, a cab driver, missed driving in the big city. So, one day, as they walked along the beach, they found a genie's lamp and were given each a wish. The rancher went first and wished he was back on his ranch and poof, he was gone. The cab driver went next and wished he was back driving cab in the big city and poof, he was gone. The third guy, who kind of liked life with the other guys in spite of the hardship, was lonely and wished that the other 2 guys were back with him again, and proof, it was so.

In 1996, Billy Graham made a speech on the occasion of receiving the highest civilian award, the Golden Congressional medal. In this speech he claimed that the 3 biggest problems facing mankind today are loneliness, guilt and fear of death. But, he stated, God has provided for help in these areas and noted that we must live out our faith.

With the Lord as our shepherd, we will never be alone or lonely, he stated. Furthermore, faith in God negates our fear of death. The example he used was like traveling through a heavy fog, when glimpses of the sun would give us temporary respite. In the same way, a stranger's smile or the love of a friend help us know that darkness and death will not destroy forever but that everything will eventually be ok.

He also said that God restores our souls and leads us in paths of righteousness to free us of our guilt. A pastor was in a hurry to complete his visitations as he had some pressing business at home. But he remembered that he had to get a couple of things first at the grocery store. As he was leaving the store he realized that the clerk had given him too much change. But he went back anyway and confronted the clerk. She said she gave him too much on purpose to see if he practiced his preaching on honesty of the Sunday before.

Lessons on God – Part 3 of 7

Text: John 15:1-4

Key verse: John 15:2bc "…, while every branch that does bear fruit he prunes so that it will be even more fruitful."

A guy was having a little trouble deciding what to have at one of his favorite restaurants, so he asked the waiter for a recommendation. The waiter suggested chicken on a bed of wild rice with green beans almondine. The guy said, "Sounds great! But how is the chicken prepared?" The waiter, who had a great sense of humor, replied," We break it to him gently and tell him that it is nothing personal."

When God does prune in our lives, it can be painful, but it is personal. God prunes us so we will be more fruitful in gaining converts for the kingdom of heaven. In the gospel according to John, Jesus compared his father to a gardener who is an expert in getting the most out of his plants. Yet, there are things we can do to make his work even more productive. These things are ensuring that the foundation of our faith is Jesus, expressing our faith in the midst of challenges and confronting our fears one step at a time.

When Bob Wieland lost both legs in Vietnam, most people would have given up. But not Bob, who took his handicap as an incentive to show people what a person could do with faith in God. He competed in the 1986 New York marathon and finished with the slowest time ever- 4 days, 2 hours, 48 minutes and 17 seconds. But he did it by planting his arms and swinging his torso forward.

Clearly, this is an extreme example but we, who are handicapped by other shortcomings, must confront them one day at a time-with God's help. And, in doing so, we give hope to others who have shortcomings.

Lessons on God - Part 4 of 7

Text: Acts 16:16-34

Key verse: Acts 16:30b "Sirs, what must I do to be saved?"

A little boy broke the glass of a streetlamp and asked his father what he should do. The father said that he must report it and then make arrangements to pay. This wasn't what the little boy expected to hear. He thought he'd just have to ask God to forgive him.

In his mind, that would have been justice. Indeed, our concept of justice and God's are probably very different- particularly as it relates to us. Indeed, how often do we wish that justice be done to someone who has wronged us while we pray for mercy for ourselves?

In today's lesson, Paul and Silas get in trouble for casting out a demon from a fortune teller. Although this could be considered a good thing from our perspective, from the men who profited from her powers, it was a very bad thing. The legal authorities apparently agreed and put Paul and Silas in prison. How fair was this? Yet Paul and Silas accepted their fate gracefully and used it to testify to the Lordship of Jesus. Perhaps we might be tempted to complain about this outcome if it were us. But Paul and Silas had the Christian maturity to trust God to bring things out right- as must we.

We cannot expect the world to understand this, however, because the world's priorities are often much different than ours. Consider this illustration: a Florida man was upset about the drug-dealing going on in his neighborhood. So, he called the sheriff's office to report it and was told that they needed proof in order to act. So, the guy bought a $4 bag of marijuana and called the sheriff's office to report it. The sheriff's office then came out and arrested him for possession.

Lessons on God – Part 5 of 7

Text: Luke 23 :39-43

Key verse: Luke 23:43b "..., today you will be with me in paradise."

A lady asks the produce clerk if she can buy a half-head of lettuce. He says that it usually isn't done that way, but he would ask the store manager. He goes up to the manager and says, "There's this stupid lady asking if she can buy a half-head of lettuce" and then, noticing that the lady is right behind her, continues, "and this lovely lady here wants to buy the other half." The manager approves the sale, the lady goes on her way, then the manager says, "That's the smoothest example I've ever seen of thinking on your feet. Where did you learn that?" "I grew up in Grand Rapids, Michigan-the home of ugly women and great hockey teams." "Hey, my wife is from Grand Rapids!" "Oh, what hockey team did she play on?"

When one considers the love of God, one doesn't have to be careful of who is listening because he loves all of us, all the time. Yet, we often miss it because it may not look the way we think it should or we miss it because we think we're unworthy of it. Indeed, we are unworthy of it. But that doesn't stop God from loving us, anyway.

In today's lesson, the thieves on the cross both want the love of God but only one thinks to ask for it. This is an important concept! Often times, people disqualify themselves for the love of God when it has been there all the time. It's not a matter of being smooth enough or good enough. And it's not a matter of God only giving us good things.

When Robert Schuller's daughter lost a leg in a horrible skiing accident, he was concerned about its impact on her faith. But when he gave her a rose from his garden, she said, "This is to my heavenly father", and taking one petal off at a time, she said, "He loves me, he loves me, he loves me," and so he does.

Lessons on God - Part 6 of 7

Text: 2 Corinthians 12:7-10

Key verse: 2 Corinthians 12:9a "My grace is sufficient for you,..."

As they prepared for their first parachute jump, a group of soldiers listened as the jumpmaster explained the procedure: "When the green light comes on, everyone will stand up, hook up, jump out and count to 4. If your main chute doesn't open, pull the cord for the emergency chute. Then, after you land, a bus will take you back to main post." One soldier, however, followed procedure but neither his main or emergency chute deployed. As he continued downward, he thought to himself, "This is just great! Probably the bus won't be there, either."

Stories such as this are rampant in the services because things don't always go as planned. Even so, we did not come to this cynicism by accident, it is a natural phenomenon when people don't deliver on their promises. And, unfortunately, many people come to assume the same thing about God. They end up not trusting him when he doesn't come through for them. They fail to appreciate God's sovereignty.

In today's lesson, Paul has asked God on 3 separate occasions to remove some affliction from him. In each case, God's answer was no- that his grace was sufficient for him. This probably confuses some folks because they figure that God would surely grant someone like Paul's requests- for all Paul had done for the sake of the gospel. But they, too, do not consider the sovereignty of God- that God will do what God will do- that God has purposes that we cannot understand. Indeed, it takes a great deal of Christian maturity to consider God's no as Paul did- that in Paul's weakness that God was rendered strong.

Joseph Criven, the writer of one of our greatest hymns, "What a Friend We Have in Jesus", had a shock that few of us could handle successfully: on the night before his scheduled wedding, his fiancée' drowned. Yet, instead of being angry at God, he devoted the rest of his life to helping others. Would we similarly turn our scars into stars.

Lessons on God - Part 7of 7

Text: 1 Corinthians 2:7-10

Key verse: 1 Corinthians 2:14a "The man without the Spirit does not accept the things that come from the Spirit of God, for they are foolishness to him…"

The Mexican criminal who robbed many banks in Texas was being hotly pursued by the Texas Rangers. Finally, they caught him in a Texas border town restaurant. The man leading the Rangers had the bad guy's waiter translate their message: Tell us where the money is, or we'll have to shoot you where you are! The bad guy quickly told the waiter where the money was located. Then the waiter said, "He says he'll never tell, and you can start shooting."

Obviously, the waiter knew what the Rangers wanted to know, but he decided to keep it to himself. God, on the other hand, does not want his wisdom hidden from us-he shares it with his Spirit, who will make it known as we seek God's wisdom from prayer and Bible reading. In today's lesson, Paul, in writing to the church at Corinth, advises that his teaching is not in the form and content of other speakers they have heard for his words have come from God's Spirit. As such, they are to be followed closely and not changed or added to.

God is omniscient-he knows everything. So, when we seek God's wisdom, it is always right. However, it is often hidden and not easily discerned. A man was following a series of cars down the road and could not understand why the guy 2 cars down was staying so far back. What he could not see was that the car in question was following a truck with a long, low trailer attached. You see, God knows those things as well as those other things that are not physically discerned. That's why we must trust him.

REFLECTIONS

Grace

For me, grace is a relatively new concept, albeit a crucial one for the Christian faith. Growing up in western Pennsylvania during the 50's and 60's, we were conditioned to admire the persons who were able to "pick themselves up by their own bootstraps"- the rugged individualists. Nevertheless, this is in direct opposition to the concept of grace getting something that we could never deserve. You see, we acted (and some of us still acted!) as if we could earn our way into the Kingdom of Heaven. This is similar to the religious leaders of Jesus' day who felt that if they could keep the 10 Commandments perfectly, they would not need any help getting in- that they would be worthy. And although Jesus tried to show them that their hopes were based on a faulty assumption (that they only had to follow the letter of the law and not the Spirit), they never did "get It." We need to be careful that we don't fall into the same trap. We need to show others that we are just "sinners saved by grace", so they don't feel as if they have to be perfect.

Lessons on Grace - Part 1 of 7

Text: Zechariah 4:6

Key verse: Zechariah 4:6 "Not by might nor by power, but by my Spirit," says the Lord Almighty.

A man dies and goes to heaven. St. Peter meets him at the gates of heaven and explains it this way: "You need 100 points to get in. You tell me all the good things you've done in life, and I'll assign points to each." So, the man tells how faithful he was to his wife and church and the good he did for others in his community and St. Peter commends him and says, "that's worth 6 points." "Is that all?" Says the man. "At this rate, the only way I'll be able to get into heaven is by the Grace of God." "Bingo!", said St. Peter," that's 100 points! Come on in!"

Too many people believe that as long as they do more good things than bad, they'll get in. This is one of the devil's worst lies. We cannot earn our way into the Kingdom of Heaven. This is the essence of today's scripture verse. It is what God has done-not us- that gets us in.

It has been suggested that God has 3 kinds of servants in the world: slaves, mercenaries and sons and daughters. The first serve God because they don't know any better. This corresponds to our service when we are children. Our parents got us started, to church so we went-trusting in their wisdom. The second type serve God out of his ability to help us in some way. If we do such and such, he is obligated to do such and such for me. Some people never go any farther and fall short of God's kingdom because they believe they can earn their way in. However, some people finally realize that they can never do enough or be good enough on their own and accept their need for a savior. Once they do this, they are welcomed in. It is not their righteousness that got them there- but Jesus'.

Lessons on Grace - Part 2 of 7

Text: Matthew 20:1-16

Key verse: Matthew 20:16 "So the last will be first, and the first will be last."

After 20 years of shaving himself every morning, a guy decided that he would treat himself to a shave at the town's barber shop. This barbershop, which was owned by the pastor of the town's Baptist church, employed the pastor's wife, Grace. And, as she was working that day, she gave the man his shave. When it was completed, he was told that the shave would cost $20. He thought that was a little high but paid it anyway, since he had not asked how much before she began. When he awakened the next day, he was surprised that his face was still smooth and would require no shave. But he was even more surprised when his face was still smooth 2 weeks later. So, he went back to the barber shop to investigate. The barber (and pastor) told him he shouldn't be so surprised. When he asked why, he was told," you were shaved by Grace. Once shaved, always shaved."

The guy thought he paid too much for his shave until he saw how long it lasted. In today's lesson, the laborers hired at the start of the day thought they made a good deal until they found that the laborers hired at the end of the day got the same amount. It wasn't fair, they reasoned. From the standpoint of work done, it wasn't fair. But, since the laborers had agreed to the amount they would get, it was. But we must be careful when we compare apples to oranges. What is being discussed here is grace- which provides for the same reward regardless of when we experience it. Our response, then, to grace should not be anger but happiness for any who become saved, regardless of the lateness of the hour. We must remember that grace, by virtue of its definition, can never be earned or deserved. Therefore, we must be thankful that we have received it, as well.

Lessons on Grace - Part 3 of 7

Text: Ruth

Key verse: Ruth 2:10b "Why have I found favor in your eyes that you notice me- a foreigner?"

A Sunday School teacher asked her class of young children, "Would I get into heaven if I sold my house and car and gave all the money to the church?" "No!", they responded. "Well, what if I cleaned the church every day and cut its grass and continually kept it neat and tidy-would that get me in?" Again, the answer was a resounding "No!". "Well, then, how do I get in?" You have to be dead!" answered one little boy.

Actually, you have to have grace. And we see grace in the story of Ruth and Naomi. They received it because of nothing they did on their own. It was an undeserved gift. When Ruth and Naomi returned home, they had no land and no social status as widows. They were completely dependent on the kindness of strangers and on any work that they could get.as such, the odds for survival were not in their favor. But, of course, odds mean nothing to God, and he did provide- as he still does today.

A construction crew was building a road through a rural area, knocking trees down as they came through. A supervisor, however, noticed that 1 particular tree had a nest with birds in it that could not fly. So, he marked that tree to be spared. Several weeks later, he came back, saw the nest was empty and ordered the tree cut down. When the tree came down, the nest flew clear and along with it the materials that the birds had used to make it. Among those materials was a scrap from a Sunday School pamphlet that said: he cares for you. The birds had done nothing to merit being spared. And so, it is with each of us. The gift of grace is eternal life through the sacrificial death of a savior- Jesus Christ.

Lessons on Grace - Part 4 of 7

Text: 2 Samuel 9

Key verse: 2 Samuel 9:8 "What is your servant, that you should notice a dead dog like me?"

A carpenter was nailing shingles on a roof and lost his footing. As he started to slide down, he prayed, "Lord, please help me!" Suddenly, his pants got stuck on a nail-which stopped his fall. "Never mind, Lord," said the carpenter, "The nail has me now." His response is often our response as well. Since we want to earn the help we get, we don't want to be beholden to anyone-even God. Yet, since grace is undeserved merit, we have to be beholden. And that takes the realization that what God provides, we can never be worthy of.

In today's lesson, Mephibosheth, the son of Jonathan, was honored by King David for the kindness that was shown to David by Jonathan. Mephibosheth was surprised at this because such kindness was rare. Indeed, he had done nothing to deserve it and would not have accepted it unless David insisted.

A seminary professor wanted to illustrate the concept of grace to his class. So in passing out his final exam, he explained that the choices the students had were 3: they could take the test as is and receive the grade the results showed; they could decide not to take the test at all and receive an f, or they could sign their name to the statement at the end of the test, asking for grace, and receive an a. As crazy as it may sound, there were some students who turned their test in unsigned and some who took the test-which was very hard, by the way. Does this not show many people's attitude toward grace? It is a prideful thing that can have eternal, unnecessary consequences.

Lessons on Grace - Part 5 of 7

Text: John 14:1-6

Key verse: John 14:6 "I am the way the truth and the life. No one comes to the father except through me."

An older woman was talking about her relationship with her husband, who was an archaeologist. "I think the older I get, the better he likes me."

In saying this, she was saying that his love for her was in direct correlation to his job. In today's lesson, Jesus is saying that our relation to God is in direct correlation to our relation to Jesus. In other words, Jesus is the gift of grace from the father. To not accept him is to not accept God's offer of salvation.

A young woman was "sweating out" the first meeting she was to have with her boyfriend's parents. But when the dad met them at the curb, smiled, kissed her on the cheek and gave her a big hug, she felt accepted because of the relationship she had with the son.

Unfortunately, we often put too much emphasis on the feeling of acceptance. Our relationship to God through Jesus is based on fact. Back in 1863, when the Emancipation Proclamation was issued, the majority of slaves kept on living as if nothing had changed. Although the proclamation was law, they didn't feel as if they were free.

So, in effect, we must by faith believe that our relationship with Jesus has reconciled our alienation from God. We are accepted by the father because of our relationship with the son.

Lessons on Grace - Part 6 of 7

Text: Romans 6:1-2

Key verse: Romans 6:1b "Shall we go on sinning that grace may increase?"

A man bought a parrot from a pet store but, upon bringing it home, was discouraged because it seemed to say nothing but swear words. So, he warned the parrot that swearing was not acceptable and, if it continued, he would put the parrot in the freezer. Apparently, the parrot didn't believe the threat and continued to swear, so the man put it in the freezer for an hour. When he opened the freezer, the bird was almost frozen but said he wouldn't swear anymore. He just wanted to know one thing: "w-w-what d-d-did the t-t-turkey do?"

You might say the parrot got the wrong message- that freezers were for punishment. Yet it is even more critical that we do not get the wrong message from the word of God. In today's lesson, the Romans did as they felt that more sinning would lead to more grace. Paul was quick to eliminate that confusion, but we worry that others might think the same thing today.

When we consider why people get the wrong message, we have to start with our sin nature- that we are apt to believe what is in our best interests to believe. How that plays out with the concept of grace is that we mistakenly think that we have earned it. Until we correct that misinterpretation, we will "get it wrong" every time. No, the correct interpretation is that grace is something we could never deserve and thus, we become grateful for it.

We are not likely to come upon this gratitude naturally or overnight, but we can get there. News commentator Eric Sevareid and his crew had to parachute from a disabled army transport plane over the border between Burma and India during WW2. They had to hike through very difficult terrain during the muggy, monsoon season and found the travel exceedingly hard-especially with injuries sustained in the parachute jump. But they could get to the next ridge or the next friendly village to spend the night. Ultimately, they made "the next mile" and we can, too.

Lessons on Grace - Part 7 of 7

Text: Ephesians 2:8,9

Key verse: (message) Ephesians 2:8,9 "Saving is all his idea, and all his work. All we do is trust him enough to let him do it."

A guy was in an accident and put in a coma. When he woke up, the first person he saw was his wife. And this is what he said, "Judy, you've always been right there whenever I've had trouble. You were there when I failed out of school; you were there when I couldn't get a job; you were there when I lost out in the stock market; you were there when my company got down-sized, and they let me go and you're right here now". At this point his wife started to get tears in her eyes and then he said, "There's just one thing i want to say to you: Judy, you're just plain bad luck!"

Not what you were expecting, was it? Clearly, the guy couldn't see that he was the recipient of grace from his wife. He just couldn't bear to admit he might have had something to do with his misfortune. And this is the prevailing problem among unbelievers today. If they don't deserve grace, they don't want it. They don't want to be beholden.

There are three parts to grace that we must understand: by faith, gift of God and not of works. By faith means that we must believe what God's word says: that all have sinned and come short of the Kingdom of God. Gift of God means that we must believe that God provided the only acceptable means to get our sins forgiven-his son, Jesus Christ. It is a gift that God gave so that we could all be together in eternity as a family. And finally, not of works means that we can never deserve this gift or do anything to earn it ourselves. Indeed, once we can fully understand these three parts, we cannot help but be beholden.

For many, this goes completely "against the grain". We've been conditioned to think we must earn our way. But with God, his standard is perfection, so we can't do it ourselves. It must be his way.

REFLECTIONS

Gratitude

Gratitude is one of the most important qualities a person - not just a Christian-can have. Yet it does not naturally develop in us. It must be carefully and persistently encouraged. Family and church environments should be places where this happens. But sadly, in many such surroundings, it is not. The Bible admonishes us to be thankful in all circumstances. This is hard advice to follow. But please note that it says in all circumstances and not for all circumstances. Obviously, there is much in this life that we can hardly be thankful for. But since thankfulness should not be dependent on outward circumstances, it is possible to be thankful in difficult times. I did not learn this lesson until much later in my adult life. And, without an accompanying greater interest in the Spiritual, it probably would not have happened at all. I believe that God specializes in bringing good out of bad. Yet, to even come to this conclusion, one must first believe that God is good and wants the best for us. Without that, I cannot be optimistic about how most people will be able to reconcile reality with the goodness of God.

Lessons on Gratitude - Part 1 of 7

Text: Psalm 100

Key verse: Psalm 100:4a "Enter his gates with thanksgiving and his courts with praise;…"

A little boy was asked to list what he was thankful for, but his teacher wanted clarification of his answer. She said, "You put down that you were thankful for your glasses. Is it because they help you to see better?" "No," he replied, "They keep the other boys from hitting me and the girls from kissing me."

Psalm 100 tells us to give thanks to God and praise his name. My guess, then, is that we should give thanks for the little things-like glasses- as well as the big things- like health, work and family. And I think that cheerfulness is part of that. When we give with joy and thankfulness, the quality and quantity of the gift is not the important thing.

A Puerto Rican woman who knew little English came to Christ at an inner-city church. She didn't feel she had much to offer but she wanted to serve in some way. So, she volunteered to ride the church bus into city neighborhoods to pick up children for church. She would invariably look for the worst-looking child, put them in her lap and tell them over and over again that she loved them, and Jesus loved them. Over her months of faithful, joyful service, she became attached to one little boy who did not speak. Finally, though, as a result of her telling him of her love and that of Jesus, he said he loved her, too. Just a little gift, given with great joy and thankfulness, made a big difference. And it can be for you!

Lessons on Gratitude - Part 2 of 7

Text: Luke 17:11-19

Key verse: Luke 17;17b "Where are the other 9?"

A single young man spotted an attractive single woman and wanted to ask her out on a date but was hesitant about doing so because he was low on cash. Then, suddenly, she sneezes, and her glass eye flies out of its socket. He catches it and hands it to her." I'm so embarrassed", she says, "would you like to come to dinner with me?" He says yes and they have a great time. They then take in a movie, and she pays for everything. At the end of the date, she gives him a kiss and agrees to go out with him again. At this point, he's feeling very grateful but has to ask just one question: "Are you always this nice to guys that you just meet?" "Not usually", she says, "but you just caught my eye."

He was right to be grateful but there are times when we should be but aren't. Such is the case in today's lesson- the story of the 10 lepers who were cleansed. In the time of Jesus, leprosy had no known cure, so to receive that diagnosis was about the same as receiving a death sentence. If this were not bad enough, people with leprosy had to seclude themselves from others and yell "Unclean! Unclean!" Whenever they drew near other people. They were thought to be cursed of God. This was the setting for Jesus' miracle. Undoubtedly, they had heard the stories about his healing miracles and so they called out to him: "Jesus, Master, have pity on us!" He told the lepers to show themselves to the priest and as they were going, they saw that they had been healed. Yet only one of them returned to give thanks.

Such behavior might not even raise eyebrows today. A number of years ago, when Orel Hershiser was pitching for the Dodgers, tv cameras caught him singing in the dugout before coming out to pitch in the 9th inning of the final game. When talk show host, Johnny Carson, asked him what he was singing, he said the doxology. For once, the great Carson was speechless as was the audience. Such thankfulness was unheard of. Let that not be said of us.

Lessons on Gratitude - Part 3 of 7

Text: 2 Timothy 3:1-5

Key verse: 2 Timothy 3:1 "There will be terrible times in the last days."

Three guys were walking along by a river when they noticed someone walking on the water coming toward them. "Who are you?", asked the first guy. "I'm Jesus". "Jesus", said the first guy, "Can you heal my back?" Jesus touched the guy's back and, immediately, it was good as new. "Jesus," said the second guy," Can you heal my poor eyesight?" Jesus touched the guy's eyes and, just like that, he had perfect vision. The third guy didn't say anything although he walked with a pronounced limp. "Can't I do something for you? "Jesus asked the third guy. "Don't touch me, I'm on disability!", he said.

Of course, this is not a true story, although I could believe it. I know there are people who would rather stay disabled than to have to do something worthwhile. I know people who would rather stay disabled rather than be grateful to someone who made them well. The Bible says in today's lesson that in the last days, there will be many such people. Yet, even now, there are many people who will not accept Jesus' sacrifice for their sin because they'd rather earn it for themselves or because they'd not want to be beholden to someone else.

That is not to say that there haven't been ungrateful people throughout history. During WW1, C.S. Lewis made friends with a man who feared that if he were killed that no one would care for his wife and young daughter. C.S. Lewis promised the guy that if he made it and his friend didn't, he would care for them. As it worked out, the guy did die, and Lewis kept his word- but not because the man's wife made it easy. She was completely ungrateful, but Lewis continued to forgive her rude behavior because of the promise he had made to his friend.

This was Jesus' attitude as well. Although roughly and wrongfully treated by the Roman soldiers as he neared death, he asked for God's forgiveness for them. This is a hard thing. but when we show his love to others whether they deserve it or not, we show our gratitude for his love of us.

Lessons on Gratitude – Part 4 of 7

Text: John 12:1-8

Key verse: Colossians 4:2 "Devote yourselves to prayer, being watchful and thankful"

A lady got a call at work from the babysitter that her daughter seemed to be very sick. So, she left work and stopped along the way at a pharmacy to get some medicine. However, in her upset state of mind, she locked her keys in her car. She called the babysitter to explain her problem then went back to the pharmacy to ask if anyone could help. But no one knew what to do. So, she prayed to God for help and within minutes a guy came over, looking very much like a hell's angel and asked her if she needed any help. Desperate about now, she cried, "Yes, please," and got out a wire hanger. Within minutes he opened the door, and she thanked the guy and gave him a big hug, saying, "You are a nice fellow"! "Not really," said the guy," I just got out of prison today for stealing cars." After he left, then, she bowed her head and prayed, "Thank you, Lord, for helping me and sending a professional to do it."

In today's lesson, Mary, the sister of Lazarus, was thankful for Jesus and his raising her brother from the dead. And she showed her thanks by pouring very expensive ointment over the feet of Jesus and drying his feet with her hair. At least one viewing this thought her thankfulness to be a little too extravagant and complained about its being wasteful. Yet, to her, nothing was too good to use in showing her thanks.

A missionary doctor made a visit to a woman on whom he had successfully operated. She then invited him to lunch-which he accepted- to be held in about an hour. So, he made one more call before returning. Then, upon entering the house, the meal she prepared was a rabbit and 2 chickens, their entire means of livelihood, as it was commensurate to her thankfulness. What does that say about our thankfulness and what it should be?

Lessons on Gratitude – Part 5 of 7

Text: Romans 1 :18-23

Key verse: Romans 1:21 "For although they knew God, they neither glorified him as God nor gave thanks to him, but their thinking became futile, and their foolish hearts were darkened."

Two guys were taking a short cut through a farmer's field when they came across a bull headed right for them. Immediately, they made a beeline for the closest fence. But it soon became apparent that they weren't going to make it and so one friend yelled for the other to put up a prayer for them both. The other friend said he couldn't because he had never prayed before publicly. As the bull got closer, though, he changed his mind and said, "For what we are about to receive, dear Lord, let us be truly grateful!"

Not an appropriate prayer, was it? Yet, for people who aren't very grateful, it is understandable that they wouldn't know one. Apparently, the apostle Paul was referring to those types of people in today's lesson. They think that what good they receive is either because of good luck or their own hard work. Conversely, I suspect that when bad things happen, they chalk it up to their bad luck or that someone "Had it in for them."

A lady was driving a loaner car by a grocery store one rainy day when she was flagged down by an elderly lady she didn't even know. But she stopped while the lady put her groceries and herself in and said where she wanted to go. Amazed at her nerve but still willing to help, she drove the woman to her house-where she requested help in getting the groceries in. Thinking that she had done this much, she complied and having got the last bag in, got the door slammed in her face. Now, very upset at being taken advantage of and not even thanked, she told her husband who said it must have been the sign she had on her car-free courtesy car. Being self-centered, she figured the car was for her use. As Christians, we cannot afford to think this way.

Lessons on Gratitude - Part 6 of 7

Text:1 Thessalonians 5:18

Key verse: 1 Thessalonians 5:18 "Give thanks in all circumstances,.."

A guy buys a lottery ticket and wins the grand prize-$20 million dollars. When he goes to claim his prize, however, he finds he must take 1 million a year for 20 years. This upsets him, so he says," if you can't give me my $20million, then give me my dollar back!"

Unfortunately, there are too many people who have to have things all their way. And, like this guy, act like they'd readily "cut their nose off to spite their face". This is not a Christian sentiment-indeed, far from it, when one considers today's key verse. The question, then, becomes how can they get from there to here? The quick answer is that they must move from earn to grace. And that is a difficult journey in our society.

A story is told of a liberated slave who goes to see President Lincoln to pay him back for his freedom. And, to prove his point, lays a silver dollar on Lincoln's desk. The president, realizing that a lesson on grace was in order, escorted the man to his window facing Arlington cemetery. Then Lincoln said, "How will your money pay back the lives that were given to make your freedom possible?"

By the same token, until we get to the place where we realize that there is no way we can pay back what Jesus did at Calvary, we will never learn the true meaning of gratitude. Because it is only grace that allows us to be grateful in all circumstances.

Lessons on Gratitude-part 7 of 7

Text: Colossians 3:17

Key verse: Colossians 3:17 "And whatever you do, whether in word or deed, do it all in the name of the Lord Jesus, giving thanks to God the father through him."

A man urgently needed to get to town but had no transportation. So, he asked his neighbor, who was a pastor, if he could borrow his horse. The pastor said yes, but the neighbor needed to understand how to make the horse go and stop. "It isn't in the usual way," he began. To get him to go, you must say thank God and to get him to stop you must say amen. Do you understand?" "Yeah, I've got it," and off he went when he said, "Thank God". But since he was in a hurry, he said thank God several times until the horse was in full gallop. Now there was one big bend on the way to town and the guy realized that they'd never make it going this fast, but, for the life of him, he couldn't remember what to say to get the horse to stop. Yet just before they got to the bend, He remembered to say "Amen" and the horse dug in its hoofs in time to stop-just inches from a big cliff. The guy gave a big sigh and said-what? "Thank God"

Certainly, it is easy to thank God when we're in trouble, but what about when things are good? Should we not be thankful then, too? In writing to the church at Colosse, Paul reminds Christians there that they represent Christ to unsaved people and so their example is critical-as it is today. That is, unless unsaved people see something in us that helps get us through good times as well as bad, they are not inclined to change their ways.

A couple at church decided to give a memorial to the church in honor of their son, who was killed in combat. But another couple whose son had been in combat but made it safely home, was touched by that gift so much that they decided to give a gift also- out of gratitude for their son being spared. So may we find it to be so out of our obedience to today's word.

REFLECTIONS

Halloween

Some people may disagree with a section in a devotional about Halloween because of its being associated with the occult. Even so, a student of the historical origins of Halloween could easily point to the opposite- a celebration of All Hallows Eve. For me it was always a fun time to get dressed up and get candy- not that we needed it. And I have always been amazed at the creativity in the costumes. A wise person once said that one's outfit for Halloween was like a Rorschach test-giving clue to a person's innermost ambitions or, conversely, a clue to the type of person most far from their actual self-evaluation. Regardless, I believe that Halloween has the potential for good or evil, just like most other things. Thus, its inclusion or exclusion is principle a matter of perspective.

Lessons on Halloween - Part 1 of 7

Text and key verse: Joshua 24:15 "But as for me and my household, we will serve the Lord."

A new Methodist pastor was called by an undertaker to perform a funeral. The problem was the guy was a Baptist and the Methodist pastor was unsure if by performing the ceremony if he would be overstepping his authority. So, he called his District Superintendent who told him to go ahead as they should be burying all the Baptists they could.

Seriously, many people make big distinctions between different denominations whereas the differences are actually not that important. In a Halloween parade, there usually are many pirates and minions and superheroes

But those differences are in appearance only-which is pretty much the case with denominations.

The fact of the matter is that although there are some differences in what we do in the service and the way we govern ourselves the essence of our faith reflects these commonalities:

All have sinned and fallen short of the kingdom of God.

The wage of sin is death; but the gift of God is eternal life through the sacrifice of his only son, the perfect Jesus Christ.

Thus, we should feel blessed to be a part of a denomination whose teachings will lead us to heaven. There are many that don't- like the Church of Universal Wisdom (which features communication with aliens) or the Embassy of Heaven (which considers all governments illegitimate and issues its own license plates).

Indeed, this is the essence of the great task before us- to befriend those who hold such precepts as valid or hold no precepts at all, to share the truth of our experience and to turn them to a better understanding of God's word. That doesn't mean that they have to be a carbon copy of us. They just need those aforementioned commonalities of faith.

Lessons on Halloween-part 2 of 7

Text and key verse: Isaiah 49:16 "See, I have written your name on the palm of my hand,…"

A couple from the east always dreamed of having a cattle ranch. And so, when they retired, they bought a ranch in Texas along with a number of head of cattle. Friends from back home sometime later, went down to see how they were making out. So, after a short time of relaxation and a tour of the ranch, the two couples sat down to talk. "What did you decide to name the ranch? was the first question the visitors wanted to know. "Well, we had some trouble deciding on that, so we compromised on the double r, lazy l, triple horseshow, bar 7, flying 11, lucky diamond ranch." "Where are the cattle? "Was the next question. "None of them survived the branding".

At Halloween it is assumed that a person somehow identifies with the type of person that the costume depicts. But as far as God's identification with us, there is no need for assumptions. Today's scripture verse clearly shows how he feels about us. Yet he allows us free choice as to whether or not we desire to identify with him. Thus, many people only associate themselves with God when they are in trouble, or they desperately want him to provide something. His identification with us, conversely, is unconditional.

The Sydney Swans of the Australian Rules Football League were clearly the worst team in the league, so most of their home games were played before mostly empty stands. But when a new coach came in along with several new players, the team started to win, and so more people started coming to the games. It finally got to the point where tickets to the games were hard to get. So, on one Sunday afternoon when the Swans were playing another good team, the tv cameras chose to focus on one fan who held up this sign: I was here when nobody else was.

Such is God's relationship to us. When we were still sinners, he loved us and gave his son for us

Lessons on Halloween - Part 3 of 7

Text: Acts 2:43-47

Key verse: Acts 2:46c "People in general liked what they saw."

A guy bought a pick-up truck "as is "from a dealer and asked as he was leaving what he should do if he broke down on the way home. The dealer told him to take their name off the truck.

Obviously, they didn't want to identify with junk. At Halloween kids usually dress up like a character they admire. So, is it surprising when people want to identify with churches that they admire? The question then becomes "how do we become that kind of church?"

The New Testament church after Pentecost had much to like. It started its day with worship and teaching followed by meals together-people gladly sharing what they had. The Bible records that the church at that time grew by "leaps and bounds".

I think that the reason the church got that kind of response was because people saw a connection between what happened on Sunday with what went on the rest of the week. This is a primary disconnect today, according to many 18 to 29-year-olds. They see the church in general as hypocritical.

Thus, we need to stop doing church and start being the church. And I think we do this by finding ways to connect with people in helpful, sharing ways as a way of life-not just a Sunday "thing". That includes a re-examination of our values and priorities to make sure they communicate what truly is most important in our life. And I think we do this by remembering "our first love" of God and getting back to the disciplines of daily prayer and Bible reading and meditation.

Lessons on Halloween - Part 4 of 7

Text and key verse:1 Corinthians 9:19 "For though I am free from all men, I have made myself a servant to all, that i might win the more."

A Catholic priest was walking down the alley next to his church, when a robber stepped out and demanded his money. The priest quickly got out his wallet and handed it over to the robber. But in doing so, the priest revealed his clerical collar. The robber asked, "are you a priest?" "Why yes I am", replied to the priest. "Then put away your wallet. I don't rob priests." Greatly relieved, the priest got out 2 cigars and offered one to the robber. "I can't," said the robber, "Smoking is wrong and I can't believe you'd do such a wicked thing."

It is easy to find churches that vigorously oppose Halloween on the grounds that it is satanic. And although there may be some Halloween practices that are clearly not Christian, I personally see no harm with most of it. And I believe this because it falls into the category of things that could go either way. So, if I join the dissenters, I have cut off any possibility of engaging in helpful communication that could lead to sharing the good news of the gospel. I believe that this was the mindset of the apostle Paul in today's scripture verse.

In effect, then, I will not openly condemn my brothers and sisters in Christ for their stance on Halloween so that I can keep the lines of communication open for more important issues even though I believe their stance is erroneous. And I will extend that same courtesy to those outside the church for the same reason. In so doing, I believe Halloween can present an opportunity to build relationships from which good can come.

Lessons on Halloween - Part 5 of 7

Text: Galatians 6:4 "Each one should test their own actions. Then they can take pride in themselves alone, without comparing themselves with someone else."

A midwestern farmer was describing his lifestyle to a group of tourists from an urban area. "One of the benefits of life on the farm is that we have built-in weather predictors", he said. When asked to explain, he elaborated that when all the cows were standing up, that it wouldn't rain for the next 24 hours and that when the cows were all lying down that it would rain shortly. "Well, what can you tell if half are standing and half are lying down?", he was asked. "That half of them is wrong."

False identity is part and parcel of Halloween, but real-life identity is more important-particularly for the Christian. We must strive to be what we say we are all the time. When Christians act a certain way among some people and another among another, there is great confusion.

The apostle Paul encountered this in the Galatian church where Jewish Christians were urging Gentile Christians to convert to the rules and regulations of the Jewish religion if they wanted to be real Christians. In doing so, the Jewish Christians were making their Gentile brothers carry a load they themselves could not carry. It was never meant to be that hard.

How then can we stay true to our faith? We need to surround ourselves with Christians who do not lead double lives in their faith walk-as there are many that do. We also need to become more familiar with the word of God, because it is our guidebook to the example of Jesus Christ and his teaching, which is the way of life.

Lessons on Halloween - Part 6 of 7

Text and key verse: Galatians 2:20 "...I myself no longer live; but Christ lives in me.'

A man went to a Halloween party dressed as the devil. The party was not far from his home, so he decided to walk. But while on his way a sudden storm took him by surprise, and he began to look for a place where he could wait out the storm. He found a church that was open and went in. Much to his and the congregation's surprise, there was a service going on and when they saw who it was that came in there was chaos with everybody heading for the nearest exit that was not where the devil was. All made it except for an older lady who had fallen. When he got to where she was to help her up, she said to him, "Satan, although I've come to this church for 30 years, I want you to know that I was really on your side the whole time."

So much for her identification with Christ. Although it is rare for people to say that they are on the devil's side, the way people live declare it loud and clear. Indeed, most people seem to want to keep their religious practices secret so as not to be thought of as fanatical. That's why the apostle's words in Galatians are so refreshing-he makes no apologies for Christ. He says that he has no identity at all except for Christ who lives in him.

It wasn't that long ago when Paul identified himself with his standing among Jews-his being of the tribe of Benjamin and being a part of the Pharisees. The attention some folks give in their obituaries to church membership sounds somewhat similar. But Paul came to realize that such affiliation means nothing outside of our relationship to Christ. That is what we must realize as well. Being on the fence means not being all in. And not being all in is being nowhere with God.

Lessons on Halloween – Part 7 of 7

Text and key verse: Galatians 3:28 "There is neither Jew nor gentile, slave nor free, male nor female, for you are all one in Christ Jesus."

A famous evangelist made a visit to a nursing home where many people were happy for his visit. What he didn't realize, however, was that some people's memory skills were not that good. So, when he asked a lady," Do you know who I am?', she responded, "No, I don't. But if you ask the lady at the front desk, she can tell you."

As we have been talking about Halloween, we determined that, in a larger sense, it is a lot about false identities. Specifically, as Christians, however, there should be no confusion.

Recently the President of France proposed a decree that would ban anyone from wearing religious symbols of any kind. He specifically was targeting the large Muslim female population within his country who wore the full-faced veil. He reasoned that France was being divided by the diversity in religions practiced there and that the French were wondering what it meant to be French. He hoped the people would unite behind the flag. But the Bible suggests that we unite under the banner of Christ.

One of my mentors in the Christian faith talked about the address his father would make to all my mentor's brothers as they would be preparing to go out on the weekends. And he would say, "Remember that you are Kramer's and what the family stands for." By the same token, we must do the same as Christians. As we are a relational people and our faith must be shared out of relationships, we must be careful not to cast aspersions on what it means to be a Christian.

REFLECTIONS

Holy Spirit

In my Spiritual development, the Holy Spirit was not really emphasized until my involvement with the Assembly of God church. I'm not sure why that was in that the Holy Spirit has such a big role to play in our Christian faith. I mean the Holy Spirit's influence convicts us of sin, fills us with not only power but peace and helps us to pray when we don't know what to say or how to say it. Perhaps that is why the Pentecostal movement seems to be growing at a much higher level than mainline denominations-particularly in third world nations. However, their emphasis on speaking in tongues can be counterproductive if not divisive. A proper interpretation of the gift of tongues reveals that not everyone has that gift or the necessary gift of interpretation of tongues, which must accompany them. In effect, it can leave the people without those gifts "on the outside looking in". We cannot afford to do that.

Lessons on the Holy Spirit - Part 1 of 7

Text: 1 Samuel 17

Key verse: Acts 1:8a "but ye shall receive power when the Holy Spirit has come upon you"

An executive was called for jury duty for a case that looked like it might drag on for some time. So, he asked the judge to excuse him. The judge called him into his chambers for a private talk. "You remind me of one of those businessmen with an exaggerated opinion of themselves. You don't think your company can get along without you. Is that right?" "No, your honor," he said, "I know they can get along without me. I just don't want them to know how well."

Similarly, many Christian leaders are afraid of letting their churches know how well they could do without them- particularly when they lead without the Holy Spirit. Although it might seem unusual to start our conversation about the Holy Spirit in the Old Testament, it is appropriate to show the power of the Holy Spirit in one of its finest moments- David's killing of Goliath. You see, David, upon being anointed as the next king of Israel, received the Holy Spirit and its power. I know that some people would like to point to David as the ultimate example of what a person with confidence can do, but I think the reality is somewhat different. I believe that David is an example of what any one of us could do in facing life's goliaths in the power of the Holy Spirit.

In a more important sense, however, David's killing of Goliath is an example of how we can overcome our sin nature by the care and nurture we give the Holy Spirit. I believe David's conquest actually began in his faithful watching of his father's sheep. Left by himself much of the time, he meditated on God's protection and provision. He composed poetry and music about God as well as honing his slingshot ability.

A young brave asked his grandfather about the battle between good and evil that seemed to be going on within him. He wanted to know which force win-to which his grandfather would say, "the one you feed is the one who will win." The same is true in our lives.

Lessons on the Holy Spirit - Part 2 of 7

Text: Acts 2:4

Key verse: psalms 46:10 "Be still and know that I am God."

A man who regularly prayed began to have doubts whether or not God actually heard his prayers. So, one day as he was praying, he stopped and said, "God, if you're up there, make yourself known!" No response came, so he called again, "God, if you're really up there, tell me what you want me to do with my life." Then a voice boomed from heaven, "I want you to help the needy and give your life to the cause of peace!" Faced with more of a challenge than he expected, the man said, "That's ok, Lord, I was just checking." Then the Lord answered, "that's ok, I was just checking to see if you were really serious about doing something meaningful."

That's the real fear, isn't it? We want God to talk to us but we're afraid that we might not want to do what he wants. Regardless, God does talk to us through the Holy Spirit. It's just a matter of being still and quiet enough to hear. From today's text, we know that the Holy Spirit did allow people to speak languages they did not know to be heard by people who would understand because it was their native tongue. This is not generally the way the Holy Spirit works today- although he could. It can be as we meditate on God's word or talk with another Christian or hear a child explain something. Again, the idea is to be open and listen to it.

A mom and dad were sitting down to eat with their little daughter. The parents had had a tough day but had not received any sympathy from the other and were upset- upset enough that the daughter was aware of it. So, as was their custom, they bowed their heads and awaited their daughter's recitation of grace. But instead, the little girl said, "Hi, God, it's me, Emily. I'm doing fine but mom and dad are mad. I'm not sure why as we have birds and toys and mashed potatoes and each other. But maybe you can get them from being mad. Because if you don't, it'll be just you and me that has any fun tonight. Amen." Do you see what I mean?

Lessons on the Holy Spirit - Part 3 of 7

Text: Acts 2

Key verse: Matthew 7:7 "Ask and it shall be given unto you; seek and ye shall find; knock and the door will be opened unto you."

A little girl had a daddy who was a pastor and so she asked him, "Daddy, how do you know what to preach on Sunday?" "God tells me, honey," he explained. "Well then why do you crinkle up so many wads of paper and throw them into the garbage can?"

Good question, yes? Especially since the pastor knew God does provide discernment through the Holy Spirit. Today's key verse tells us that. Nevertheless, our problem, often times is that discernment can take more time than we are willing to give it. As a pastor, I know I want to complete my sermon by a certain time and God may have a different timetable.

In today's Bible lesson, the followers of Jesus showed excellent discernment in waiting on the Holy Spirit before engaging in ministry after the ascension of Jesus. You see, Jesus didn't say exactly when the Holy Spirit was going to come. They had to wait but used the time productively by coming together and praying. When we do that, the results can be amazing –as they were at that first Pentecost.

Discernment can also be useful in our dealing with those we don't know. A story is told of a man and his son who were traveling on a bus. The son was "out of control', running and yelling and generally disrupting the other passengers. The father just sat there, unkempt and half asleep. So, a man seated nearby took it upon himself to advise the father to do something about it. The father seemed to awaken from his stupor and said, "You know, you're right. It's just that the boy's mother-my wife-just died after suffering all night and I just haven't figured out how to tell him."

Lessons on the Holy Spirit - Part 4 of 7

Text: 1 John 4:1-3

Key verse: John 16:13 "When the Spirit of truth comes, he will guide you into all truth."

An old country doctor had to go pretty far out into the "sticks" to deliver a baby. And when he got there, he found that there was no electricity and only the 5-year-old son was available to help. So, he had the boy hold a lantern way up high so he could see what he was doing. After a short period of labor, the lady delivered a baby boy- which the doctor lifted by the feet and spanked its bottom to get it to breathe. When the doctor asked the little boy what he thought of his new baby brother, he said, "Spank him again! He shouldn't have crawled up in there in the first place."

That, of course, wasn't the truth, but it was for the little boy. Similarly, some unusual explanations may be truth for some people, but how do we know if it's really the truth? Today's Bible lesson advises us to "test the Spirits". Actually, the Bible is asking us to pray for the leading of the Holy Spirit- the Spirit of truth. The Holy Spirit will never mislead us and so when we feel assured by the Spirit that what we're testing is true, we can move confidently forward.

The point is, we can't always rely on our senses to tell us the truth. Nor can we be sure that what we want to believe is true. The first day of medical school, the professor came in and said, "Observation is the key to medicine." To prove his point, he got out a test tube of yellow liquid and explained, "This is human urine. Many times, a patient's condition can be determined by how it smells and tastes." With that he dipped a finger into the test tube and then put a finger into his mouth. That freaked a few of the new med students out but not as much as when he passed the test tube down the rows, instructing them to do as he had done. Obviously, there were many groans along the way until the test tube came back to the professor. Then he said, "You have just had your first lesson in observation. But what you didn't notice was that I put a different finger in my mouth than what I put into the test tube.

Lessons on the Holy Spirit - Part 5 of 7

Text: Galatians 3

Key verse: Galatians 3:3 "Are you so foolish? After beginning with the Spirit, are you now trying to obtain your goal by human effort?"

A man returned to his car in the parking lot and found this note under the windshield wiper: "I just smashed into your car. The people who saw me do it are watching me write this note. They probably assume that I am writing my name, address and phone number down for you. But they are wrong."

Clearly, he didn't take responsibility for his actions. When this happens with Christians, however, they begin to feel conflicted. And this conflict comes from the Holy Spirit. It acts like a double check to make sure we are abiding in God's word.

Yet sometimes, the convicting power of the Holy Spirit is not enough to change behavior. Such was the case in the church in Galatia. At first, they had accepted Christ as a gift of grace but then had apparently felt that that was too easy and now were trying to add works to the equation. They were not feeling the conviction they should, so Paul had to help them see it.

This responsibility may also fall to us as Christians. And it may put us in danger of greater condemnation as people hate having their sins exposed. Nevertheless, we can't let people continue to believe a lie- particularly when it impacts their salvation.

Today a growing number of people refuse to take responsibility for their actions. What's worse is that the court lets them "get away with it" far too often. Consider the case of a teenage boy in Washington, DC, who was acquitted of murder because of being "morally handicapped". Friends, where will they learn to take responsibility for their sins and to be self-corrected by the Holy Spirit, if not from us?

Lessons on the Holy Spirit - Part 6 of 7
Text:1 Corinthians 12
Key verse: 1 Corinthians 12:7 "Now to each one the manifestation of the Spirit is given for the common good."

A young woman came to the welfare office to apply for medical assistance. After she filled out the forms, she was told her husband would have to sign. She looked like she wanted to use the phone in the interview booth to call her husband, so the caseworker told her to dial 9 to get out. She dialed 9 then put down the receiver, went out of the office and brought her husband in. After he signed the form, she asked the caseworker if she had to dial 9 again, to get out.

Of course, the caseworker only was referring to the use of the telephone in asking her to call 9, but she didn't get it. Some might say, then, that she wasn't very smart. Others might say that she was not given the gift of wisdom. Yet, she did have at least one Spiritual gift, as this is what the Bible tells us. Although they are not always used in this way, the intended use of Spiritual gifts is for the building up of the church.

Although we tend to think of Spiritual gifts in terms of the New Testament, there is evidence of them in the old as well. Specifically, Exodus tells us that certain people had been given gifts in building the tabernacle. Even so, the tragedy of gifts has always been in the case where people have been unaware of them.

During the Depression, a man by the name of Yates had a sheep ranch that didn't make him much money. As a matter of fact, he was doing so poorly that he was in constant danger of having his ranch sold out from under him. So, every day, as he grazed his sheep, he could think of little else. Then, one day, an oil drilling crew asked permission to drill a well on his property and a contract was signed. They hit oil at 1115 feet, which netted some 80,000 barrels of oil a day- making Mr. Yates a multi-millionaire. Yet, all this time, with all this wealth laying beneath his feet, he lived in poverty. So, it is with those of us who are unaware of our Spiritual gifts.

Lessons on the Holy Spirit - Part 7 of 7

Text: Acts 19:1-6

Key verse: acts 19:2b "No, we have not even heard that there is a Holy Spirit."

The Sunday School teacher was trying to teach her class of 5th and 6th graders about the Trinity and asked if anyone could name the three entities that make it up. One little boy said he thought he knew and said, "God the father, God the son and Andy." "Wait a minute," said the teacher, "who's this Andy?" "you know, teacher," he said, "Andy walks with me; Andy talks with me."

Unfortunately, the third person of the Trinity often gets a "short shrift". And not only is it unfortunate, but it is also tragic as the Holy Spirit has so much to offer. In today's lesson, Paul comes across some followers of Jesus who had not even heard of the Holy Spirit or the power that the Spirit provides. Up to that point, they had been trying to live a Christ- centered life without it. They didn't realize what a losing proposition this was.

On June 12th, 1979, a young man-made aviation history by flying a pedal-powered plane across the English Channel. Yet, in spite of his achievement, he proved that non-powered flight would never be practical, as this flight completely exhausted him. By the same token, we can never hope to be successful in our own strength of serving our Lord.

It is, indeed, wonder-working power. Let us, then, praise God that this power is so easily accessed.

REFLECTIONS

Hope

Hope has always been that which keeps us going. It is as essential as air to our lungs, or water and food to our bodies. We may hope for different things at different times of our lives, but we have always craved it and sought it out. In my life, however, the basis of hope changed when my Christian faith matured. Up until that time, I had hoped for luck, hard work and the basic goodness in people. Over time, I saw that those things could not be counted on and that I needed a surer foundation for hope. I found that in the promises of God. I came to realize that it wasn't about me- that God didn't exist just to meet my needs but that I existed in order to serve and glorify him. That didn't mean that I would have no hardship, but that I could always count on His presence and help to get through them.

Lessons on Hope – Part 1 of 7

Text: 1 Kings 19:19-21

Key verse: Ecclesiastes 12:13c "Fear God and keep his commandments, for this the whole duty of man."

A woman walked into the bathroom as her husband was standing on the bathroom scale, sucking his stomach in. "That's not going to help," said the woman. "It already has, "he replied. "Now I can see the numbers."

Particularly, as we grow older, we get on the scale in the morning in hopes that something has happened during the night that results in some kind of weight loss. Yet, if we've done nothing to promote weight loss, this is just wishful thinking. In today's lesson, when Elijah threw his cloak over Elisha, he was doing more than wishful thinking about Elisha's taking over for him someday. God had given him the leading to do it. Similarly, God leaves nothing to chance and so if we depend on his guidance, we have a solid foundation for hope.

Yet this is not enough for many people, who would rather trust in their own strength to achieve their goal. This may work for a time but ultimately will end badly. Such was the case for Spanish conquistador Cortez, who defeated the Aztecs and claimed Mexico for Spain. Despite his success, his strength alone was never enough to guarantee his happiness, nor was it a guarantee that his hope for everlasting fame and acclaim would be achieved.

It has been famously said that those who do not learn from history are doomed to repeat it. This is true for Bible as well as world history and we would do well to learn it, too. God is the true foundation for hope.

Lessons on Hope – Part 2 of 7

Text: Job 19:21-27

Key verse: Job 19:25a "I know my redeemer lives;"

A guy was going by a used bookstore and saw a book in the window with the words from hardship to hope and decided to buy it since he had been going through some difficult times recently. But when he got it home, he discovered that it was just that part of an encyclopedia set that dealt with the words between hardship and hope.

Unfortunately, there are no easy answers or quick fixes for the problems we routinely face. What keeps us going, however, is the hope we have in God. There is no better place to look in the Old Testament for that hope than in the life of a Job. As we find in the book of the same name, Job was a good man that God allowed to be tested by Satan. And despite, the trials he faced, he clung ferociously to his innocence and his faith in God.

Of course, this is easier said than done. But we do have a modern-day inspiration in the life of Martin Luther King. He lived in constant fear for his own life and those of his family. He suffered threats and time in jail for his work on civil rights. Finally, his life was taken by an assassin's bullet on April 4th, 1968. The autopsy that was done revealed a 60-year-old heart in a 39-year-old body-due to the emotional and mental trauma he so faithfully faced.

This is not to suggest that we must face those kinds of trials. Yet, the hope that sustained both Job and Martin Luther King, is also available to us and is easily accessed. It is as close as a prayer.

Lessons on Hope – Part 3 of 7

Text; 1 Samuel 1:11-28

Key verse: Psalms 62:5 "Find rest, o my soul, in God alone; my hope comes from him."

The Amish family went to the big city to see the sights. They saw many wondrous things, but the dad was most impressed with the elevator. What really got his attention was when an elderly lady stepped into the elevator and the next time the elevator door opened, a beautiful young woman stepped out. "Quick, boy!", said the father, "Go get your ma!"

In today's lesson, Hannah has no such basis for her hope. Her hope is solely directed to God and his mercy- which is, as we know, a much surer basis than the Amish dad's. Even so, she is not sure that God will answer her request. She just believes that God loves her too much to leave her in the misery that she is in.

This is the essential reason that we turn to God instead of luck or whatever. We are never certain that things will turn out the way we hope but we know that God loves us and wants what's best for us. And that's enough. It's just too bad that more people don't see it that way.

A number of years ago, when I worked for public welfare, I was required to attend a training session in an underprivileged neighborhood. And in that neighborhood, there was a restaurant/ lottery sales establishment that did a brisk lottery business with people who were not placing their hope in God. I remember one fellow in particular that very much liked his chances to win based on a dream he had the night before in which a particular number was prominent.

Friends, I believe God wants to bless us and I believe he could do it any way he chooses-even the lottery. Nevertheless, to place our hope in God's helping the way we envision is not in our best interest. God is sovereign and works in mysterious ways-ways that are far beyond our understanding. Just because he may not help us the way we want does not mean he is not willing or able to help.

0Lessons on Hope – Part 4 of 7

Text: Jonah

Key verse: Jonah 3:10 "When God saw what they did and how they turned from their evil ways, he had compassion and did not bring upon them the destruction he had threatened."

A woman took her hard-of-hearing husband to the doctor. After his exam, the doctor told the woman that her husband had a serious infection. The husband then asked the woman what the doctor said, and she replied, "He said you're sick." Then the doctor explained that if she would be nice to him and not yell at him and make his favorite meals whenever she could for the next 6 months, that he expected that her husband would make a full recovery. On the way home, the husband asked her again what the doctor had said. This time she said, "He said you're gonna die."

So much for hope. Be that as it may, today's lesson provides excellent examples of hope that is placed in God. First, it shows that there is hope for people who disobey God and then repent. As the story shows, Jonah went the opposite way when God called him to prophecy against Ninevah. Second, it shows hope for condemned people who repent of their sin. When Nineveh repented for their sin in ashes and sackcloth, God had compassion.

The beauty of this story, I believe, is that we can see a little of ourselves in both Jonah and the people of Ninevah. My guess is that, for most of us, there were periods in our life when we were disobedient to God because we couldn't care less or because it didn't suit our purposes. The fact, then, that God's love is relentless to both should give great hope.

This is hope we can take to the bank. It is not at all like the hope baseball fans have at the beginning of the season for their teams to win. Being a long-time Pittsburgh Pirate fan, I know all about this.

Lessons on Hope – Part 5 of 7

Text: Matthew 25:14-30

Key verse: Matthew 25:21a "Well done, good and faithful servant!"

"I just don't understand my parents," "lamented one college student to another," "I ask for the money for a chair and they send me a chair!" Obviously, the parents felt that their child would spend the money on something else. It was a classic case of failure to communicate. And the fault for that often goes both ways. In addition, the problem is made worse because it has a dampening effect on the hopes of each. Clearly both sides need to express their hopes to the other.

Consider the graduation gifts that are often received by the high school graduate headed off to college. When I graduated, I got a briefcase because that's what serious college students were thought to carry. Now I never asked for nor wanted a briefcase- nor did any college student at my school ever carry one. Graduation gifts today are much different but still communicate the same thing-study hard so you can get a job and be a productive (and hopefully independent) citizen. Today computers and calculators, as gifts, express the same sentiment-although the hopes are often left unsaid.

In today's lesson, the hope of the master is that his servants will be good stewards of what has been entrusted to them. The hope of the servants is that they will be rewarded for how they have cared for the master's property. Now the master had different hopes for each servant, presumably based on their varying abilities. These hopes, however, were left unsaid-although 2 of the servants apparently "got it", anyway.

The question that we must answer, then, is: are we aware of the hopes God has for us? The answer is: we should because they are clearly stated in Micah 6:8:"What does the Lord require of you? To act justly, to love mercy and to walk humbly with your God."

Lessons on Hope – Part 6 of 7

Text: Mark 9:2-9

Key verse: John 1:14b "We have seen his glory, the glory of the one and only son, who came from the father, full of grace and truth."

The sea captain, in trying to cheer up the sea-sick passenger, said, "Cheer up, no one has ever died from seasickness!" "Don't tell me that," said the passenger, still leaning over the rail, "It's only the hope of dying that has kept me alive this long."

Today's lesson on transfiguration is also about hope-just not so morbidly so. I believe Jesus hoped that this event would help sustain his inner circle of disciples when he was no longer with them. It was, to say the least, an amazing occurrence. Yet, it's significance seemed to be lost on Peter, James and John until much later. After the crucifixion, they seemed to forget how even the father had testified about Jesus.

As Christians, we are constantly faced with the need to walk by faith and not by sight. And so, when we are able to see the events that vividly display what our faith would tell us was so, it should be truly memorable. Yet I believe that we can have a "transfiguring" influence on others, if we are open to God using us that way.

Several years ago, a teacher assigned to visit and teach children in a large city hospital received what she thought was a routine request to teach nouns and adverbs to a particular child so that they wouldn't get too far behind the rest of their class. But nobody prepared her for the horribly burnt and critically ill young boy she visited. When she saw him, she wanted to run but instead focused herself on her assignment and completed it. When she returned the next day, the nurse on duty on the floor confronted her and asked her what she had done to that boy. Thinking she had made some mistake, she was relieved to hear that he now was "fighting back", since teachers don't come to teach dying boys, do they?

Lessons on Hope – Part 7 of 7

Text: Luke 1:26-38

Key verse: Luke 1;38 "Behold the handmaid of the Lord,..."

A parishioner took his pastor on the pastor's first airplane ride. But the pastor's fear of heights got to him, and he quickly asked to be taken back down. The parishioner kidded the pastor in saying, "What happened up there, pastor? Didn't you think that the Lord was with you?" "Well," the pastor said, "The correct quotation reads" Lo, I am with you always."

After the angel gave Mary the news of what part she would play in the Christmas story, she had hope but she just wasn't sure as to how some things, like her fiancés or family's reaction, would go. But she knew that her cousin, Elizabeth, would be accepting and decided to visit her. This is an important piece of hope-that we can be with someone who will be the good news to us.

Such was the case with Bill. Bill was an ex-alcoholic who had been converted at the city mission. Bill had been considered a "hopeless" case, but after his conversion, everything changed. He became the most caring person there-no job he was asked to do was beneath him. He even helped feed and care for other alcoholics who could not care for themselves. One evening after the mission director delivered his evangelistic message, one of the mission dwellers came forward to pray at the altar. He cried out to God, pleading with him to help him change. Over and over again, he'd say, "Lord, make me like Bill! Make me like Bill!" The mission director came over to him and suggested, "Wouldn't it be better to say, "make me like Jesus?" The guy thought about that for a couple of moments, then asked, "Is he like Bill?"

Thus, we have to ask ourselves, "Are we being the good news to others?" Bill and Elizabeth were. They realized that good news needs good people to make it real.

REFLECTIONS

Humility

I don't belief there is any concept so close to the heart of God but farther from human desire than humility. Humility and humble are mentioned 64 times in the Bible, and almost all of them are in a good or preferable context. Yet, the culture in which we live glorifies the "rugged individual" – the one who is able to "pull himself up by his own bootstraps".

Considering our own upbringing, the Dornan's should have been humbler. But we believed the "American" ideal and thought that we, too, could achieve great and noble things, despite our socioeconomic status- or lack of it. For one, I am grateful that I didn't constantly eliminate myself from opportunities to "better myself". Nevertheless, I am also grateful for the realization that some people were better suited for a task and that I didn't embarrass myself out of pride.

Most of all, I believe that humility in the presence of an Almighty God is an absolute essential to successful Christianity. As the apostle Paul once said: "For when I am weak, then I am strong."

Lessons on Humility - Part 1 of 7

Text: Judges 16:4-20

Key verse: Isaiah 64:8b, c "…,we are the clay, you are the potter; we are all the work of your hand."

A pastor was starting a new appointment and wanted to show the church secretary that he was a "take-charge" kind of guy, so he got on the phone as if he was talking to the bishop. "No, bishop, nothing to worry about. And I will have no problem coordinating your new project in addition to my responsibilities here. But thank you for your concern. Talk to you soon. Bye." Then, looking up, said to the church secretary, "Can I help you?" "No, pastor," she said, "I just wanted to tell you your phone will be hooked up tomorrow."

So much for first impressions! But seriously, we all like to think of ourselves as being very capable and independent-whereas, we would be so much better off remembering our dependence on God. In today's lesson, Samson takes the blessings of God for granted and finds that his disobedience and inattention to God has serious consequences-which he realizes much too late.

Similarly, when God places a course of action before us, we would do well to commit our response to him- so that we might follow both what, how and when of his will. When the new hope United Methodist church was planning to move to a new worship facility, it represented the culmination of many people's prayers over a 7-year period of time. Yet, the closer the church came to making the move, the smaller peripheral concerns came to light-threatening to divide the church. Without a dependence on God, these are the kind of issues that can thwart the work of the church. If we can but humbly remember who is ultimately in charge, such confrontations can and will be overcome.

Lessons on Humility - Part 2 of 7

Text: Mark 10:35-45

Key verse: Deuteronomy 30:11 "Now what I'm commanding you today is not too difficult for you or beyond your reach."

Two women spent all afternoon quoting scripture to one another-each trying to outdo the other. When the visiting woman left, the woman who remained said, "She is a good Christian woman, but I think I live closer to the Lord. "The husband, to whom this remark was addressed and who was turned off by their "holier-than-thou" attitude replied, "I don't think either of you is crowding him any."

It would appear that neither woman had a humble Spirit. And I think we could say the same thing about James and John in today's lesson. They ask Jesus for places of honor when he came into his kingdom. The fact that they asked such a thing is evidence that they didn't get Jesus' words or his example. Perhaps they listened selectively to what he said. We have to be careful that we don't do the same thing.

A few years ago, when I worked for a county welfare office, my friend and I would regularly go through the drive-thru at McDonald's for coffee (or in my case, tea). So, on this particular day, the usual question came through the speaker, "Welcome to McDonald's. How can I serve you?" When I said, "just a second", they answered, "that'll be 48 cents. Please pull around to the next window." Apparently, they thought I said "Just a Sanka" because they heard what they were conditioned to hear.

By the same token, we often listen in the same way. This is a dangerous practice-especially when God is doing the talking. What God is saying will not be too difficult to understand (as our key verse indicates), but we must be sure we focus so that we get the message right.

Lessons on Humility - Part 3 of 7

Text: Mark 12: 41-44

Key verse: Isaiah 40:25 "To whom will you compare me?"

At a daycare center, the children were bragging about their siblings. One said, "My brother takes horseback riding lessons." Another said, "my sister takes gymnastics." Another child, not to be outdone, said, "my sister takes antibiotics."

This comparison seems to be normal behavior, but it can lead to trouble. After all, for the Christian, it's only God's evaluation that matters. In today's lesson, Jesus and his disciples were watching the people putting their money into the temple treasury. He saw many put in more than an old widow woman but noted that she gave all she had to live on- and thus gave more than the rest.

Thankfully, our getting into heaven will not be about comparisons, whatsoever. We will only get in on the basis of whether or not we have accepted Jesus' work at calvary as being sufficient. We will not be compared with other Christians, although we may be embarrassed by how we have used the gifts and graces for ministry that we ourselves have been given.

Unfortunately, many people today feel that God's decisions about heaven will have everything to do with comparisons-that they are so much better than this one or not nearly as bad as that one. In essence, they believe that God will "grade on the curve". Friend, the devil has no bigger lie! That's why we must have a greater sense of urgency about sharing the truth about salvation. Jesus says, "I am the way, the truth and the life. No man cometh unto the father but by me."

Lessons on Humility - Part 4 of 7

Text: Luke 10:25-37

Key verse: James 2:26b "…,so faith without works is dead."

A man tells his wife that he is no longer physically able to work around the house, so she schedules a physical for him. After the physical is done and tests results have come back, the doctor calls the man into his office. The man says, "just give it to me straight, doc. I can take it." "Well, in plain English," the doctor begins, "There's nothing wrong with you. You're just lazy!" The man thinks a moment and then says, "Doctor, give me a medical term for that so I can tell my wife."

In today's lesson, the priest and the Levite wouldn't help a person in need, although they were able. So perhaps they could use a medical term to express their problem. Even so, it is clear that there was no adequate excuse for not helping. Clearly, this parable has a much wider application, however. It means that as we have the ability and opportunity to help, so must we. There is no adequate excuse for us not to.

In the old west, a stagecoach allowed for 3 classes of tickets: first-class, second-class and third-class. If you had a first-class ticket, you could keep your seat regardless of any trouble the stagecoach would encounter. If you had a second-class ticket, you could keep your seat unless the stagecoach had a problem. Then you had to get off and stand aside while someone else fixed the problem. But if you had a third-class ticket, you could keep your seat unless the stagecoach had a problem. But then you had to help fix the problem.

The analogy is clear: the priest and Levite considered themselves first or second-class ticket holders, who did not have to help. But in the parable, Jesus is indicating that there are no first- or second-class tickets for the Christian. We are obligated to help those in need. Our failure to do so shows others that our faith is not alive but dead. That is, if others can't see it, then it doesn't do much good.

Lessons on Humility - Part 5 of 7

Text: Luke 18:10-14

Key verse: romans 2:11 "There is no respect of persons with God."

The old church was getting ready for its 200th anniversary when the church's bell ringer was called out of town for an emergency. So, the pastor immediately put out word for a replacement. The problem was this person had to climb up stairs to get where the bell was in order to ring it-some150 ft. above the ground. Obviously, it had to be a person in good health. Fortunately, a man meeting the pastor's specifications showed up pretty quickly. The pastor, then, took the guy up the stairs to where the bell was but just as they got to the bell, the guy tripped and went face-first into the bell-bong! Well, the guy was so stunned that he fell backward into the railing-which let go and the guy fell all the way to the ground. Again, fortunately, the man was uninjured, just shook up. To be on the safe side, the pastor called for an ambulance. And when the ambulance arrived, the emt wanted the guy's name, to which the pastor replied, "I don't know his name, but his face sure rings a bell."

You might say the pastor wasn't as interested in who the guy was as long as he could ring the bell. In today's lesson, you might say that God was not as interested in who the person was as he was in the condition of his heart. In this lesson, a religious leader and a tax collector go into the temple to pray. Immediately the religious leader, a pharisee, points up the difference between him and the tax collector in terms of righteousness- inferring that he needed a whole lot less forgiveness than the other guy. The tax collector, however, just knows that he is a sinner and asks God for mercy. Yet, he is the one who goes home forgiven. The lesson, I believe, is clear: sin is sin, regardless of who commits it and must be confessed in addition to really trying to do better.

Robert E. Lee, the confederate general, had it right. Criticized for taking communion next to a black person, he said, "All ground is level beneath the cross."

Lessons on Humility - Part 6 of 7

Text: Romans 15:1-7

Key verse: romans 15:2 "Each of us should please his neighbor for his good, to build him up."

Jim Dunn was the pastor of a small church. His wife, Gladys, who was naturally a pleasant person, did her best after each service to speak to as many visitors as possible, to make them feel welcome. However, on one particular Sunday morning, her husband went on quite a bit longer than usual- causing some people to fidget in their seats or check their watches or simply fall asleep. So, as she made her rounds, she came across an old gentleman who seemed to be adjusting his hearing aid. "Hi, I'm Gladys Dunn", she said. "Me, too, "He replied. "I never thought he'd get finished."

It takes humility to greet, but you never know what response you might get. That should not discourage us, however, as the result can be well worth the effort. In today's lesson, Paul's letter to the roman church reflects the need for Christians to "get out of their comfort level "And talk to people they don't normally associate with to look for common ground. That church was a diverse church, and that effort was necessary to make those folks feel welcome, despite their differences.

In our own churches, it is every bit as important to do this, even though we are often not so diverse as the Roman church. Because when we're not sociable, we are sending the message that new folks are not welcome here. Obviously, we cannot afford this attitude.

When the boys in my neighborhood were growing up, we were often so exclusive that we made new kids who wanted to play ball with us not feel welcome. I don't think we were aware of our exclusivity, but the effect was just the same. It doesn't take a "rocket scientist" to realize that the same could be said in any grouping of people. As Christians who are determined to reflect Jesus to others, we have to be better than that.

Lessons on Humility - Part 7 of 7

Text: Philippians 2:1-11

Key verse: Phil. 2:3 "Do nothing out of selfish ambition or vain conceit, but in humility consider others better than yourselves."

Tv newsman Tom Brokaw was wandering through Bloomingdale's department store in New York City one day, shortly after his promotion to co-host of the "Today" show. He was feeling pretty good about himself after "climbing the corporate ladder" from Omaha, Nebraska to where he was now. It was in this happy mood that he encountered a stranger who seemed to recognize him. "Tom Brokaw, right?" "Yes, that's me." "You used to do the news on KMTV in Omaha, right?" "Yes, that's right", Brokaw said, expecting an accolade. "Well, whatever happened to you?" That brought him back to earth, as it would any of us. That's not to say we can't be happy when we have achieved something significant. It's just that something that's not good, called pride, is very close to that emotion-something that we must be careful to guard against.

In today's lesson, the apostle Paul gives us some handy advice about this. He says that we should consider others as being better than ourselves. With that attitude, we can more easily follow the example of Christ. And it's not just Christ's example. Paul himself exhibited this mindset in his writings: referring to himself alternatively as "The least of the apostles", "The least of the saints" and the" foremost of sinners'.

But Paul did not learn this overnight. And neither will we. It is only the result of the kind of personal discipline we need to improve other areas of our faith, like prayer and Bible reading. Just realize that the better we get at it, the closer we get to "blowing it". Golda Meir, the former prime minister of Israel recognized this in a person and let them know it: "Don't be so humble, you're not that great!"

REFLECTIONS

Jesus

I'm not sure when I began to consider Jesus to be the central figure in the history of the world. I just know that for a long time, he was the right answer to most Sunday School teacher's questions. He was mentioned prominently at Christmas and Easter. His name was used frequently by mean old and young rebellious men- but not in nice or honorable way. You might say I really didn't know who Jesus was-or, more importantly, what he did for me.

The change must have started sometime after I started to attend a small Assembly of God church in Anita, PA. after college. I began to listen to what the pastor said and began to read the Bible myself. Isn't it ironic, though, that we assume that just because we are raised in Christian household that our kids should automatically be Christians, too? Nevertheless, it soon became clear who Jesus really was and his significance to me. He was nothing less than God in the flesh sent, not only to be the only acceptable sacrifice for our sins, but also a model of God's love for us and a model of the way we, as followers, should live.

Lessons on Jesus - Part 1 of 7

Text: Mark 8:27-30

Key verse: Mark 8:29b "Who do you say that I am?"

A Texan visiting England attended a Protestant church service there and was amazed how quiet and reserved people seemed to be. Nevertheless, when the pastor got to a part that the Texan thought was compelling, he shouted, "Amen!" Immediately, he was the center of many disapproving looks and an usher rushed over to advise him not to speak out loud again. "But" said the Texan, "I have a personal relationship to Christ." "Well," replied the usher," You didn't get it here."

Unfortunately, I believe there are many "so-called" Christians who fail to give passion to their faith. And, as such, show precious little that people would want to emulate. Fearing this and knowing that his time on earth would be short, Jesus, in today's lesson, needed to gauge the Spiritual temperature of his disciples. If they didn't see him as the son of God, their ministry would not be effective.

In other words, unless a person can appreciate and accept Christ's sacrificial death as their only way to obtain forgiveness of their sin, that person will never have what he needs to be a disciple or a disciple-maker, himself. For many people, it takes a "teachable moment" to bring this about.

For golfer Paul Azinger, it was a brush with cancer. He had to come face-to-face with his own mortality to understand the timeless quality of grace that the life and death of Christ presents. Indeed, especially for someone as successful as Azinger, it had to be that special. Nothing and no one else would do.

Lessons on Jesus - Part 2 of 7

Text: Mark 13:24-37

Key verse: Mark 13:32a "No one knows about that day or hour…"

A Cardinal was approached one day in the cathedral by a very excited young priest. "Your eminence," began the young priest, "a woman claims to have seen the savior in the chapel. What should we do?" "Look busy," said the Cardinal, "Look busy."

In today's lesson, Jesus talks about the things that will precede his second coming. Yet because only the Father knows when these things will happen, he tells us to be alert, so we're not caught off guard.

Unfortunately, often times, we tend to get lazy unless we are sufficiently afraid. And this the devil takes full advantage of. "You've got lots of time" he says. And many believe him.

We've seen many historical precedents in areas other than our Spiritual readiness. Among these is the great Galveston hurricane of 1900. When Isaac Cline, then chief of the U.S. weather bureau, found that a major hurricane was headed to his home in Galveston, he got on his horse to warn as many townsfolk as he could to head to higher ground. But few listened and some 6,000 people were killed, our deadliest natural disaster in history. And to think that much of this could have been avoided.

Yet as horrible as that natural disaster was, it will pale in significance to the tragedy of souls lost in hell that could have been saved just by heeding our savior's warning. This should spur us on with a greater sense of urgency in sharing the good news of the gospel. But will it?

Lessons on Jesus - Part 3 of 7

Text: Luke 8:22-25

Key verse: Luke 8:25c "He commands even the winds and the water, and they obey him."

A psychiatrist was talking to the person seated next to him on a cross-country flight a few years before airplane security is what it is now. And the guy was explaining how he had overcome his fear of flying. He said that his fear started when he heard of a guy bringing a bomb on a flight to kill his mother-in-law. So, he took one of those classes that addressed the problem of fear of flying and found that the odds of a person bringing a bomb on a flight was 1 in 10,000-which he considered too great. But then he also found out that the odds of 2 people carrying a bomb on a flight was 1 in 100 million-which he felt was acceptable. "Well, how did that information help you?" The psychiatrist asked. "Well, since then, I always bring 1 bomb on a flight, myself."

I wonder what the odds of anyone getting the wind and waves to obey them. In today's lesson, this is what Jesus does. A minute before it appeared that the boat that carried Jesus and his disciples was going to capsize. Anyone not named Jesus should have been worried. But because it was Jesus, he asked the disciples where their faith was. That would be a good question for us, as well, in whatever we face, as Jesus is with us, too.

I believe that, although we soldier on with whatever faith we have, we have to exercise that faith to get it to the place where we rely on it. And hand-in-hand with faith, must be our consistent prayer life. A Christian sea captain was at the helm of his ship in a terrible storm. A passenger, beside himself with fear, burst into the wheelhouse and yelled at the captain, "Why aren't you praying?" And the captain answered, "I pray during the calm so I can sail my ship in the storm." So, it should be for us.

Lessons on Jesus - Part 4 of 7

Text: John 10:11-18

Key verse; John 10:11b "The good shepherd lays down his life for the sheep."

A guy travelling through an unfamiliar area lost control of his car and went into a ditch. Fortunately, a local farmer saw his accident and hurried over to the scene with his big plow horse, Buddy. So, with the guy's permission, the farmer hitched up his horse to the car. First, he yelled, "Pull, Nellie , pull!" But nothing happened. Then the farmer yelled, "Pull, Coco pull!" But again, nothing happened. Then the farmer yelled, "Pull, Buddy, pull!" And the car was easily brought back up on the road. The traveler, elated but curious, asked the farmer why he called the 2 other names. "That's easy," said the farmer, "Buddy's blind, but if he thought he was pulling alone, he wouldn't even try.

In today's world of business, the need to cajole or fool people into helping seems almost second nature. But this was not Jesus' leadership style. In today's lesson, he characterizes himself as "the good shepherd", and goes on to explain what that means. In essence, it means that he knows each sheep individually but loves them all the same. It means he would do anything for them-even giving up his own life. In other words, he puts their needs and safety above his own.

The famous evangelist, Charles Spurgeon, understood what that meant. Spurgeon liked to visit Monaco for its beautiful gardens. But after talking to a friend who felt the same, he stopped going. The friend explained that he had encountered the owner of the adjoining casino and that the friend had told the owner that he was going to stop visiting the gardens because he couldn't support the casino's gambling. At which time the owner told him not to stop because other people, in seeing the gardens, were led to try the casino as well. Spurgeon, realizing that his enjoying of the gardens might place others of weaker resolve in harm's way, thought better of it and quit going.

Lessons on Jesus - Part 5 of 7

Text: John 14:1-6

Key verse: John 14:6 "I am the way, the truth and the life. No one comes to the father except through me."

An 83-year-old man, who had been a bachelor all his life, called his 3 nephews together to tell them he was getting married. Not surprisingly, they wanted to know why he was marrying now. "Is she beautiful?", asked one. "Is she rich?", asked another. "Is she a great cook?" Asked the third. "Nope", said the uncle, "she's none of those things". "Well, why then?" they asked. "She drives at night", answered the uncle.

It was reason enough for him. It was, he reasoned, a way to keep things the way he wanted them. Unfortunately, too many of us want to do the same thing with our Christian walk- to keep things comfortable. But this is not what Christ calls us to, as is indicated in today's scripture lesson. It's not our way, but his way.

A pastor had just finished preaching in a slum area in New York City and was feeling pretty good about it. Many had come forward to commit their lives to God. But then he saw him, or should I say, smelled him. A rough looking homeless guy was walking right toward him, and he could not escape, although the guy's rank smell made him feel that way. The guy said his name was David and he had been living on the street for the last 6 years. The pastor quickly assumed that to give him money would get rid of him. But when he got his wallet out, David said he didn't want the pastor's money, but the Jesus that he had been preaching about. He said that he thought he would die on the street and wanted to have Jesus before that happened. The pastor was instantly convicted of his sin and asked God for forgiveness and began to cry. David did too and with the pastor's help, found peace, forgiveness and hope. The Lord then admonished the pastor by whispering to the pastor's heart: "If you don't love this smell, I can't use you!" It was the way the pastor was to go- like it or not.

Lessons on Jesus - Part 6 of 7

Text: Hebrews 7:25-28

Key verse: 1 Timothy 2:5 "For there is one God, and one mediator between God and men, the man Jesus Christ."

An employee went to a fellow worker at his office with a prayer request, knowing that that worker kept an ongoing list of 10 people she would pray for daily. In presenting his urgent prayer request, he asked if there was room for him. And she responded that yes there was because 3 of the people she had been praying for had died.

My guess is that he would have hoped for better results from an intercessor. Nevertheless, we do have the ultimate intercessor for us in Jesus Christ-for he loves us and has experienced all the temptations that we have. Today's lesson substantiates this claim, as it points out Jesus' qualifications and great pleasure in helping us in this way.

A story tells of the value of intercession. A man who could not speak Spanish went to live in Columbia and work as an intercessor. He did not convert a single person but obediently and faithfully prayed for the people in his town until his death, 18 years later. When experienced missionaries came to that town after the guy's death, they expected the worst, as they usually did. But this time, revival broke out, thanks to the prayer work that was done before.

The value, then, of intercessory prayer should be self-evident as there can be no significant Spiritual work accomplished without it. It has been said that prayer changes things. But the change that is most clearly demonstrated is in us- the change that Jesus makes in our heart.

Lessons on Jesus - Part 7 of 7

Text: Philippians 2:8

Key verse: phil. 2:8b "..., he humbled himself and became obedient unto death-even death on a cross!"

A young boy was asked by his mother to go to the neighbor's and borrow an iron, as theirs was broken. But just before he left, his mother warned him about a snake called a black racer, that allegedly could chase and bite him.so, on the way to the neighbor's, he carefully watched both sides of the path, but saw no snake. On the way back, however, he did become aware of something trailing behind him that was both long and slender. So, he took off running and almost made it home before realizing that what he thought was a black racer was actually the electric cord of the iron.

At least you could say he was obedient- which is more than you can say for us, at times. Yet we have an excellent example of obedience in our Lord and savior, Jesus Christ. As today's lesson indicates, he was obedient to the father's will- even unto death. Not that that was easy for him. He just accepted that it was what was needed for our sins to be forgiven. Although he might have preferred an easier way, he obeyed because it was the father's way.

From our study of scriptures, we get a pretty good idea as to what God wants. But because we have free will, the decision to obey or go our own way is still ours to make. In a modern-day context, football quarterback Roger Staubach faced a similar dilemma. His coach, Tom Landry, called all the plays-which greatly frustrated Staubach. After all, Staubach had been a star quarterback in the navy and had served as an officer in that service. He was used to taking charge. But, in his words, "once I learned to obey, there was harmony, fulfillment and victory."

I believe that we will be able to say the same thing, once we learn to obey. And most of that will come once we realize that God has a much better perspective than we do.

REFLECTIONS

July 4th

Growing up, the holiday known as July the 4th never meant too much to me other than a parade and fireworks. It didn't seem like much of a holiday because it didn't interrupt school or change my summers in any appreciable way. It did mark the middle of summer break but as so much more remained, it was no big deal.

But being a sort of history buff and being part of a family where the father and all the sons served in the military, I came to appreciate the idea of commemorating our nation's freedom on July 4th. I'm not sure where that came from, but the idea of protecting our way of life through military action has always been somewhat of an interest. As a boy, those things always seemed so glorious. But when Vietnam claimed the lives and futures of so many that I knew, and when the combat veterans returning from Vietnam (who were conducting my basic training at Fort Polk, Louisiana) urged us to speak out against that war, I began to think otherwise. Yet, I have never regretted my military service and like to think that our country's maintenance of a strong military is the best means of promoting peace.

Lessons on July 4ᵗʰ - Part 1 of 7

Text: 1 Corinthians 10:23-33

Key verse: 1 Corinthians 10:23b "...I have the right to do anything- but not everything is constructive."

Two guys were walking through a forest when they came upon a grizzly bear. Instinctively, they began to run. But they had only covered a short distance when one of them stopped to tie his shoes. "What are you doing?", asked the one. "I'm tying my shoes so I can run faster", said the other. "What difference will that make? We can't outrun a grizzly bear." "I don't have to outrun the bear, "he said. "I only have to outrun you!"

With friends like that, we'd never need enemies, right? And if he were able to make it out of that predicament, no one could blame him for not wanting that guy as a friend. That's called freedom of choice- one of the many freedoms we enjoy in this great country. But freedom of choice is not democracy- a difference not easily discerned.

Democracy, or rule by the people, is a long-cherished freedom that we have come to think of as the best possible way for people to live. However, in our nation-building efforts in many third-world countries, that idea has often not been easily accepted. And that is because the underlying assumptions of democracy are not shared. What are those assumptions? They are that the strong are not supposed to exploit the weak; that every life is worthwhile and capable of greatness; that no one is more worthy than anyone else; and that no type of government can make one compassionate.

The point is, then, from a Christian perspective, that the concept of Christian freedom must also have some underlying assumptions. This is what the apostle Paul is pointing out to the Corinthian church in the matter of eating foods offered to idols. He says that, even if there is nothing wrong in eating this food, that he would abstain for the sake of someone that thought it was wrong. The assumption underlying this behavior was that not all things are beneficial or constructive or good for others.

Lessons on July 4th - Part 2 of 7

Text: Joshua 4:1-9

Key verse: Joshua 4 :7c "these stones are to be a memorial to the people of Israel forever."

An elderly man and an elderly woman lived fairly close to one another in a trailer court and, over the years, had gotten to know each other pretty well. Finally, the old guy got up the nerve to ask her if she would marry him. And, after thinking about it for a few moments, said, "I will." They said a few more pleasantries to one another and then went their separate ways. The next day when the old guy got up, he couldn't remember if she had said yes or no. So, he called and asked her-to which she said, "I do remember saying I would but I'm awfully glad you called because I had forgotten who asked me."

It has been said that a mind is a terrible thing to waste. And, although I agree, I see evidence fairly frequently that such a thing is possible. We just have to be careful that we do remember the most important things-like the celebration of our country's independence.

Today's lesson shows us Joshua's plan for remembrance, and it was a good one. He had an elder from every tribe of Israel pick up a stone from the middle of the temporarily dry Jordan river to place as a memorial to God's dividing that body of water so the nation of Israel could pass through. The biblical account does not say if his efforts were successful- but at least he tried.

Similarly, many people wear a cross to remind them of the sacrifice that Jesus made to gain us forgiveness of sin. Our churches also have crosses prominently displayed. But, again, I'm not sure of their effectiveness in helping us remember- just as I'm not sure that our American flag invokes patriotic feelings as it should. So, my guess is that we need something stronger than a symbol to remind us. We need a grateful heart.

Lessons on July 4th - Part 3 of 7

Text and Key verse: Jeremiah 16:20 "Do people make their own Gods? Yes, but they are not Gods!"

The teacher was watching as the children prepared to recite the Pledge of Allegiance. But when she saw that little Johnny had his hand on his butt instead of his heart, she stopped the pledge. "We will not start again until Johnny put his hand on his heart." "But, teacher, it is!" "What makes you think that that is where your heart is?" "Every time grandma comes to visit, she picks me up, pats me there, and says, "Bless your little heart."

Certainly, teaching children to recite the Pledge of Allegiance is a good start toward teaching them about the virtues and responsibilities of freedom. But this litany must be matched with solid teaching about our history and with tangible examples of people who have helped our nation bring this freedom about. Two such historical figures are displayed prominently on Mount Rushmore: George Washington and Thomas Jefferson. This monument is a symbol of American pride and as these two men figured prominently in establishing our country and the freedom we enjoy; it is only right that they be presented there. They have attributes that all Americans should aspire to.

Yet, making monuments is something that people have always been about-even from the time of the tower of Babel. The only problem with that, however, is when the people have moved from seeing the monument as a symbol to seeing it as a God. Clearly, both Washington and Jefferson had their faults and as such, were not worthy of worship. By the same token, there are no mere humans worthy of worship, and we would do well to remember that.

That brings me to an interesting concept that I heard about recently. A man was talking about his personal Mount Rushmore. On that imaginary monument, he was talking about putting a sports figure on because he thought so much of him. And, without consciously putting it that way, I think that we do the same with people in our lives. Thus, we must be careful that we don't put them on a plane with God, because only he should be there.

Lessons on July 4ᵗʰ - Part 4 of 7

Text: 1 Corinthians 12: 1-14

Key verse: 1 Corinthians 12:14 "Certainly the body is not one part but many."

A duck walked into a pharmacy and asked the pharmacist if he had any grapes. The pharmacist said no but that they did at the grocery store two blocks down. The next day, the duck walks into the pharmacy and asked the pharmacist the same thing. A little annoyed, the pharmacist replied that he didn't and that the grocery store down the street did. The next day, the duck walks back into the same pharmacy and asks the same pharmacist the same question. This time the pharmacist lets him have it: "This is the third time you've come in here asking for something I told you we don't have. Now if you come in here again asking for grapes, I'm going to nail your little webbed feet to the floor." Believe it or not, the duck walks into the pharmacy the next day, but with a little more fear than he has before, and again approaches the pharmacist and meekly asks: "Do you have any nails?" "No" "Well then, do you have any grapes?"

In a free country, I guess you're allowed to ask stupid questions, but people don't have to be happy to answer them. But, in a free country, there has to be a general willingness to contribute what talents we do have to keep it that way.

In 1 Corinthians 12, we learn about the gifts of the Spirit and their use in the church- to make it the best it can be. Similarly, this country needs its parts to contribute to the whole to make it the best it can be. Unfortunately, the contributions to our country's greatness are being made by fewer and fewer people- what with the all-volunteer military services, and the comparatively few people who are involved in non-military government service. As a result, fewer and fewer people feel the need to give anything back.

I'm not sure how we can affect the needed change in a majority of the people, but we must. Surely, if one were honest with themselves, they would have to admit they are truly blessed to live in such a country. And, as a result, to love it, obey its laws and defend it against all enemies, foreign and domestic.

Lessons on July 4th - Part 5 of 7

Text: Numbers: 13:1-2,21, 25-33

Key verse: numbers 13:18 "See what the land is like and whether the people who live there are weak or strong, few or many."

Two guys were standing outside the gates of heaven waiting to get in when St. Peter approached them and said, "Only one mansion is finished at this point, so I'll have to detain one of you here for a little while. So, the one I'll let in now is the one of you who has done the bravest thing in death." The first guy said he had cancer for the last year but kept his fears to himself so that his family would not worry. The second guy said that he had not done anything that worthy. The bravest thing he'd done was to finally get up the nerve to tell his wife that he didn't like her backseat driving. "When did you do that?", St. Peter asked. "About two minutes ago", replied the second guy.

It is only fitting that, on July 4th, we remember the bravery of those people who have risked their lives for us. In today's lesson, moses selects 12 men to spy out the Promised Land for 40 days and bring back a report. This, indeed, called for bravery as their detection would have surely meant their execution and jeopardized the safety of the Israelites who waited behind. Yet, when they returned, bravery was also required in those making a report if it went against the analysis of the majority. In this case, only 2 spies, Joshua and Caleb had the courage to give a contradictory report.

From a non-military viewpoint, missionaries must show great bravery. Such was the case for David Livingston, who spent the majority of his adult life serving as missionary to primitive Africa during the 1800's. Once he received a letter from home indicating that his supporting agency was about to send some help if a good road could be found into where he was. And he replied not to send them if they had to wait for good roads. He wanted only the ones who were willing to come even if they had no roads at all. This is the kind of bravery that sets missionaries and fighting men apart and earns them our undying respect.

Lessons on July 4th - Part 6 of 7

Text: Matthew 4:18-22

Key verse: Matthew 4:19a "Come, follow me,"…

The pastor of a church which didn't give much money felt that something drastic needed to be done. So, before the annual meeting of the church where the giving pledges were received, he got together with an electrician and wired all the pews. At the meeting, then, he announced, "All pledges will be done by standing up when I give a money amount. So, let's get started: will all those who pledge $10/week, stand up." Then, he turned a dial, sending electricity all through the pews, causing half the congregation to stand up. The ushers then hurried and took down their names and amounts. Next the pastor asked for all those who would donate $20/ week to stand up. Again he turned the dial, sending a higher jolt of electricity through the pews, causing several more people to stand. Again the ushers recorded all the names and amounts. He did this several more times, each time increasing the voltage. After the service, he and his staff congratulated themselves on their success while adding up the pledges. But their joy evaporated when a couple of the ushers came back to inform the pastor that several people in the congregation had been electrocuted because they refused to stand up.

The beauty of celebrating July 4th and the people that made it possible is the fact that they did not have to be coerced into fighting for our freedom. They knew that their participation might lead to death. But they'd rather be dead if they could not be free.

Jesus did not have to coerce his followers, either. But they were not sure where their participation would lead them. Yet, in time, they, too, realized the possible costs of discipleship and willingly made the sacrifice.

The only difference between the two, then, is that one followed our nation's leaders for a life that was free and the other followed our Spiritual leader for a life that was both free and eternal- both good reasons to "follow me."

Text: Ephesians 4:7-16

Key verse: Ephesians 4:7 "But that doesn't mean that you should all look and speak and act the same."

A pig and a chicken are walking down the road together when the chicken says to the pig, "Let's open a restaurant." "What will we call it?" "How about ham and eggs?" The pig thinks about it for a moment, then says, "No thanks. For you it would only be an involvement, but for me it would be a total commitment."

One's level of involvement in something is something that should be decided at an early stage. When it comes to what we do to ensure the continuation of our nation's freedom, this is particularly important. When I was growing up, our nation had a draft where all but those who had a good reason for not serving in the military, served. But now we have an all-volunteer service, so only the ones who want to, serve. So far that has worked fairly well except that pride in our nation has deteriorated. It's not that we have any less reason to be proud of our country, but the lack of participation seems to have had a weakening effect.

In today's scripture, the apostle Paul is addressing the church at Ephesus re: the varied roles for service that exist and should be filled in relation to each one's Spiritual gift. It seems that our nation's needs could be addressed similarly. That is, not everyone has the gifts and graces to be a warrior. But there should be some alternative available to allow all to participate. And the reason is similar. The church spreads its responsibilities wide enough to allow all to have some sense of ownership. This is lacking in our government service.

REFLECTIONS

Labor Day

As a student, I always regarded Labor Day as the last gasp of summer and the start of the school year. That did not necessarily have a negative connotation for me although, like most kids, I would miss summer vacation. Labor Day, instead, is a holiday that causes me to reflect on my work history rather than on the holiday itself. My work history was largely unremarkable other than the summer factory work that helped me decide what I didn't want to do. After college, I took a civil service position as a caseworker in the public welfare field. This was to be my primary life's work. As it turned out, it was a job that gave me the opportunity to help people but in a work environment that did not foster one's best efforts. Fortunately for me, I was blessed with some interesting and challenging part-time work-first as a logistics officer in the National Guard and then as a pastor at several small rural churches. Reflecting, I was blessed to have had a strong work ethic instilled at an early age and some diverse work opportunities that helped give me a well-rounded perspective on work and its benefits.

Lessons on Labor Day – Part 1 of 7

Text: Genesis 43:1-14

Key verse: Genesis 43:9 "I myself will guarantee his safety…"

A man had been out of work for a long time and had just about given up about finding work. So, one day, deciding to take a break from his job search, he went to the zoo. But when he got there, he, out of habit, asked the zookeeper if there were any job openings. "It's ironic that you should ask that today", he replied. "Our gorilla died last night and until we get another one, we need someone to put on a gorilla outfit and act like a gorilla. If you're willing to do this, we'll pay you $10/hour. It will mean a lot to the kids who really enjoy seeing a gorilla." The guy thought about it for a minute and decided to take the job. And it went very well-so well that he decided to show off a little when the kids came by after school. In fact, he swung so high on the tire swing in his cage that he swung over into the lion's cage-where the swing broke. Now he really started to scream and rattle the cage as the lion slowly made its way over to investigate. Just about the time the guy thought he had had it, the lion whispered to him, "Hey buddy, you'd better shut up or we'll both get fired."

It only stands to reason that we do the best work we can, regardless of what it is. Otherwise, we'll lose the ability to gain the respect of those we hope to reach for Christ. Doing our best is part of what gives us integrity.

When Israel asked his sons to return to Egypt to bring back grain because of the famine, they advised their dad that they could not return unless they brought their youngest brother Benjamin. Israel did not initially agree until Judah, Israel's oldest son agreed to vouch for his safety.

For us Christians, our word is our bond. If we show we can't be trusted to keep our word, we have little hope of becoming the Christian influence we hope to be.

Commercial vehicles often carry the offer to report to them if their driving is substandard. Similarly, we, as Christians need to live our lives in such a way that we could give those around us that same offer.

Lessons on Labor Day – Part 2 of 7

Text and key verse: psalm 90:17 "…; yes, establish the work of our hands."

A man going to work was pulled over one day by a state troper, who asked, "Didn't you see that stop sign back there?" "Listen, officer, I've been traveling this same road for 20 years and have never stopped at that stop sign." "Well, you will now!", the policeman replied and gave him a ticket. The next morning, that same trooper was called to investigate an accident at that same stop sign. This time, the guy he had stopped the previous day had been rear-ended by another driver. When the trooper asked the second driver how it had happened, he said, "It's not my fault, officer. I've been following this guy for the last 20 years and he never stopped at that stop sign before."

Just because we do the same thing for an extended period of time doesn't make it right. When we ask God to establish the work of our hands, we need to make sure we're doing things correctly. We are creatures of habit and, as such, we can pick up bad habits just as easily as good ones.

But there is another good reason to do our work as well as we can: our integrity is a critical factor in enabling us to reach out to unbelieving co-workers. If we shortchange our work, someone else has to pick up the slack and that makes for hard feelings. You can hardly blame someone for not being attentive to anything a "slacker" is selling.

Certainly, Jesus lived what he taught. That's why his life continues to inspire people today. And it's also the reason that Christianity has such a bad name among people who see that many so-called Christians do not live Christ-like lives. That's why we need to ask God to establish the Christian work we do as well as the secular.

Lessons on Labor Day - Part 3 of 7

Text and key verse; Colossians 3:23 "Work hard and cheerfully at all you do, just as though you were working for the Lord and not merely for your masters."

A young lawyer had just set up private practice and was waiting for his first real client. His office was just a desk with a phone and a bookcase with legal volumes. Nevertheless, he hoped to make a good first impression. And so, it was as he looked out the window on his first day, that he spotted a guy coming across the street toward his office and opened the door to come in. The lawyer immediately picked up the phone and started a conversation with an imaginary client, making important points while the visitor looked on, waiting patiently. When the phone call was completed, the young lawyer looked up and asked, "How can i help you?' the guy replied, "I'm here from the phone company to set up your phone service."

Not the best first impression, right? The point is we all want people to think that we are competent. We just don't always know the best way to do that. Some reason is that if they make a lot of money that people will think they are successful. It is a measure of success, but is it the best measure? A young apprentice named Harry worked for a Scottish cobbler named Dan. Harry's job was to pound out and dry leather for the soles of the shoes. It seemed to Harry like an endless, boring job but particularly so when he came across another cobbler who put the leather on wet. When Harry asked that cobbler why he did it that way, he replied that the shoes came back quicker for repair that way. When Harry shared that with his employer, Dan replied, "I don't make shoes for the money, Harry. I make them for the glory of God. If I do less than my best, I can't expect to hear "well done".

Some work as if they will never answer to a higher authority. As Christians, we need to help them to see things differently.

Lessons on Labor Day – Part 4 of 7

Text and key verse: Ecclesiastes 5:18 "Well, one thing, at least is good: it is for a man to eat well, drink a good glass of wine, accept his position in life and enjoy his work whatever his job may be, for however long the Lord may allow him to live."

The mayor of a small city was driving around when he spotted 2 city employees doing something unusual-one was digging holes while the other was filling them in. So, he stopped asking them about it. "It's this way, Mr. Mayor, there are usually 3 people on this team: one digs the hole, one plants the tree, and one puts dirt around it. Today our tree planter was sick, but we wanted to work anyway."

Today's scripture text was written by a cynical old man at the end of his life. In summing everything up he said that everything seemed so futile to him-everything, that is, except for doing your work. I believe that old age can tend to make one cynical- but, in Christ, our attitudes can be much more positive.

Indeed, God provided work for Adam to do in the garden of Eden, so he must have thought it had a benefit. However, as our work has become so specialized, it is harder to appreciate what part we do of it. Henry Ford, in starting his assembly lines, tried to address the problem by increasing the hourly wage, but in the end, it did not make up for the loss that specialization brought.

Thus, we must strive to find the meaning in the seemingly meaningless. To do this we must catch hold of the human factor in our work- the camaraderie, the teamwork and the shared experience of doing a good day's work. With that comes the realization that the human factor is our most important product.

Judson Taylor, the famous China missionary, tells a story about a young man who drowned because the fishing vessel who could have saved him valued their catch of fish over the young man's life. We must be careful not to do the same.

Lessons on Labor Day – Part 5 of 7

Text and key verse; Acts 1:11 "You Galileans-why do you just stand here looking up at an empty sky?"

A church called a new pastor at 60 years of age. His first sermon was 15 minutes long. Kinda short but fine for the folks. The deacons met with the pastor to see if there was anything they could do to make he and his wife more comfortable. So, the pastor asked them to make the parsonage bathroom a little larger. The next week he preached for 20 minutes. That was ok, too. After the service, the deacons came again and made the same request. The pastor again reminded them about the bathroom, but once again the deacons didn't get around to doing anything. But the following week he preached for an hour and 45 minutes. The deacons pulled him off to the side demanding an answer for such an atrocity. He said, "Well, you know that parsonage bathroom is so small and my wife and I were running late this morning and we got mixed up and I accidently put her false teeth in by mistake and once you get those things a goin' you just can't get 'em to stop." At the next deacon's meeting it was recommended to get a bigger bathroom in the parsonage.

When it comes to procrastinating, it's hard to tell the sinners from the saints. And today's scripture verse reminds us that the disciples were not immune. The angels admonished them for wasting time when there was work to do. Whether we like it or not, people who help us to focus our efforts are really doing us a favor-particularly when we are doing the Lord's work.

Albert Einstein once said, "The world is a dangerous place-not because of the people who are evil, but because of the people who do nothing about it." This is the reason that we must be diligent in our good work. This is the reason that we cannot afford to wait.

Lessons on Labor Day – Part 6 of 7

Text and key verse: Deuteronomy 5:13 "Six days you shall labor and do all your work."

A preacher rode by one Sunday morning to see a farmer and church member at work harvesting. "Brother", said the preacher, "Don't you know that the creator made the world in six days and rested on the seventh?" "Yes, I know all about that," the farmer replied, "but he got his work finished and i didn't."

It has been said that the savings bank of human existence is the weekly sabbath. Unfortunately, many people don't practice it-oftentimes to their own detriment. In the Challenger space shuttle disaster, key NASA officials made the ill-fated decision to go ahead with the launch after working 20 hours straight and getting only 2 hours of sleep the night before. Their error in judgment cost the lives of seven astronauts and nearly killed the Us space program. If we ignore our need for rest and renewal, we do so at the peril of others and ourselves.

God realized this and the need we have to get things done. But he also knows how we are made and so commanded us to have a day's rest each week- the benefit of which we all have experienced. For example, it is a common experience that a problem difficult at night is resolved in the morning after the committee of sleep has worked on it. It is also a common experience for us to be able to approach even the least engaging job with a more positive attitude when we've received adequate rest.

Perhaps most important with that positive attitude is the realization that if we are doing our work as unto God, we are enabled to see our work for the higher calling that it could be. Christopher Wren, who designed St. Paul's cathedral in London, wrote about the reactions of construction workers working on that building. Although some saw their work as laying bricks or carrying stones, one replied that he was building a great cathedral. Without adequate rest we are unlikely to have such a lofty view.

Lessons on Labor Day – Part 7 of 7

Text and key verse: Haggai 2:4 "…and now get to work, for I am with you, says the Lord of heaven's armies."

The human services director was taken aback by the applicant's salary request and said, "You certainly expect to be compensated well for a beginner." "Well, yeah", the applicant said, "work's a lot harder when you don't know what you're doing."

In today's lesson, the people who had returned from exile to rebuild the walls of Jerusalem had seemed to have lost their purpose and fallen down on the job. So Haggai the prophet was trying to "light a fire" under them to finish the job. For the people, they had not forgotten how to do the job, but got comfortable in not doing it, which is just about as bad. Certainly, the work would seem hard at first after their lay off but they knew it was important. They just had to be reminded. We should be able to relate. We, too, know that the work of the church is important and must not be stopped. We just get lazy at times and need to be reminded.

During the D-day invasion of World War II, much of what could go wrong did and so as Gi's huddled behind the seawall and other obstacles, many had forgotten their purpose. Because things didn't go as planned, many were paralyzed with fear. After all many people had been killed and the bullets were coming in hot and heavy. But thankfully, there were guys who remembered what was expected and set the example of moving ahead toward their objectives.

Similarly, when we go to battle with Satan, he does his best to disrupt our plans and paralyze us with fear. At times like these, we must remember who is with us and trust his help. He will help us accomplish our mission.

REFLECTIONS

Love

Probably more so than any other concept, we must be careful to define our terms when it comes to love. As we know, love is different between a man and a woman, between a parent and a child, between siblings and between friends. It is possible to love one's work or hobby or even some material things. I have been blessed in my life to have been able to experience all these different types of love and they have all been wonderful in their own right. But I feel that it is absolutely essential for a person to first experience the love of parents and to be able to express their love back to them in order to be fully prepared to experience the rest. I submit that if this first love is somehow restricted or stunted, their capacity to love in all ways will be seriously compromised. They will likely be less inclined to trust that emotion if they feel that it may prove painful again. Nevertheless, I further submit that the love of God can heal that pain for the love of God is perfect. As 1st Corinthians 13 describes it; it is not self-seeking but always protecting, always trusting, always hoping and always persevering. I have also experienced that love in my life and know that this claim is true.

Lessons on Love - Part 1 of 7

Text: Ruth 1:16-17

Key verse: Ruth 1:16c "Your people will be my people and your God my God."

The wife woke up one morning and said to her husband, "Honey, I had a dream last night where you gave me a gold necklace. What do you think that means?" "Well, Monday's your birthday. Maybe you'll find out then." The next morning, when she awoke, she told her husband that she had a dream where he gave her a pearl necklace and wondered what that meant. And he told her to wait 'til her birthday and then she'd know. Finally, on Monday morning, she woke up and told her husband that she had had a dream where he gave her a diamond necklace and, again, wondered what it meant. To which he told her, "Wait until tonight!" When he got home that night, he gave her a package, which she eagerly opened, only to find a book, entitled "The Meaning of Dreams."

Often times, human love can and does disappoint. But in today's lesson, Ruth shows a love for her mother-in-law that shows that it doesn't have to be this way- that human, at times, can be capable of a love that is almost divine. As the story goes, Naomi and her husband and 2 sons leave Judah for Moab, a foreign territory due to a famine. While there, disaster strikes in the form of the death of her husband, and 2 sons, who, by that time, had taken 2 wives, Orpah and Ruth. Naomi then decides to go home again but knows her prospects there are not good. So, she releases her daughters-in-law from any obligation to her and allows them to return to their home, presumably to get remarried. But Ruth refuses to leave her and Ruth's great loyalty and faithfulness are rewarded.

This lesson is an oft-quoted example of loyalty and love that we are encouraged to emulate. And, although the Bible also gives us examples of behavior that we should avoid, it is well that we see the best and worst of which we are capable.

Lessons on Love - Part 2 of 7

Text: Hosea

Key verse: John 3:16 "For God so loved the world that he gave his only begotten son, that whosoever believeth in him shall not perish but have everlasting life."

Jimmy receives this note: "Dearest Jimmy- I made a terrible mistake in breaking our engagement and pray that you'll take me back. No one could ever take your place in my heart. Yours forever, Marie"

Ps: Congratulations on winning the lottery!

The question is: Can true love ever be answered by what's in it for me? If so, maybe there is hope for Jimmy and Marie. In a more important sense, however, this is a question that many would-be Christians ask prior to taking the leap. Yet, I'm thankful that God doesn't ask that same question, as it appears to be a rather lopsided deal. Praise God that his love is not like ours! Despite our fickleness, he giveth and giveth and giveth again. It is a love that is rarely, if ever, seen this side of heaven.

This kind of love is depicted in the life of the prophet Hosea and his marriage to Gomer. She was a prostitute when he married her, but his marriage to her did not change her orientation to infidelity. It was a perfect metaphor for the way the Israelites acted toward God, despite his many loving actions toward them. Nevertheless, God advised Hosea to take her back and try to work things out, as this was his desire for the Israelites.

The question then becomes what this looks like in the church today. A few years ago, Jim Bakker was a very successful tv pastor. But he got in trouble for diverting ministry money for his own use and was sent to prison. When he got out, he had no place to go. So, Billy and Ruth Graham took him in and supported him, despite what some people might think about that association. The Bible says, "Go and do thou likewise." Could we?

Lessons on Love - Part 3 of 7

Text: John 13:1-17

Key verse: John 13:15 "I have set you an example that you should do as I have done for you."

A second-grade schoolteacher intercepted a note and passed it on to the mother of the little girl who wrote it. The note said: Dear Billy-if you don't say you love me and walk with me to the bus stop, i will kill myself and beat you up. I love you and want to marry you soon. Suzy. That was when Suzy was 8 but 16 years later, at the rehearsal dinner for Billy and Suzy's wedding, Suzy's mother got the note out and shared it with the pastor. So, the pastor included the following in Suzy's wedding vows: I, Suzy, promise to never kill myself or beat you up. After the ceremony, the pastor remarked that if Suzy's faithfulness to Billy and the laughs that vow got in the wedding were any indication, their life together should be happy ever after.

You see, even kids understand that love should be demonstrated as well as expressed. AND THIS IS THE ESSENTIAL MESSAGE of today's lesson. Not long before Jesus was to die, he washed the disciple's feet- a task usually reserved for servants. But he wished to set an example for them in doing this- that a servant- mentality was absolutely essential to effective and compassionate service.

But how does this look in everyday life? A Christian man from India who lived in a big college town decided to open his home to foreign students going to school there for dinner. Yet, despite his opportunity to do so, he never shared his faith with them, out of his respect for their faith-which was obviously different from his. That is, he didn't share his faith until they asked him why he did it.

This, then, appears to be the key for us as well. When people's resistance is broken down and their trust in us built up, they can see our love and are attracted to it.

Lessons on Love - Part 4 of 7

Text: 1 Corinthians 13

Key verse: 1 Corinthians 13:8a "Love never fails."

A poem:

I climbed up the door,

And I shut the stairs.

I said my shoes and took off my prayers.

I shut off my bed,

And climbed into the light.

And all because she kissed me good night.

That's romantic love for you. And it is a wonderful thing. Yet there is another love that exceeds even this- and that is the love of God.

In today's lesson, the apostle Paul talks about this love. And although many try to portray this as human love, we know that human love can only aspire to this.

God's love is relentless. A little boy was playing at his father's knee while his dad was reading the paper. All of a sudden, the little boy's love for his daddy welled up and he proclaimed to his dad, "I love you, daddy!" The father looked up from his paper and patted the boy's head, saying, "I love you, too, son." Then he went back to his paper. Apparently, that wasn't good enough for his son, who went back and took a flying leap into his daddy's lap and said, "And I've just got to do something about it."

God's love sees us, not as we are, but as we could be. When sea-captain and former slave trader, John Newton, asked Polly Catlett to marry him, her family and friends all objected. They said the two of them were too different and that she'd hate being a sea-captain's wife. But she saw something in him that no one else could see, and made it work.

Lessons on Love - Part 5 of 7

Text: Galatians 6:2

Key verse: Galatians 6:2 "Carry each other's burdens, and in this way, you will fulfill the law of Christ."

One winter day, a kindergarten teacher was helping one of her students get on his boots. This was much harder than it sounds and so when she finally helped get them on, the little boy said, "Teacher, they're on the wrong foot!" So back off they came, then, back on again. Yet, after completing this tiresome task, the little boy said, "Teacher, they're not my boots." After once again getting them off, the little boy explained that the boots were his brother's but that his mother had said he could wear them today. So, once again, she tugged and pulled to get them on. But this time the little boy said, "My mittens are in the toes of the boots."

Thankfully, helping will not always be that hard but burden-bearing can be just that. That's why it falls under the category of love. Christians who risk having a partner with whom they can be accountable are a good example of what that love looks like.

Paul realized that he was swearing too much and asked his friend, William, to help him stop. The system they devised provided for Paul to give William $5 to put into the church offering plate for each time he swore during the week. The first week, this amounted to $100. But each week since, Paul had made progress. But by the 4th week, William could see what a burden it was becoming, and so changed the system. Now each time Paul swore, William would pay the $5. Now the burden was even heavier on Paul since he didn't want his friend to give up so much money. And this helped him to stop much faster than he ever would have, otherwise.

This is also a great example for the grace Jesus shows to each of us as the Bible says that we crucify Christ anew whenever we knowingly participate in sin. Hopefully, in appreciating such an effect on Jesus who loves us so, we too are constrained to do our utmost in abstaining from sin.

Lessons on Love - Part 6 of 7

Text: Romans 10:12

Key verse: Romans 10:12 "For there is no difference between Jew and Gentile-the same Lord is Lord of all and richly blesses all who call on him."

Two young engineers applied for the same position at a particular company. And since they had the same qualifications, the HR director gave them a five-question test. When the tests were scored, the HR director told the first applicant that they were going to give the job to the second applicant. "But we both only missed one question", said the first. "How does that make him the better candidate?" "Easy," said the HR director. "On the question that you both missed, he wrote I don't know, and you wrote, neither do I."

No two people are the same and we must remember this in dealing with them. God loves everyone but sees each for their unique gifts, graces and shortcomings. Our scripture verse spells this out clearly, as well. Our problem comes when we like one over the other or dislike one over the other.

I had this problem when I worked for the state welfare department many years ago. There would be some people who would come in demanding this benefit or that while others were humbler in their approach. I liked the humbler clients but had to administer benefits based on financial eligibility. That meant that their approach meant nothing —only their eligibility, whether I liked them or not. As I think back on it, this was a wise course of action because it protected the clients from worker discrimination.

In the early church, there were pockets of discrimination between Gentiles and Jews-the Jews feeling that the Gentiles should adopt more Jewish customs before being considered for salvation or leadership positions in the church. But God, through his Spirit, made no distinction between the two. Thus, neither should we.

Lessons on Love - Part 7 of 7

Text:1 John 4:21

Key verse: Philippians 4:9 "Those things, which ye have both learned and received and heard and seen in me, do."

Two well-known pastors, driving down the road, came upon a guy who told them that the bridge ahead had been recently washed out and immediately decided to make a sign to warn oncoming traffic. So, they put these words on the sign: the end is near! Turn yourself around before it's too late. But when they held up the sign, most of the motorists just rolled down their windows and called them religious fanatics and went on to their demise. So, the one pastor turned to the other and said, "Do you think we just should have put, "bridge out"?

I suppose it can be hard to pass on a good turn but that does not relieve us of the responsibility of doing so. It is clearly an important way of showing our love. Indeed, it is the strong recommendation of today's scripture verse. And it was the clear example of Jesus, who, in the last day of his life, washed the feet of his disciples. Thus, we, who are Christian followers, must also become of a servant mentality, so we are less likely to miss those opportunities where we can show Christ's love.

A farmer was sitting on his porch when his newspaper boy came by to deliver his newspaper. The newspaper boy noticed a sign that the farmer had out advertising puppies for sale. When the newspaper boy asked to see them, the farmer whistled and four puppies came around the porch, yapping and playing, as puppies are inclined to do. Yet still later another puppy came around the porch, dragging one leg behind. The newspaper boy asked the farmer the problem with the puppy and was told it was born without one of its hip joints. Immediately the boy asked to buy the puppy. But the farmer said, "This puppy will never be able to do all the things a regular dog will be able to do. Are you sure?" At which time the boy pulled up his pantleg to reveal a brace. "Mister, "the boy said, "that puppy will need someone that understands him."

REFLECTIONS

Marriage

At the time of this writing, I have been married almost 25 years and then some 15 years before that. Yet I think I know more than I actually do. There are, however, a couple of things worth noting: people should know each other as well as possible before they get married; love, rather than lust, is the best reason to get married, and those with the greatest potential for marital success are those who have become one another's best friend.

Some explanation is in order. Although physical attraction is usually what draws one to another, it really is the personality of the prospective mate that should be what one should consider most seriously as that is what remains when the looks are faded. There are many reasons besides love that lead people to marriage: looks, money, fame, convenience, and fear of loneliness among others. But it is love that is most important of all – knowing that one's life will never be as good as it can be without that person. Over time people's feelings change and thus are a poor indicator of love. But for two people who are best friends, the continual discovery of new dimensions of a relationship ensures that things will never get stale.

Lessons on Marriage - Part 1 of 7

Text: 1 Samuel 1:1-8

Key verse: Proverbs 9:8b "…rebuke a wise man and he will love you."

A young couple was about to be married, but the bride was experiencing cold feet, in spite of the love she had for her fiancée. The pastor, having much experience in these things suggested a piece of scripture that he thought would help. It was 1 john 4: 18, which reads: "there is no fear in love as perfect love casts out fear." The bride thought that it was a good verse and asked her maid of honor to read it at the ceremony. When the time came for the maid of honor to read, however, she showed that she didn't know her Bible very well-picking john 4;18 instead, which reads: 'You have had 5 husbands and the man you now have is not your husband."

She meant to help but didn't get it right. That often happens in marriage and when it does, it isn't pretty. In today's scripture lesson, Elkanah, Samuel's father, doesn't get it in dealing with Hannah, Samuel's mother, as he fails to realize what being childless meant to her. Now when this happens in real life, it often leads to bitter arguments with much criticism that is usually not the "truth shared in love".

That's why if we can learn to handle criticism better, the outcome can become much less acrimonious. One suggestion worth consideration is a 2-phase theory where we turn the sting of the criticism over to God, then, when we have cooled down, to analyze it in terms of the acronym "think". Obviously, when criticism makes us angry, we are likely to respond in kind. That's why turning it over to God makes so much sense-if we can do it. But then the think acronym comes in. T stands for True, or is the criticism true? H stands for Helpful, or was the criticism meant to be helpful? I stand for Inspire, or was the criticism meant to inspire us to higher achievement? N stands for Necessary, or was the criticism something that had to be said right then and there? And K stands for Kindness, or was the criticism done in such a way that a bond of friendship could be maintained? Hopefully, if we can cool down enough to calmly evaluate these factors, we will have done well.

Lessons on Marriage - Part 2 of 7

Text: Proverbs 24:3

Key verse: Proverbs 24:3 "Through wisdom is a house built; and by understanding, it is established."

The pastor was visiting the 4th grade Sunday school class to talk about marriage and asked if anyone knew what God said about it. One boy indicated that he knew and said, "Father, forgive them, for they know not what they do."

Unfortunately, this anecdote seems truer than we'd like it to be. An entry in the may24th, 2007 upper room daily devotional published this excerpt from a woman "I have been married for 17 years. I am passionate about my husband. I look forward to seeing him at the end of the day. I love to cuddle with him and talk things over." She also wrote this: "I have been married for 17 years. I am indifferent to my husband. I don't want to talk to him in the evening. I'd rather do my own thing." Hardly sounds like the same woman. But it is! And she is not schizophrenic! She said she held these opposite views of marriage at different times. And I began to wonder how common such ambivalent feelings are.

Clearly, the rates of divorce are high. But i feel that God wants better results as he was the one to institute this concept, originally. As a pastor, i have the responsibility of counseling young couples about to be married. And i consistently advise them that it is a covenant that was to be forever and one that requires constant watchfulness and care and that God, and the church were meant to be an important part of that.

I am not the best example of this as I have been a divorced person. But my relationship to God was not what it should have been then and so i and those involved paid the price. Yet not everyone has to learn the hard way. That's the benefit of sharing one's experience.

The other piece, of course, is seeing marriage as a house with the need for a strong foundation. That is the essence of today's scripture lesson. God must be that foundation. And, if he is, he will help those who turn to him restore that which is in need of repair.

Lessons on Marriage - Part 3 of 7

Text: John 15:16

Key verse: john 15:16 "You did not choose me, but I chose you and appointed you to go and bear fruit"

A woman seemed to be very depressed and so her concerned husband brought her in to see a psychiatrist. After hearing them talk for a little while about their relationship, the doctor said, "The treatment that i am prescribing is really quite simple." And with that, he gathered the man's wife up in his arms and gave her a big kiss, then, standing back from her so her husband could see her big smile, the doctor said, "See. That's not so hard. Do that and she'll be good as new!" Expressionless, the husband replied, "Ok doc. I can bring her on Tuesdays and Thursdays."

He didn't get it, did he? The doctor could see what the husband could not: the woman just needed some tender, loving care. It seems so simple, but it is surprising how often people can't see this. And this lack of attention only gets stronger as the couple gets older. They assume the other knows that they love them so the need to say it or show it seems unnecessary.

What couples often don't appreciate, however, is that their kids need to see their parents' care for one another. How else will they learn what they should do when they find a mate?

A story is told of a 6th grade boy whose class was learning to square dance. As the boys had to pick a girl partner, they would usually pick the prettiest or most popular one. But this time the teacher whispered to the boy to pick Mary. The boy really didn't want to, but his better nature made him reconsider. Now Mary wasn't pretty or popular. She was heavy and still suffered from a childhood case of polio. So, when the boy got his chance, he picked her and got a smile so wide from her, he had to look away-it was so lovely, and he knew he didn't deserve it. For once, she got picked first.

By the same token, God didn't have to pick us to save-but he did. And we, like Mary, should be forever grateful.

Lessons on Marriage - Part 4 of 7

Text: Mmark 10:6-9

Key verse: Mark 10:9 "Therefore what God has joined together, let man not separate."

A pastor was preparing his remarks for an upcoming wedding when the groom unexpectedly showed up at the pastor's study. He asked the pastor to change the wedding vows to reflect his unwillingness to honoring and obeying and gave him $100 to do so. When the big day came, however, and the pastor asked the groom to answer, he put the vow this way: "will you promise to bow down before her, obey her every command and wish, serve her breakfast in bed every morning of your life and swear before God, these witnesses and your lovely wife that you will not even look at another woman as long as you both shall live?" The groom gulped and said he would in a very small voice. Then he whispered to the pastor, "I thought we had a deal." The pastor then handed back his $100 and said, "She made a better one."

Of course, no pastor worth his salt would consider changing the marriage vows. That doesn't mean, however, that people won't try to get them too. In today's culture, people seem to be looking for the easy way out.

Today's scripture lesson makes very clear how God views the marriage vows. Yet it is generally the older folks who get this. One such older guy, when a friend commented on how long their 50 years together seemed to be, responded, "Not nearly as long as it would have been without her."

Our job as Christians, then, is to encourage young people to know their mates as well as possible before marrying them-to even become the other's best friend, if possible. But we also must do a better job teaching them about the importance that God puts on the marriage covenant.

Lessons on Marriage - Part 5 of 7

Text: Ephesians 5:25-33

Key verse: Ephesians 5:33 "However, each one of you also must love his wife as he loves himself, and the wife must respect her husband."

A little country church abruptly stopped using the office supply company that they had used for years and so the office supply manager called the pastor to ask him why. "I'll tell you why," the pastor said. "It was because of those little pencils you sent us for use in the pews." "What about them?" The store manager asked. "They were all stamped with the words: play golf next Sunday"

Obviously, the pastor wanted products that would support his church's ministry. No Christian would want to discourage a potential church attender. And no Christian should want to discourage a young couple who married in the church to re consider the marriage covenant formed there. Indeed, Jesus compared the marriage covenant to the covenant that church members should have with their church.

Personally, I like the analogy of going to church for better or worse, for richer or poorer and in sickness and in health. And I especially like that one vows "with all that they are and all that they have" to honor the church. We need to be careful, then, that we are not sending out mixed messages.

Certainly, Jesus didn't. He said that marriage with the church is characterized by giving, not getting. He says that everything a person who loves his church does is designed to bring out the best in it. And he treats it as he does his own body. So, clearly, the loved one has for the church should mirror the loved one has for his or her spouse and vice versa.

Lessons on Marriage - Part 6 of 7

Text: Matthew 25:14-29

Key verse: romans 14:12 "So then, each of us will give an account of himself to God."

A man left work on Friday but didn't go home as he usually did. He went fishing with some friends without telling his wife and stayed out all weekend. When he came home on Sunday night, he was confronted by his understandably angry wife. "How would you like it if you didn't see me for 2 or 3 days?", she asked. "I'd like that just fine", he replied. Well, Monday, then Tuesday went by without seeing her, then Wednesday, as well. But by Thursday, the swelling went down just enough for him to see her out of the corner of one eye.

I guess you might say he was being held accountable for his failure to be a good husband. But not all accountability is so painful-especially if we're doing what we are supposed to do. And that is as true for marriage as it is for anything else.

Today's Bible lesson is about the parable of the talents. In this parable, 3 servants are held accountable for how they handle their master's assets. When two of them do well, they are rewarded. But when the third does poorly, he is punished. I believe we should consider marriage as an asset. As such, then, we should handle it with care and responsibility, as if we will give an accounting for our marital efforts.

It is my experience that holding people accountable makes sense in more ways than just money or marriage. As a company commander, battalion logistics officer and chief of logistics for the training site at Fort Indiantown gap, I routinely assigned tasks for people to accomplish and checked to make sure they carried them out. But that checking process also became part of the basis of determining who would get promoted. So, it had a positive benefit as well. It is as the Bible says in 1st Corinthians 12:31, a more excellent way.

Lessons on Marriage - Part 7 of 7

Text: Genesis 4:4-22

Key verse: genesis 2:18 "It is not good for the man to be alone. I will make a helper suitable for him."

A story is told that it was eve that God made first, and it was eve that came to God asking for help with her loneliness. At which point God gave her the pros and cons of what the man would be like. In spite of the shortcomings, she urged God to go ahead. "There's just I more thing", God said. "you'll have to let him think that he was made first."

Although that story would answer some things, it is not how the Bible reads. Nevertheless, it is clear that both man and woman were pleased to be put together. Yet, it is over the long haul that the relationship must be evaluated.it seems apparent, then, that one must not just find the right mate but be the right mate.

Toward that end, there must be at least 3 traits in abundance: trust, adaptability and communication. In far too few relationships, however, this is not the case. But even then, these traits can be increased or improved upon if the couple wants to make it work. Their relationship to God can be a crucial element to this as the Christian couple operates from the position that divorce is not an option.

In addition, the married couple must maintain their relationship through the seasons of life. That's where their basic friendship becomes most critical. I believe that's why it's said that although marriages may be made in heaven, they must be maintained on earth. That's probably the most difficult idea to get through to young couples preparing to marry. The stars in their eyes do lose their luster over time and trial; it's the taking of the next step and the living of the next day that can be the most trying. That's why God's help and guidance is such an important aspect of successful marriages.

REFIECRTIONS

Memorial Day

Memorial Day has always carried a positive connotation for me because it has always coincided with the end of school and the beginning of summer vacation. In Monongahela, Pennsylvania (my hometown) Memorial Day was marked by a parade and a lot of do-what-you want. It was, to be sure, a day to celebrate. But, as I grew older, I began to appreciate Memorial Day for something much more needful- to remember and give honor and thanks for the sacrifices that were made to maintain our nation's freedom. Visits to relative's graves brought me closer to the fact that many young lives were "snuffed out" much too soon because of war. All my brothers and I serving in the military also gave me a profound sense of loyalty and love for our country and its war heroes. I am concerned, however, as to how the next generation will view Memorial Day-especially in the age of the all-volunteer army. Until all citizens come to the place where they realize freedom has a price, I'm not sure they'll get it.

Lessons on Memorial Day – Part 1 of 7

Text: Joshua 4:1-7

Key verse: Joshua 4:7c "These stones are to be a memorial to the people of Israel forever."

Two elderly women were out for a drive when they went through a stoplight. The lady that was in the passenger seat thought that she imagined it, as her friend was surely a better driver than that. So, she told herself to focus to see if it happened again. So, when the next light was red, she felt sure her friend would stop but, no, she went through again. "grace", she exclaimed, "you just went through 2 stoplights!" "oh", said grace, "Am I driving?"

Clearly, this is a little extreme but to forget what Memorial Day all is about is very bad. One way to remember, then, is to have a symbol to remind us. A united states flag might be one, but it wouldn't have to be that. In today's lesson, the Israelites were directed to put 12 stones from the middle of the Jordan in a tower to be a memorial of the deliverance of God in getting across that great river.

We do not ever find out if this worked or not, but we do have evidence of the Israelites forgetting God's deliverances at other times. So, I am not sure that symbols always work. I mean, consider the cross as a symbol. It stands alone as probably the greatest symbol of God's love and provision that anyone has ever had. But does it remind people sufficiently to keep them from doing the wrong or sinful thing? Unfortunately, not!

In the same way, the flag doesn't seem to be any more successful in helping people to remember the sacrifices that were made by the martyrs of previous wars. So, it would appear that we need more than symbols. We need grateful hearts. And nothing encourages this more than regular Bible reading, meditation and prayer. And, as for Memorial Day, let us regularly reflect on those lives that were given much too soon that we might have the freedom we have today.

Lessons on Memorial Day – Part 2 of 7

Text: 2 Samuel 1:19-27

Key verse: 2 Samuel 1:27a "How the mighty have fallen!"

An elderly woman died and, having never married, requested no male pallbearers. In her handwritten instructions regarding her funeral, she wrote," they wouldn't take me out while I was alive and so they won't take me out when i'm dead."

When we follow a person's last requests, we give them honor. But if there have been no last requests, as is often the case of young people who are killed in combat, we need to honor them at least for the freedoms their lives have purchased. Such is the case for Memorial Day.

And such was the case for Jonathan and Saul, as they, too, gave their lives for the cause of Israel. David, who knew and cared for them both, wrote a lament that was to be sung and remembered for posterity and for their everlasting honor.

We, as Christians, have another "hall-of-fame", as it were, in Hebrews, chapter 11. It is the "hall-of-fame" of faith.in this chapter, we have a list of persons who exemplified faith in the course of their lives for the cause of God. And it is their example that we are urged to follow as it is faith that changes lives in showing the power and provision of God.

Abraham Lincoln once declared in his famous Gettysburg address, "The world will little note, nor long remember what we say here, but it can never forget what they did here." The same is true of faith. We may not be famous for it, but God will not forget it-nor the people who have been encouraged or saved by it.

Lessons on Memorial Day - Part 3 of 7

Text: psalm 77

Key verse: psalm 77:7 "Will the Lord reject forever? Will he never show his favor again?"

A man came to the Lutheran church and asked to see the pastor. When he came into the pastor's office, he asked him, "Pastor, my dog died, and I'd like to have a Christian burial for him." The pastor replied," I'm sorry but we Lutherans don't do funerals for dogs. Maybe you should see the Baptist pastor. The Baptists will do most anything." The man turned sadly away but said before leaving, "I'm sorry you won't do it and so I will go to the Baptist church. But, before I go, please advise me as to the proper amount to leave for a memorial to the church. I was thinking of $10,000." "Why didn't you say your dog was a Lutheran? I think we can arrange services, after all."

As you know, memorials do help in remembering a lost loved one, whether they be man or beast. And some of the most impressive memorials we have in this country are those dedicated to our war dead. Yet, often times, people still have trouble appreciating the sacrifices made on their behalf. The same can be said about that which God has done for them.

In today's lesson, the Psalmist is going through some difficult time and questions where God is in this. But, in remembering what God has done in the past (not just for him but for his people), he finds his answer. Would we learn to do the same.

In the novel, Robinson Crusoe, the main character finds himself shipwrecked on a deserted island. So, the first thing he does is make a list of the positives and negatives of his situation. What he finds is that there is a positive for every negative and thus is something for which to be thankful. If memorials don't help us remember, maybe making a list of positives and negatives will.

Lessons on Memorial Day - Part 4 of 7

Text: exodus 3,4

Key verse: 1 Timothy 4:12a "Don't let anyone look down on you because you are young,.."

When the man found that his work was going to require that he would have to be away for long periods of time, he decided that his wife could use a watch dog. So, he went to the pet store and told the owner what he wanted. The pet store owner said, "I have just the dog for you", and brought out a little Pekinese. "Doesn't look much like a watch dog to me," said the man. "don't let the dog's size fool you-he's a big fighter! Here, I'll show you." Then the owner said, "karate this chair!", and the little dog reduced it to matchsticks in no time. The man was impressed and took the dog home. But when he brought it in, his wife became very skeptical. And before he could explain that the little dog was a karate expert, she loudly complained, "Karate, my foot."

When I was growing up, I was particularly impressed with people who had lots of medals. I, at that point, didn't understand that medals weren't necessarily the measure of a man. Similarly, many folks do not appreciate the bravery of a lot of people whose graves they pass on Memorial Day. And I might say, we may not have been particularly impressed with the people that God decided to use to promote his earthly work. In today's lesson, Moses, upon being selected by God to rescue his chosen people from slavery, complains loud and long that he was not the guy. Perhaps, we would have agreed. But God sees what we cannot-the heart of a person. In the New Testament, Paul sees great promise in timothy, despite his young age.

More importantly, when God selects us for a particular work, he sees that we have what we need to get the job done-even if we can't. Like with moses and timothy, God is with us- and that makes all the difference. We have long been warned not to "judge a book by its cover". But that is especially true in the work that God commissions.

Lessons on Memorial Day - Part 5 of 7

Text: Acts 4:32-35

Key verse: Acts 4:34a "There were no needy persons among them."

One Sunday morning, the pastor saw a young parishioner looking at the memorial plaque in the foyer. Since he had been staring at it for some time, the pastor went over to see if he had any questions. "what's this plaque about, Pastor?", little Alex asked. "It's a listing of all the young men and women who lost their lives in the service," the Pastor replied. "Which one?", Alex asked. "The 9:00 one or the 10:30?"

No wonder Alex was so concerned. Yet, for the most part, the people who have served in time of war almost universally downplay their part. For them it was just doing their duty. We, as adults, know better. For to be successful in any big endeavor takes the 'little' contributions of many.

Such was the case at the New Testament church right after Pentecost. No one claimed any possession as their own but liberally shared everything they had. As a result, there were no needy among them. Unfortunately, this state of affairs has never been successfully achieved since. Even so, we could all benefit from a greater willingness to share-even if it's a little.

During World War 2, an allied bomber, accompanied by a contingent of American and British fighter planes, made a bombing run over German territory. But, on the way back, the bomber encountered a squadron of German fighters. And despite the most heroic efforts by its protecting planes, suffered what appeared to be several critical damaging shots. Yet, it made it back. Upon landing, an investigation found five nearly perfect but crumpled, unexploded bullets. When the bullets were opened, a note was found that was signed by several polish pow's. Translated into English, it read, "We are polish pow's forced to make bullets. But when the guards aren't looking, we don't put gunpowder in. It isn't much but is the best we can do." A little contribution.

Lessons on Memorial Day - Part 6 of 7

Text: John 15:9-17

Key verse: John 15:13 "Greater love hath no man than this, that he lay down his life for his friends."

Three sisters lived together but each depended on the others because of occasional lapses of memory. For example, one evening, sister one was going up the stairs to go to bed when she forgot whether she was going up the stairs or down. When she asked her sisters, the second sister said, "You were going up the stairs to go to bed." The second sister went into the kitchen to make herself a sandwich. But when she got out there, she forgot why she was there. When she asked for help, the third sister replied that she was in the kitchen making herself a sandwich. The third sister was feeling pretty proud of herself for not being as forgetful as her other sisters and knocked on wood. At hearing it, however, she called out, "Who's there?"

Regardless of our age, there are some things that we would do well to forget- but Memorial Day isn't one of them. We need to remember our war dead because it was their sacrifice that has made our freedom possible. Similarly, we need to remember the sacrifice of Jesus because it was his death that has purchased our freedom from sin.

Yet, there is a major difference between the two sacrifices. Our war dead did not have any specific person in mind that their death would save. By contrast, Jesus had each of us in mind in giving up his life. He knew that we had no hope of salvation without it- he loved us that much.

A little boy was asked to give a blood transfusion to save his sister. He, at first, hesitated (not knowing what it would entail), then, readily agreed. As the process was taking place, it was clear that his blood was restoring his sister. Then, when the process was nearly over, he asked the doctor when he would die. He didn't know that his blood supply would be re-generated. Yet he was willing to give his life so that his sister would live. That is sacrifice that Jesus willingly made for us.

Lessons on Memorial Day - Part 7 of 7

Text: 1 peter 1:12-18

Key verse: 1 peter 1:12a "So I will always remind you of these things,"

A little 4-year-old boy was standing in line during the spring of 1924, waiting to meet the president of the United States, Calvin Coolidge. And he noticed that the president said something to each person in line. So as the line grew shorter, he was anxious to hear what the president would say to him. Finally, the big moment arrived. And what did the president say to him? "Move along."

For him, then, this is how Coolidge will always be remembered. I would think, however, that we would want someone's memory of us to be a lot better than that. But on this Memorial Day, the question is, "How will our war dead be remembered?" Certainly, they deserve a lot better than Coolidge. Indeed, they should be remembered in the best possible light. But how do we accomplish this?

The apostle peter was concerned about how Jesus and his teachings would be remembered. He reminds his readers that the stories of Jesus were not some cleverly invented tales but documented facts, backed up by eyewitnesses. And he knew how false teachers worked to discredit that witness and confuse would-be believers. But he also knew that there was power available to fight against those evil influences.

In 1947, Jackie Robinson broke the color line in major league baseball. He was a rough, tough-minded athlete, but he was not without feelings. And he had to take a lot of

Harassment and mistreatment that no one should have had to take. But the strength he had in facing these did not solely come from within. He had a teammate, Pee Wee Reese, who stood by him in the power of love.

Similarly, it is the power of love that ensures that the teachings and example of Jesus Christ stands today. You see, false teachers cannot duplicate the power of love. It is a power that none can resist or deny. That's why God tells us that his word will not return to him void but accomplish his purposes. And it is the reason that our war dead's legacy will not be forgotten. It was a gift given in love.

REFLECTIONS

Mothers

Mother's Day causes me to reflect on the impact my mother had in my life. For me, that impact was tremendous. Not only did my mother love me unconditionally, but she also saw the best in me. That acceptance very much influenced how I saw myself. There were negative aspects, as well, like her not making me do more for myself or her handling of disputes or negative behavior by silence. Yet I feel that the good far outweighed the bad. Indeed, I tend to evaluate other mothering behavior by my mother's. Upon further reflection, though, this is probably a biased opinion as everyone has different life experiences and influences that cause them to react in one way rather than another. Even so, my bias was also held by my other siblings and my childhood friends, who also felt well about my mother. Of course, my mother's faith helped shape my openness toward the Spiritual as well as my basic outlook that most people have something good about them, unless they prove themselves unworthy of that acceptance. All in all, she gave me a great start in life and one that still helps me today.

Lessons on Mothers - Part 1 of 7

Text and key verse: Exodus 20:12 "Honor thy father and thy mother, that thy days be long on the land that the Lord thy God giveth thee."

A teacher gave her class of 2nd graders a lesson on magnets, then a quiz to see if they had been listening. One of the questions on the quiz went like this: "My full name has 6 letters, starting with "M". I pick up things. What is my name? "The teacher, though, was surprised to see that ½ the class put down "mother".

Today's scripture lesson advises us to honor our mothers, but it certainly is for more than her picking things up. My guess is that it is more about honoring the things that good mothers have always stood for. But it could also be for how they impressed upon us those things that we should stand for.

A mother visited her son at college. Upon entering the room, her eyes swept the walls of his dormitory room, which was covered with a dozen or more of suggestive pin-ups. Her heart was grieved, but she said nothing. Several days later, the young man received a gift from his mother- a beautifully- framed picture of the head of Christ. Proudly, he hung the picture above his desk. But the pin-ups closest to that picture didn't look right, so he took them down. In the days following, he did the same to the rest of the pin-ups, until the picture of Christ was the only wall-hanging left.

Similarly, it was a mother's loving influence that impacted many famous lives, as well. Thomas Edison claimed that his mother was the "making of him". And Abraham Lincoln's mother made him promise to never drink or smoke. And it was anna Jarvis's great love for her mother that caused her to tirelessly campaign for the establishment of Mother's Day.

As for me, my mother will always be remembered for how far she could make a chicken, as well as the family money go. Growing up, we were well aware that we weren't rich, but neither did we consider ourselves poor. And I will always remember how she always looked for the best in people. That, particularly, was a trait that I wish we all could show more of.

Lessons on Mothers - Part 2 of 7

Text: 1 Samuel 1,2:19-21

Key verse: 1 Samuel 1:22c "After the boy is weaned, I will take him to present before the Lord, and he will stay there always."

One night when mom went to a PTA meeting, dad and the kids decided to clean the kitchen to surprise her. But when mom came home, she didn't say anything about it, choosing to join the rest of the family in the den to watch some tv. The fact that she didn't say anything surprised the husband, as he didn't do that sort of thing too often. So, he said, "Honey, did you notice that the kitchen was clean?" "Yes, I noticed," she replied. "Well, why didn't you say thank you or something?" "Why should I," she answered, "it is a thankless job, isn't it?"

Clearly, moms have always suffered from a lack of appreciation. And it seems evident that Hannah's married life reflected this, as well. She was not able to have a child but since her husband's other wife could, he thought nothing about it. He did not consider how humiliated she felt. However, when the Lord answered her prayer for a son, she did not renege on her vow to take the child and dedicate him to the Lord's work for the rest of his life.

This puts her on a higher plane than most mothers today-even most Christian mothers. Nevertheless, sacrifice seems to come with the territory as far as motherhood is concerned- but it is not as thankless as most imagine. I feel that most children count their mothers as one of their biggest blessings. I know I do. It's just too bad the appreciation had to come so late.

I remember how my mother would routinely take the clothes from the hamper upstairs to the basement, where she would put the clothes in the washer and then through the wringer. Then she would haul the ones that didn't need ironing out to the back yard to hang up to dry. Then she'd do the ironing and hang those things up to be taken upstairs again to be hung up-which she usually had to do herself. That I didn't do more shames me when i think of it. Yet, I can honestly say that, for her, it was a labor of love- a love that I wish I had said thanks for more often.

Lessons on Mothers - Part 3 of 7

Text: 1 Samuel 10:8; 13:4-14

Kley verse: 1 Samuel 13:13b "You have not kept the command the Lord your God gave you; if you had, he would have established your kingdom over Israel for all time."

A little boy was talking to a neighbor girl about what he could give his mother for Mother's Day. She suggested that he could keep his room clean and orderly, brush his teeth after eating without being asked or stop fighting with his brothers and sisters, especially at the dinner table. "No!" he said, "I mean something practical."

What mother wouldn't want her son to be obedient? And that also goes for God. But the reality is always more than we want to commit to and so we try to please God in some other way.

Such was the case in today's lesson. The prophet Samuel gave king Saul specific instructions re: how he was to approach the upcoming confrontation with the enemy philistines. But when Samuel didn't come at the specified time, Saul took the matter into his own hands, making a sacrifice that he was not qualified to make. In short, he was disobedient- something that a leader of God's people must avoid at all costs.

In our lives, God has appointed people that are entrusted with our proper nurturing- people that we should obey- people like mothers. And when we are disobedient, we "pay the price".

One of the stories my mother liked to tell was about the time my brother john tried to ride a bike that was too big for him. She had warned him not to do it, but he tried, anyway, and ended up with a broken arm. And her story always ended the same way: with my brother's words, "I'm sorry I didn't mind you, mama."

Lessons on Mothers - Part 4 of 7

Text: Psalms 40:1-5

Key verse: Psalms 40:5d "…; were I to speak and tell of your deeds, they would be too many to declare."

A guy was cleaning out his attic and came across an old lamp. When he began to clean it off, however, a genie appeared and offered him one wish for setting him free. The guy thought for a minute, then said, "I've always wanted to see Hawaii, but I hate boats and planes. Could you build me a highway over, so I could drive it?" "That's impossible- even for me. Is there something else?" "Well, I've always wanted to be able to know what a woman was thinking so I could get a date easier. How about that?" "How many lanes do you want, one or two?"

From the stories that I've heard, some mothers have achieved some virtually impossible things. Yet, the ones who have achieved the best results have been the ones who have used the Bible for their mothering example.

Today's scripture is describing the attributes of God, but , to a much more limited yet still significant extent, the best mothers have also reminded us of the nature of God by their love. Specifically, the scriptures that best describe these moms would be those that talk about hearing our cries and lifting us out of miry places, giving us a new song and their trusting of the Lord.

Early African converts to Christianity were earnest and regular in their devotion to their private devotions. As a result, they would find their own place in the thicket where they would pour their heart out to God. Over time, these paths would become rather well-worn. However, when someone would fall away from their prayer life, the path would reveal it and they would say, "brother or sister, the grass grows on your path." This is how I see our moms-and their reminder to us to get us back on track.

Lessons on Mothers - Part 5 of 7

Text and key verse: Daniel 12:3 "Men and women who have lived wisely and well will shine brilliantly, like the cloudless, star-strewn night skies. And those who put others on the right path to life will glow like stars forever."

A man was putting a tin roof on his barn when, all of a sudden, he slipped and started to slide down the roof. So, he cried out to God to help him. But no sooner did he get the words out of his mouth, than a nail caught his pants and stopped him. When he stopped, he said, "never mind, God, i took care of it."

I wonder how many times our mothers have saved us without getting any credit. Be that as it may, on Mother's Day, they do get some measure of credit-just not enough for what they do or have done.

Unquestionably, mothers have played a crucial role in our nation's Christian education. Not only have they been the major supporters of the Sunday school movement, but they have also often provided the only encouragement the children have ever received to go to church at all. Indeed, in mothers' children see the closest translation of what the Bible and Godliness are about.

You see, mothers are most influential because they are always there- because they show up day in-day out regardless. Erma Bombeck, famous American humorist, originally saw her role of mother as a temporary one. But she realized that, later on, she still was a major force in their lives-making them finish what they started, forgetting it when they said they hated her and generally sharing their good times and bad. She realized that her influence was like a steadying light. And so, like with Mrs. Bombeck, mothers' lights will continue to shed their beams to help us avoid future reefs and light our way to worthy goals and aspirations.

Lessons on Mothers - Part 6 of 7

Text: Matthew 27:19

Key verse: Genesis 2:18 "It is not good for the man to be alone."

A man and his wife were awakened at 3 am by a loud pounding on their door. When the man investigates, he finds a drunken guy in the pouring rain asking for a push. "Not a chance!", says the man, "It's 3 am1" and slams the door. When he returned to bed, his wife asked him what it was about, and he told her. "Well, did you help him?" "No, "he replied, "it's pouring down rain and 3 o'clock in the morning!" "Well,", she said, "you must have a short memory." "What do you mean?" "Don't you remember how those 2 guys helped us when we broke down on vacation? I think you should help him." So, the man got dressed and went down and opened the door and called, "are you still there?" "Yes" "Do you still need a push?" "Yes, please." "Well, where are you?" "Over here on the swing."

This little anecdote helps to shed some light on how men and women react to things. Even though one spouse might have some impression about a particular situation, it may not be the right one. That's why one can complement the other.

Certainly, this appears to be God's thinking as well in recognizing the potential that the right mate can bring to the spouse. And it plays out again in today's scripture: the interplay between Pilate and his wife prior to the trial of Jesus. She senses that Jesus is innocent and that his conviction will be a big mistake. And Pilate himself senses that there has been no crime punishable by death. Yet, his fear of criticism by the local Jewish leaders coming to the attention of Caesar causes him to do other than what he knows is right.

My point is that he could have and should have followed his wife's instincts, regardless of the outcome. Yet this same kind of dilemma often comes up in the life of a Christian- where it is more convenient to do the less honorable thing. And it is often the wife's instincts or intuition that could have helped the man in his decision- if only he would have listened. And, not coincidentally, it would have made her feel more valued.

Lessons on Mothers - Part 7 of 7

Text: 1 Corinthians 3:5-9

Key verse: 1 Corinthians 3:6 "I planted the seed, apollos watered it, but God has been making it grow."

A young mother was out walking with her 4-year-old daughter, when the little one bent down to pick up a piece of candy that was lying on the sidewalk. "don't pick that up, honey. It's full of dirty germs." The little girl looked up at her mother and said, with awe, "how do you know these things?" "All mommies know them, honey. It's on the mommy test. If you don't pass it, they don't let you be a mommy." They continued their little walk as the daughter processed this new information. Finally, the little girl said, "i get it now! If you don't pass the mommy test, you have to be the daddy." The young mother considered this briefly, then said, "exactly."

The story has a certain amount of relevance. That is, moms have a crucial role to play in providing the environment for children to grow. It's not a guarantee that it will happen, but it provides for a certain amount of possibility.

Certainly, this analogy fits in today's scripture lesson: if we help provide the right environment for Christian growth to take place, there is a better possibility of its happening. This is the essence of the apostle Paul's statement in assessing the growth of the Corinthian church. He had a part to play as did apollos. But God caused the actual growth to take place.

So, in today's society, moms are put in a unique position to provide their children with some of the building blocks of a stable, loving culture. But other factors are important, too, like dads, churches, schools, families, neighbors and society in general. Even so, without God's influence, these factors can all go for naught. This ought to give us more than adequate incentive to take our molding opportunities seriously. Unfortunately, however, it seems like the moms have been forced to do more than they should be expected to. Perhaps we, too, should be given a test to ensure we do our part.

REFLECTIONS

Obedience

Obedience in the Dornan household was reinforced largely by our mother. It was a job that my father basically abdicated. In those days, my dad felt that by bringing home financial support, he was doing his part of the job. My older brothers and sister advised me, however, that this was a better situation than theirs in that my dad could be rather heavy-handed at times. Be that as it may, it was easy to tell when you had been disobedient: you either got a paddling or you were given the "silent treatment". In retrospect, the punishment that we received for being disobedient was never out of proportion to the crime and it had no lasting negative effects. Indeed, I am sure it had a very positive effect. Yet, as we grew older, we understood the purpose of the punishment was to make us better people and citizens and help bring honor to the family.

More importantly, helping us to become obedient had even more benefit in terms of our Christian Walk. Because my parents enforced our obedience, God didn't have as much correcting to do, and we could more fully enjoy his blessings. Let's face it: the sooner we learn the lesson of obedience, the better.

Lessons on Obedience - Part 1 of 7

Text: Matthew 4:18-22

Key verse: Matthew 4:18 "Come, follow me and I will make you fishers of men."

Ed and Doris went camping and took their dog, Ralph. But because it was raining, Doris decided to make the best of things by going over the commands that Ralph would have to accomplish to graduate from obedience school. And so, all evening in the tent, it was "Sit, Ralph" or "Stay, Ralph" or "Roll over, Ralph." The people at the next campsite did not see the dog, so they assumed that Doris was giving those commands to her husband. The next day, the neighbor came over to borrow a hatchet and when ed handed it to him, he smiled and said, "Thanks, Ralph."

He smiled because it seemed funny that a wife would have her husband so well trained. In a sense, it also seems unusual for the men Jesus called to be so instantly obedient. Yet today's scripture records that they immediately dropped what they were doing and followed.

Of course, there is application to our situation today-that Jesus continues to call us to follow. And so, we are confronted with a question of obedience: do we immediately follow or not? Jesus is concerned, however, with both our availability and our durability-that we hang in for the long haul.

A basketball player from the championship team was being interviewed after winning the game and was asked if it was hard to follow the coach's direction in that the whole team was so athletically gifted. And the player answered, "Oh no, his way has always been our way." And so, it must be for us.

Lessons on Obedience - Part 2 of 7

Text: Daniel 3

Key verse: Daniel 3:25 "Look! I see 4 men, unbound, walking around inside the fire, and they aren't hurt! And the fourth one looks like one of the Gods."

A man died and was met at the pearly gates by St. Peter, who said, "we've been reviewing your case and are not quite decided as to whether or not to allow you in. Is there any thing you'd like to tell us to help make up our minds?" "well,", said the guy, "A little while ago i came upon a tough- looking set of bikers who appeared to be harassing a woman. I went up to the toughest looking one and ripped out the ring he had in his nose and told him that if he and his gang didn't leave the woman alone, they'd have to deal with me." "Pretty impressive!", said St. Peter, "when did that happen?" "About 2 minutes ago."

We can find many stories of courage in the Bible, but the story of Shadrach, Meshach and Abednego in the fiery furnace is one of the best. When Judah was defeated by the Babylonians, the Babylonians took the best and brightest young people to Babylon to train to be administrators. Among these were Shadrach, Meshach and Abednego. However, there were some Babylonians who did not approve of this practice and looked for ways to discredit them. So, when the king had made a 90-foot golden statue of himself made for people to bow down to, and the 3 jews didn't bow down, they were brought to the king- who sentenced them to be burned in the fiery furnace. But God rescued them, and they suffered no ill effects, which gained them the respect of the king.

We have had many heroes in our nation's history, but we need more who will stand up for their faith. John Wesley, the founder of our denomination, put it this way, "give me a hundred men who fear nothing but sin and desire nothing but God…and I will shake the gates of hell and set up the kingdom of heaven on earth" do we dare to take that pledge?

Lessons on Obedience - Part 3 of 7

Text: Genesis 6-9

Key verse: Genesis 6:22 "Noah did everything exactly as God commanded him."

As he approached his 16th birthday, the son asked his dad for permission to use the family car when he passed his driver's test. The father said, "Son, driving is a very responsible thing, and you've not been acting very responsibly lately." "Well, dad, what do I have to do?" "Three things: get your grades up, read your Bible every day and cut your hair." The son thought it over and decided that if at least he did the first 2 things, his dad might relent on the third (as he really didn't want to cut his hair.). So, after a month, he showed his dad his improvement on his grades and his accomplished Bible reading and asked again about the use of the family car. His dad replied, "Son, you're 2/3 of the way there- get your hair cut and you've satisfied my conditions." "But, dad, Jesus had long hair!" "Yes, and Jesus walked everywhere he had to go."

In today's lesson, God gave Noah very specific instructions as to the building of the ark and in filling it. What isn't so clear is the amount of time that it took to accomplish these tasks and what problems Noah encountered in following God's commands. I imagine that during the building phase, he received a lot of verbal abuse and ridicule from his neighbors. I imagine that herding the animals into the ark could have had its moments, too. My guess is that when the ark finally came to rest, the animals and his family were very anxious to get out of the smelly ark and get started with their lives. Yet, in all these things, Noah was completely obedient to God.

It seems to me, however, that our natural inclination would be to be like the son in the first illustration than Noah in the latter. This is not good, as God 's specific instructions are meant to be followed specifically. Otherwise, it is disobedience. We see this in other biblical illustrations as well as our own life experiences. And so, when God puts a period, we should not change the punctuation.

Lessons on Obedience - Part 4 of 7

Text: Exodus 3:1-14

Key verse: exodus 3:11 "Who am I to go to Pharoah and to bring the Israelites out of Egypt?"

A woman who had never flown was going to visit her daughter in North Dakota. The daughter was concerned about her mother making her connecting flight out of Chicago and had her paged at the airport. She didn't answer the page and did not arrive on the expected flight. But finally, she did arrive and the daughter, though much relieved, asked her mother why she did not answer her page. She answered, "I heard my name called, but I didn't answer it because I didn't know anybody in Chicago."

Similarly, moses couldn't figure out who would be calling him in the desert. Perhaps he thought God had forgotten him after these forty years. Nevertheless, he was not very obedient to God's call and offered objection after objection. Did God make a mistake in choosing moses for this great task? After all, we usually expect more from a biblical leader. In retrospect we know better- that God, in looking on the heart, is better able than we are to predict success.

In effect, general Norman Schwarzkopf , commander of the allied forces in the gulf war, agreed with that sort of assessment, when he said, "You can add up all the factors of military might but unless the soldier on the ground...has the will to win, the strength of character to go into combat, the idea that his cause is just and the support of his country, all the rest is irrelevant". In other words, it's what inside those counts-and God alone knows that. You might say, then, that obedience is a choice that he knows who will make before he asks.

Lessons on Obedience - Part 5 of 7

Text: 1 Samuel 3 :1-18

Key verse: 1 Samuel 15:22 "Obedience is better than sacrifice."

An older guy was pricing hearing aids at a store that sold them and found a large variance in prices. So, he asked the salesman to explain what the highest aid would do as well as the lowest aid. The highest, which cost around $25,000, translated 3 languages. The lowest, which cost $1.50, did nothing. But, he explained, when you put the button in your ear and the cord into your shirt pocket, you'd be surprised how much louder everyone talked.

Now young Samuel wasn't hard of hearing, but the words of the Lord were rare in those days. So, Eli the priest had him listen carefully as Eli suspected the Lord was trying to make contact. The essence of what God said to Samuel had to do with the disobedience of Eli's sons and Eli's unwillingness to do anything about it. I believe this is an important point in that the standard of obedience is higher for those directly involved in God's work, as Eli was and, as such, could not expect to avoid God's punishment.

The Bible advises us to lead lives that are beyond reproach because we are examples to others and because God does not want us to be the means by which the weak fall. A story is told of a person who prayed to God over injustices that the person thought that God should have corrected. "Why didn't you do anything, Lord?", he asked. "I did do something," the Lord replied, "I made you. "And so it is that the people of God must be the agents of God's work as the Holy Spirit directs.

Lessons on Obedience - Part 6 of 7

Text: 1 Samuel 15:17-26

Key verse: 1 Samuel 15:19 "Why didn't you obey the Lord?"

A couple had been fighting over the purchase of a new vehicle. He wanted a truck, and she wanted a sports car. Finally, she said, "My birthday is coming up soon and you'd better surprise me with something that can go from 0 to 100 in less than 4 seconds if you catch my drift. Because if you don't, it will start getting very lonely for you." So, on the day of her birthday, she went out to the garage, but no car. Then she went to look for her husband, but he wasn't home. Upset, she then went into the bathroom where she spotted something on the bathroom floor with a red ribbon on it. It could go from 0-100 in under 4 seconds alright. It was a bathroom scale."

He knew what she wanted but didn't apparently think it was important enough to obey it. Instead, he did as he pleased- almost like a consultant. The problem comes, however, when we treat God as a consultant.

In today's scripture lesson, King Saul receives a directive from God through the prophet Samuel. But instead of doing exactly what God asked, he did what he wanted-what he thought was best. In return, God removed his favor from Saul.

Clearly this is an important lesson from God. He is not a consultant and hates being treated that way. To obey God means that we must do as God directs-in his way and time. Anything less is disobedience.

Lessons on Obedience - Part 7 of 7

Text: Luke 18:18-23

Key verse: Luke 18:27 "What is impossible for humans is possible for God."

Gloria, a middle-aged woman, had a heart attack and was taken to the emergency room, who rushed her into the operating room. While on the operating table, she had a near-death experience where she talked to God. "God", she said, "Is this it?" "No, gloria," said God, "you have 40 more years left." So, as you can imagine, she pulled through, and with the knowledge that she had so much time left, she took what savings she had to get a complete makeover. When everything was done and healed, she left the plastic surgeon's office on the way to her car. But as she crossed the street, an ambulance ran over her, killing her instantly. When she appeared before God, then, she asked him why she got killed when he had told her she had 40 years left. And God said, "Gloria, is that you?"

Of course, God recognizes us, and he also recognizes that which is most important to us. And that's the problem for the rich young ruler who presents himself to Jesus, wanting to inherit eternal life. Jesus, who is able to look on the heart, recognizes that the young man's wealth is his God and asks him to give it all away. At that the young man goes away sorrowful.

It is important, however, to make sure we don't misinterpret the moral of this story. Jesus is not against riches or wealth, per se, but that nothing separates us from the love of God. And he goes on to say that even though some things in our life have a real hold on us, it is still possible, with God, to break that hold.

The point is: we are usually aware of that which separates us from the love of God. We just don't want to take the steps necessary to give them up.

REFLECTIONS

Peace

When I think of the word peace, it is usually with the connotation of an absence of war. And my guess is that this has something to do with my lifelong obsession with things in the military. I myself served in the Pennsylvania Army National Guard and Army Reserve for 29 years and my father and brothers before me had all served in the Army or Marines. I'm proud of that service but am aware that a military connection with peace is not what concerns most people. Their concept of peace is a more personal one- more like the absence of worry. And it is also my guess that their concern centers around the difficulty they have in finding that place in their lives. That is not surprising in that most people accept the world's definition of peace- that is, in the striving to have more and more of the material. The Bible clearly points out that that is not the source of peace. And it is the essence of Jeremiah 6:14, "saying peace, peace-when there is no peace." True peace, then, comes from having a personal relationship with Jesus Christ. Listen to his words on the subject: "Peace I leave with you, my peace I give unto you; not as the world giveth, give I unto you. Let not your heart be troubled, neither let it be afraid."

Lessons on Peace - Part 1 of 7

Text: Exodus 18:13-23

Key verse: Exodus 18:18b "The work is too heavy for you; you cannot handle it alone."

Two hunters contracted with a pilot to fly them into the far north to do some hunting. And, once they were there, they were very successful- each bagging 3 large buck elk.so, when the pilot came back for them, they started loading up their gear-including the elk. But when the pilot saw the size and bulk of the elk, he protested that the weight was too much. The hunters countered that the previous year, the pilot had agreed and had the same size and hauling capacity as this plane. So, the pilot reluctantly agreed. But as they began to take off the pilot realized that the weight seriously endangered their ability to climb and had to crash land the plane. As one hunter climbed out of the plane, the other hunter asked him if he knew where they were. "Yes, I think so. This looks like where we crash landed last year."

They knew the plane was too heavy but somehow hoped that the result would be different. In today's lesson, Moses was trying to carry too heavy a load in hearing all the disputes of the Israelites on the road to the Promised Land. Fortunately, Jethro, Moses' father-in-law, recognized this and suggested a solution. Hopefully, we will recognize when we are carrying too heavy a load and pray for the help we need. It will increase our peace to lighten the load. This is particularly true in the church. As scripture indicates, we all have been given at least one Spiritual gift, that, put to use in the church, will help "lighten the load".

Many years ago, merchants would often overload ships in hopes of maximizing their profits. When those ships would hit bad weather, the ships would often sink-causing much loss of life and property. Finally, a Christian man by the name of Samuel Plimsoll came up with the idea of determining what a safe load for a ship would be so that a ship's hull could be marked-showing when it was overloaded. Similarly, God knows our Plimsoll mark and will help us unload accordingly when we seek him in prayer.

Lessons on Peace - Part 2 of 7

Text: 2 Peter 3:13

Key verse: 1 Peter 1:4 "...an inheritance that can never perish, spoil or fade-kept in heaven for you."

It has been said that the measure of a man's life is 20 years of his mother asking where he was going, 50 years of his wife's asking where he's been and 1 hour at his funeral with his friends asking which place he's gone. But the fact of the matter is, the measure of a man is in how he has lived. And when a man has lived his life in service to God, he has peace about where he's going.

It is a hope that has sustained many an oppressed person, both in olden times and today. That's why there are so many biblical references to it.

Yet, it is not just a Christian idea- this idea of moving on to some better place. It has been the hope of many immigrants coming to America. These were people who had known hardship and uncertainty of life who heard the stories of a second chance and wanted that for themselves, but especially for their children. When they got to Ellis Island, many thought this was the greatest place they had ever seen. And some may have thought that they had arrived. But Ellis Island was only a gateway to something better.

By the same token, many look at this life as the best it would ever be. But, as the Christian knows, this is only a gateway to a better place, a place not built with human hands. Thus, it is important to help our neighbors see beyond the physical to the Spiritual, so they won't be discouraged when life takes a negative turn, as it most surely will.

Lessons on Peace - Part 3 of 7

Text:1 Corinthians 2:9-16

Key verse: 1 Corinthians 2:10 "...but God has revealed it to us by his Spirit."

An organization in Montana offered a bounty of $5,000 for every wolf captured alive. So, Sam and Jed headed for the hills, thinking that they could make some money. For 3 days and nights they hunted for wolves but could not find them. So, discouraged and exhausted, they rolled out their sleeping bags by their campfire and went to sleep. But Sam woke up in the middle of the night and saw that they were surrounded by a pack of hungry wolves, ready to pounce. Immediately, Sam jostled Jed awake and said, "Wake up, Jed, we're going to be rich!"

That probably wouldn't be my perspective, but at least I think we could agree that one's perspective is crucial to how one handles a situation. In today's lesson, the apostle Paul is defending his presentation of the gospel to the Corinthian church in saying that the power of what he said was in the message rather than in the messenger. He knew the Corinthians were in a place and culture that was easily influenced by how a message was delivered and by whom it was delivered. This was a major cause of the errant thinking done there. Yet, we, too, can be swayed many times by the means as well and thus should not be too hasty in our judgment. As Paul explains, it was the Holy Spirit that gave the message through Paul, and it was then the Holy Spirit that should be considered than the perceived deficiency of the speaker. We would do well to remember that.

In other words, they had been given information from a higher unimpeachable authority. It's a little like the perspective of a pilot in a plane flying high above a mountainous road where a car is anxious to pass a tractor-trailer but can't see around. The pilot could tell the car's driver that it was safe if there had been a way for them to communicate. Similarly, the Holy Spirit can see our "road" and can tell us where there is peace and safety, but this message can only be Spiritually discerned.

Lessons on Peace - Part 4 of 7

Text: Acts 27

Key verse: Acts 27:25 "Be encouraged, men! I have faith in God that it will be exactly as he told me."

Mac and Todd went to the employment office to look for work. So, when Mac was called in first for an interview, he told the counselor that he was a pilot and was offered a job right away. But when Todd was called in, things did not go so well. He told the counselor he was a tree cutter and was told that no jobs existed for him at this time. "Well, why was my brother given a job?" "He's a pilot and has specialized skills," replied the counselor. "What specialized skills?" Said Todd, "I cut the wood, and he piles it."

You might call this a classic case of misunderstanding, but this is a fairly common situation when people talk of peace. For many, peace means an absence of problems. But for some, peace is evident even in the midst of trouble. Such was the case for the apostle Paul in today's lesson. He is being sent to Rome because he, as aRoman citizen, has appealed to Caesar for justice. Yet the ship has anything but a pleasant journey. Indeed, it appears that all on board will perish. But God comforts Paul that all will be spared, and he shares that information with all and encourages them to "hang in".

Yet, God's provision of peace may not necessarily mean what we think it should. During WW2, missionary Eric Barker sent his wife and 8 children home to Great Britain as conditions were so poor in the land where he ministered (Portugal). So, when he reported to his congregation that he had just received word that his family had just returned safely home, they assumed that he meant to England. But what he really meant was that a submarine had torpedoed their ship and they had all died and gone to heaven. Clearly, his peace was not something the world could understand.

Lessons on Peace - Part 5 of 7

Text: Romans 8:28

Key verse: Philippians 4:7 "The peace of God, which transcends all understanding, will guard your hearts and minds in Christ Jesus."

A young man happened to notice an elderly couple preparing to share a meal in McDonald's. Yet, as the husband began to eat, the woman just sat and watched. Thinking that perhaps they only had enough money for I meal, he asked if they would allow him to buy them another. The husband thanked him but said no- it was just that they had only one set of dentures between them, and it was his turn with them.

Clearly, there was more to this situation than met the eye. And so, it is when non-Christians see the peace with which many Christians deal with their problems.

A pastor used Romans 8:28 as his text in giving his sermon, just 10 days after his son had committed suicide. In explaining, he said this; "I cannot make my son's suicide fit into this passage. Yet somehow, I believe that when all of life is over, when God has fully worked out his perfect plan, even my son's suicide will be woven into the final tapestry of his eternal design. It's like the miracle of the shipyard. Almost every part of our great oceangoing vessels is made of steel. If you take any single part and throw it into the ocean, it will sink. Steel doesn't float! But when the shipbuilders are finished, that massive ship will be virtually unsinkable."

No doubt we all have, at one time or another, agonized over things that have happened and wondered where God was in all this. Perhaps you are facing something like this now. Even so, we must hold on to our faith even harder knowing that God loves us, is working behind the scenes on this as we continue to be sorrowful, and is faithful to his promises. That's a peace that transcends all understanding.

Lessons on Peace - Part 6 of 7

Text:1 Corinthians 1:10-12/3:5-9

Key verse: 1 Corinthians 1:10 "Now I encourage you, brothers and sisters, in the name of our Lord Jesus Christ: agree with each other and don't be divided into rival groups. Instead, be restored with the same mind and the same purpose."

A man bought a parrot at an auction after some heavy bidding. "I sure hope this parrot talks", said the man to the auctioneer. "Talk?", asked the auctioneer, "Who do you think was bidding against you the last 10 minutes?"

Clearly, the man and parrot did not see "eye-to-eye." Yet this is fairly common in churches, where you'd think people would get along much better. A story is told of a small church in the Midwest where a parishioner poisoned the after–service coffee time by putting arsenic in the coffee urn. He, as well as other people from his family, were upset with the church because they would not use the communion table that the family had donated. Many times, it does not take much.

In today's lesson, the apostle Paul is addressing the Corinthian church as the result of a report Paul had received about fighting that was taking place within the church. The problem here was that of a part of the church following the teachings of Apollos and part of the church following the teachings of Paul. I'm sure, however, that the problem was more deep-seated than that. These Corinthians seemed willing to argue just about anything, and "at the drop of a hat".

How Paul addressed the problem, though, is the piece that we must make sure we don't miss, as the same process could easily be applied to our day and time, as well. He stayed with the facts; he highlighted the differences, and he ultimately pointed the people to God, on whose behalf that he and Apollo both worked.

Lessons on Peace - Part 7 of 7

Text: Philippians 4:4-7

Key verse: Philippians 4:6a "Do not be anxious about anything..."

A man decided to come to church with his family for the first time in a long time, but after the service he complained about everything. He didn't like the music; he thought the sermon was too long; he thought some parents didn't do enough to quiet their kids; it was too warm. After that litany of complaints, his son exclaimed, "What did you expect for a dollar?"

Everyone complains at one time or another, but it is still a choice we don't have to make. In today's lesson, Paul is in prison with every reason to complain, but he does not. Indeed, this epistle is considered by many to be his most joyful. Thus, it could be argued that the reason for this may have been the result of 3 factors: his faith focus, his moral focus and his future focus. When these factors are combined, it does put us in a place where we can praise instead of complain.

First, then, let us consider his faith focus. In 2 Corinthians 11:24-27, Paul lists the sufferings that he had experienced as a result of his faith journey. But he claimed that these problems kept him centered on God.

Second, let us consider his moral focus. Paul was unstintingly correct in his morality. He abstained from the very appearance of evil. Unfortunately, not all Christian leaders have been able to say the same thing-much to the despair of the Christian followers who looked to them for a Godly example.

Third, and perhaps most importantly, he had a future focus. He did not see his life on earth as his final resting place. He looked to a home whose builder and maker was God. So, he was able to put his trials and tribulations in their proper perspective.

We cannot hope to live our Christian life in a vacuum as our faith is a relational one. Our example affects others and can give them either peace or uncertainty. Which will it be?

REFLECTIONS

Perseverance

"Hanging in" has got to be the universal advice to any who are experiencing difficulty in their lives. Yet, it does have some biblical support, as well. Many times, we are admonished to "wait on the Lord" as his timing is perfect. In thinking back over my life, I'm sure I heard it many times: through various social shortcomings, through the deaths of loved ones, through basic training, through work disappointments, etc. But, without faith, it is only like a band aid on an open wound-it doesn't do much good. Indeed, unless we can access the strength of Spirit provided through the Holy Spirit, we are doomed to just "putting one foot in front of the other" until things get better. Clearly, some people are better suited to this period of "treading water" than others. My guess is that it is in direct proportion to the amount of hope they have. Again, faith has an answer- that we who have faith will eventually "mount up with wings as eagles". The world, unfortunately, has no such answer.

Lessons on Perseverance - Part 1 of 7

Text: Genesis 6-9

Key verse: Genesis 8:13 "By the first day of the first month of Noah's six hundred and first year, the water had dried up from the earth."

The man's granddaughter was seated on his lap as he told her the story of Noah and the flood. After the story, the little girl looked up at her grandfather and asked, "Grandpa, were you on the ark?" "Why, no I wasn't", he replied. "Well, why weren't you drowned?"

It must be hard for a child to reconcile old age with ancient times, but the story of Noah has relevance for any time or age in terms of getting a perspective on perseverance. It is estimated that it took Noah 100 years to build the ark and he was on it a year until the flood waters receded enough to be able to walk on dry land again. Of course, things didn't move as fast as they do today. But any way you look at it, he had to wait a long time. Yet not only was it hard to wait, but I'm also sure that many of Noah's neighbors spent considerable time laughing at Noah's folly. That could not have been easy, either.

The question for us, then, is how well do we wait? I know I'm not much good at it. As I think back over my life, there have been many things that I just couldn't wait for: I couldn't wait to start school then couldn't wait for summer vacation, I couldn't wait to drive a car, I couldn't wait for basic training to be over, I couldn't wait for the kids to get old enough to play with, then I couldn't wait for them to play with kids their own age.

As I grow older, however, it seems like time has flown and that it would be great to be going through some of those old things again. I also have come to the conclusion that God's timing is perfect. Although I didn't have to get to age 600 to find those things out, I'm glad I finally did.

Lessons on Perseverance - Part 2 of 7

Text: Genesis 32:22-28

Key verse: Genesis 32:28 "You shall no longer be called Jacob, but Israel, because you have struggled with God and with men and have overcome."

Someone once said that persistence is like wrestling with a gorilla. You don't give up when you're tired. You give up when the gorilla is tired.

Jacob, now named Israel, must have known something about that. Although many of his problems were of his own making, the consequences of them seemed to be about ready to be unleashed. Afraid of what his brother, Esau, might do to him, he desperately wanted some reassurance that God was with him and would see him through.

I think we can all relate to this, at one time or another in our own lives. "Will you see me through this, Lord?", while we await our fate. The waiting itself seems hard enough, much less what we fear will happen to us. Yet, as Christians, we must hold fast to the promises of God-not just for our own sakes, but for those who we have counseled to do the same. Indeed, it is good that those people can hold us accountable. It just gives us that much more incentive to do what we know we must do.

Early converts to Christianity in Africa needed to be earnest and regular in their private devotions. Each had a separate spot in the thicket where they would pour out their heart to God. So, over time, these paths would become well-worn. As a result, if one of these believers began to neglect their prayer time, it became very apparent to the others, who would gently remind that person, "Brother (or Sister), the grass grows on your path."

Lessons on Perseverance - Part 3 of 7

Text: 2 Kings 2:1-2, 6-14

Key verse: 2 Kings 2:9b "Let me inherit a double portion of your blessing."

Victor Borge, famous comic musician, told a story about his Danish uncle who wanted to "strike it rich" in the soda industry. He said his uncle tried 1-up, 2-up and so forth all the way to 6-up and stopped then lamented that he did not give it one more try.

I rather suspect, in looking back over our life, that we could find similar instances where we could have demonstrated more perseverance. There are certainly many instances where people did stick with their projects, like Edison with the lightbulb or Norman Larson with WD-40(the 40 stands for the 40th try at his project!). And there are instances where a person had one idea that failed but tried another use for his product and was wildly successful (Levi Strauss).

In today's lesson, the prophet Elisha, successor to the prophet Elijah, was bound and determined to receive a double portion of the miracles that Elijah had experienced in his earthly ministry and would not leave him on the day that Elijah was going to be taken to heaven. As Elijah had been involved in seven, Elisha, then, was looking at fourteen. Seeing that Elisha would not leave him even for a moment, Elijah promised that if he saw Elijah being taken, he would receive this double blessing. And when he saw Elijah being taken in a fiery chariot, he knew he had his wish.

Would that we could display such single-minded persistence! In Elisha's case, his belief was strong. I'm sure that his was the result of much prayer and dedicated reflection to being open to God's leading. If we were willing to put in the work, I'm sure we would likewise be blessed. Yet, our perspective, too, needs work: An elderly lady was lamenting her lack of financial resources when 2 children came to her door, asking for newspapers to burn to keep warm. Feeling sorry for them, she invited them in for hot chocolate, then went back to her chores. When she checked back on them, they were ready to go and thanked the "rich" lady whose cups and saucers matched.

Lessons on Perseverance - Part 4 of 7

Text: 1 Corinthians 9:24-27

Key verse: 1 Corinthians 9:25a "Everyone who competes in the games goes into strict training."

On a cold, rainy night, the phone rang for the doctor. A man identified himself and asked that the doctor come to his house as his wife was so ill. The doctor said he was willing to come but that his car was being repaired and that he'd needed to be picked up. The man then replied, "What? In this weather?"

The apostle Paul was trying to help the church at Corinth understand the nature of the commitment to following Christ that needed to be made. He likened it to preparing to run a race and the discipline necessary to be in shape to win. The only difference was that winners in the race received a corruptible crown while Christians competed for an incorruptible one.

Clearly, this does not come easily for us. We'd rather take the "path of least resistance". But, when things begin to go badly, we have to go into a "crisis" mode. Where this is particularly dangerous is where another person's soul hangs in the balance. If that person hasn't been encouraged to "put in the air" from a Spiritual point of view, they find that they lack the resources to "run the race." That is, if they haven't developed the self –discipline of Bible reading, prayer and giving thanks, they will not be prepared to move ahead when trouble comes. Their Spiritual tires will become flat.

On a particularly difficult cruise, a passenger came into the wheelhouse and yelled to the captain, "Why aren't you praying?" And the captain replied, "I pray when the sea is calm. When the storm hits, then, I steer the boat." "This is a great analogy for the way we must operate.

Lessons on Perseverance - Part 5 of 7

Text: Hebrews 12:1-3

Key verse: Hebrews 12:3 "Consider him who endured such opposition from sinners, so you will not grow weary and lose heart."

A young man asked a friend for a cigarette. And the friend replied, "I thought you were quitting smoking." "I am . As a matter of fact, I'm now in phase 1." "What's phase 1?" asked the friend. "I quit buying!"

Our Christian walk is also a process-a long one that requires much perseverance. This is noted in today's scripture as it reminds us of the long process that Jesus went through in dealing with various sinful people.

Our process has been referred to as "living between the trees". What this refers to is the lives that Adam and Eve went through from the time they were denied access to the tree of life and that time when they died and, once again, regained that access. It is the process better known as the time between salvation and sanctification. It is more than a destination. It is a journey.

Along the way, then, we must be careful of several things. First, we must not be so focused on the future that we miss the lessons and joys of the present. Second, that we just don't stay in our comfort zone. Our faith needs stretched from time to time. Third, we cannot focus on our past failures and disappointments because that only makes us bitter. Fourth, we cannot let the world define happiness and success for us. And finally, we must continually remember that God does not just have 1 plan for us. He, as a loving God, knows that we, through our sin or error in judgment, sometimes miss the blessing he has for us along a particular path. That's why he makes provision for alternatives-as he did for Adam and Eve.

Lessons on Perseverance - Part 6 of 7

Text: Luke 18:1-8

Key verse: Luke 18:7 "Won't God provide justice to his chosen people who cry out to him day and night? Will he be slow to help them?

A story is told of a lady who got this call from a telemarketer: "May I talk to Leah Johnson?" "She's an infant." "That's ok, I'll just call back later." As much as I hate that kind of call, today's scripture seems to suggest that we, in our prayer life, ought to be more like that telemarketer.

Today's lesson, better known as the parable of the unrighteous judge, talks about an unGodly, self-centered judge who, because he is worn down by the incessant pleas for justice by a woman, grants her request just to get rid of her. Now, this was not shared as an analogy to how God works. Rather, it was told to contrast how God works with how unrighteous people work. Yet it is also a reminder that people ought to pray like the poor woman in the parable- to be that persistent.

There are many examples of people who were rewarded for their perseverance: Dr. Seuss's 1st children's book was rejected 23 times, or Coca-Cola's minimal sales the 1st year. But the point is that people tend to give up too soon on their prayers. This parable, then, says loud and clear: Don't do it!

Lessons on Perseverance - Part 7 of 7

Text:2 Peter 3:8-9

Key verse; 2 Peter 3;9 "The Lord isn't slow to keep his promise, as some think of slowness, but is patient towards you, not wanting anyone to perish but all to change their hearts and lives."

The father was bringing work home each night from the office and his first-grader son asked him why. "I just can't get all my work done, buddy", he explained. "Well, Daddy, why don't they put you in the slower group?"

Makes sense to me, Dad. Yet, I wonder, what does our use of time communicate to our kids or those we love? And is it how we'd want to be remembered?

The point seems to be that this is a task that requires our persistent attention. Children, but particularly boys, don't come with an implicit knowledge of what fatherhood should be. These tasks-to provide for and protect his family and to give moral and Spiritual guidance- must be learned from a father's example.

Consider the following: As far back as he could remember, his dad would put any change from his pockets into a pickle jar by his bed before retiring for the night. When he would ask his dad about this practice, he'd say "You'll get to college on pennies, nickels, dimes and quarters, but you'll get there, I'll see to that." And no matter how hard things got-like the summer when his dad got laid off from the mill- not a dime was ever taken from that jar. He remembered that summer because during it, the family often would only have garden beans for supper. But he also remembered that summer because each time they had beans, his father had to put ketchup on them just to get them down. Then he'd say to me, "Son, when you finish college, you'll never have to eat beans again, unless you want to. "The years passed, and he did finish college. But he remembered that pickle jar and what it stood for in terms of the perseverance that fatherhood entails.

REFLECTIONS

Plans

The Bible has much to say about plans and what that basically comes down to this: God has plans and man has plans. God's plans are plans that result in blessings. Man's plans can also bring blessings but only in conjunction with his. When man plans without God and apart from God's guidance, those plans will eventually fail.

The experience of my life would cause me to concur. I never was one to plan far in advance. What I mean is I might want to play golf or go to a game or cut grass on a particular day, but I knew that those plans would be completely dependent on the weather. Later on, I would think in terms of doing things with others but that became dependent on the people involved.

As for plans that were roughly conceived, I, like others, hoped to fall in love, get married, have children, have a good job, travel and have a nice car. And I hoped that I would be able to do these things from the standpoint of health, and lack of conflicting obligations or money. However, even though those things did happen to me, I credit God's blessing me more than my own foresight.

Lessons on Plans - Part 1 of 7

Text: Matthew 1:18-25

Key verse: Matthew 1:23 "Behold, the virgin shall be with child, and bear a son, and they shall call his name Immanuel, which is translated, "God with us."

A young man asked an old man near him on the crowded bus, 'What time is it?", but the old man refused to reply. After the young man got off the bus, the old man's friend asked the old man why he was so rude to the young man. He said, "If I would have answered, he might have kept the conversation going and I might have found myself beginning to like him. If I liked him, I would have asked him home to share dinner. And if he came to my home for dinner, he would have met my beautiful daughter and wanted to marry her. And I wouldn't want my daughter to marry a man who couldn't afford a watch."

That's planning ahead, isn't it? Yet, being human, the old man could only speculate on the future. No one but God could plan for it. And God's plan, first prophesied hundreds of years before for the salvation of mankind, forced many to change theirs. Among these were Joseph and Mary. I'm sure that, at the time of their engagement, they foresaw no unusual developments. They planned to marry, raise children, work and be a family. But when their plans came into conflict with God's, their lives would be changed forever.

Even so, history is full of instances where man's plans have proved futile because of their inability to foresee future developments or the ramifications that these plans would have. Take Alfred Nobel's invention of dynamite. He foresaw its ability in making infrastructure rather than its ability to destroy it and human life with it. Or take Henry Ford's invention of the assembly line. He had no idea what changes that invention would make for good or evil.

That's the reason God's plans are always best. He sees the future in light of the past and uniquely knows what works best. That's why our plans should be contingent upon God's.

Lessons on Plans - Part 2 of 7

Text: Matthew 22:1-14

Key verse: Matthew 22:14 "For many are called, but few are chosen."

A story is told about a football game played between the big creatures of the forest and the little creatures of the forest. As hard as it may seem to believe, the little creatures were holding their own, using their quickness to counter the big creature's size and strength. But by the end of the first half, the big creatures seemed to be wearing down the little ones and were just about to score when the little creatures called a time-out and sent in a fresh member, a centipede, to strengthen the defense. Even so, the big creatures were confident that the new player would not keep them from scoring and so they gave the ball to the elk to run it in –but he was stopped flat by the centipede. Next, they called on the mountain lion to run it in, but once again was stopped for no gain by-you guessed it- the centipede. Well, they finally decided to let bear take it in, but was tackled for a loss by the little centipede. And that's how the half ended. The coach of the big creatures was confused why the little creatures had not employed the centipede earlier in the game and so asked the coach of the little creatures why. "That's easy", said the coach, "he was still tying his shoes."

He hadn't done the pre-game planning necessary to be able to start the game. By the same token, today's lesson deals with much the same problem. It's called the parable of the wedding banquet. In this parable, the people the king has invited to his son's wedding can't come, so he has his servants go out and invite any one they can. When the king comes in to visit the invited guests, one does not have his wedding outfit on and is then asked to leave because he was not prepared.

The analogy, then, is clear: God has invited whosoever to accept his son's sacrifice for their sin and come into heaven. Yet there are some who feel they don't need that sacrifice. They will be disappointed because they are not "dressed" in the Savior's righteousness and be asked to leave.

Lessons on Plans - Part 3 of 7

Text: Mark 5: 25-34

Key verse: Mark 5:28 "If I may touch but his clothes, I shall be whole."

A guy was always late for his dental appointments. So when the office called to confirm his appointment, he said he'd probably be 15 minutes late. Then he asked if that would be ok. The receptionist said that it would but that they just wouldn't have time to give him anesthesia.

Many people have difficulty "fitting things in" to their lives. But are they the most important things? Have they prioritized correctly?

Jesus is a good example of proper prioritizing-particularly in the area of prayer. For him, prayer came first, as it should for us. Yet, for him, the mass of people coming to him for healing and direction determined his priorities, in most cases, because to them, their situation was an emergency.

Such is the case with today's scripture lesson-a lesson that combines 2 healing experiences. A Jewish religious leader first came to Jesus seeking the healing of his little daughter. This was certainly an emergency as this leader would have certainly rather have resolved the problem in a way that did not involve Jesus, as his peers were constantly trying to discredit the Savior. In the second case, a lady had been afflicted with a bleeding disorder for 18 years and felt that that problem could not continue much longer without killing her. The fact that Jesus healed both as they came seems to prove that he did not deem one case needier than the other.

We, on the other hand, must be careful to prioritize beyond prayer because we are not as discerning as Jesus and are much more easily tempted to "get off track". In an average lifetime, we spend 13 years watching tv, 24 years sleeping and 6 months waiting for red lights to turn green. But that leaves plenty of time to do the important things, if we prioritize the non-emergency things.

Lessons on Plans - Part 4 of 7

Text: Luke 10:38-42

Key verse: Luke 10:42a "One thing is necessary."

A young girl's purse had been stolen from her car. So when she got home, she made all the necessary calls but did not tell her mother- mostly because her mother always seemed to make her feel as if she had "messed up". But she knew she had to tell her, so she went quietly into the mom's room and told her what happened. The mom then asked her what purse she lost. When the girl said the green suede one, the mom sat up in bed and, turning on the light remarked, "With that dress?"

Different people, different priorities. But to what extent are we influenced by those others?

In today's lesson, Martha seems to be influenced by the society in which she lived- which advised that good hospitality dictates a clean house and an enjoyable meal. But she failed to realize that Jesus changed the equation. His teachings negated societal expectations. Yet this is a lesson that many people still miss today.

In the city of Atlanta, Georgia, there was a restaurant called the Church of God grill. It was originally a church that served meals after Sunday worship to help finance the church's ministry. But people started liking the meal better than the service and so they eliminated the service altogether. Clearly, money influenced this decision-not Jesus. In the same way, many modern singers got their start singing in church choirs, but fame influenced their later decisions- not Jesus.

We have to be careful not to let Jesus be put out of the picture because these lesser motives cannot save us when the storms of life roll in. The George Barna institute, which measures the Spiritual temperature of our times, has noted that 66% of our adult population are only casual Christians. Casual Christians don't realize that Jesus changes the equation and thus will make the same mistake that Martha did.

Lessons on Plans - Part 5 of 7

Text: Philippians 4:6-7

Key verse: Philippians 4:6a "Don't be anxious about anything…"

A guy was having a problem and asked a plumber to come to his house. The plumber said he was busy and might not be able to get to him for about 2 years. The guy then asked, "Will you be coming in the morning or afternoon?"

Sounds like he would be able to wait. But I'm not sure we would be able to say the same- particularly when we are seeking something from the Lord. Yet, today's scripture verse tells us not to worry. Our faith in God should assure us that we will get our answer in a timely way. All we need to do is ask what we want in prayer, being sure to thank God for his goodness. In reality, this does not sound like good preparation or planning, however. But it is God's way.

King Saul paid dearly for not following this advice. Early in his reign, the Israelites escaped across from the Philistines. But due to their superior numbers, many Israelites began to desert. King Saul, who had been advised to wait for Samuel the prophet, felt that he could wait no longer and offered a sacrifice that he had no right to do. Because of his disobedience, then, God withdrew his support from him.

In my Army National Guard career, we often would accuse those in authority of making us "hurry up and wait." Nevertheless, the wise soldier would try to make the best of this "downtime" to grab a snack or refill his canteen or write a letter home so that, when the order to move came down, they were ready. This is a helpful analogy to life in general. There is much that is not within our control and so we must also make the best use of our "wait-time"-trusting God's timing as being in our best interests.

Lessons on Plans - Part 6 of 7

Text: Genesis 11:1-9

Key verse; Genesis 11:7 "Come, let us go down and confuse their language so they will not understand each other."

83-yeart old Harry played a great game of golf but suffered from failing eyesight. So, not wanting to give up the game, got his friend Sam, who had excellent vision but did not play golf, to go along. The only problem was that Sam had more than his share of senior moments. In any event, on the first hole, Harry hit a great drive and asked Sam if he saw it. Sam said yes but when they started to drive out in their golf cart to the ball, Sam said he'd forgotten where it went.

And so it is, oftentimes, with our plans. When they don't fit with the will of God, they don't work out. This was the case with today's Bible lesson, the Tower of Babel. God's plan after the flood was for man to spread out and replenish the earth. This did not fit with man's plan and so the people started to build a great city in one place with a great tower that would "reach to heaven". God then intervened by giving them different languages so the work could not continue. Then, the people who could understand one another, moved off by themselves-thus accomplishing God's original plan.

The clear lesson for us, then, is consciously living within the extent of God's will, as we are led by the Holy Spirit. This does not only mean doing what he wants but doing it his way and in his time. He does not want us to ask him to bless something when we aren't giving it our best.

A high school football player asked his history teacher to give him a passing grade on his project when he hadn't given his best effort. The teacher replied that if he had run the football 99 yards from his goal line but didn't feel the need to go further, would the officials give him a touchdown, even though he had not actually got into the endzone? "Of course, not", said the player. "Then why should I give you a passing grade when you handed in a shoddy project that could easily have been done to standard?"

Lessons on Plans - Part 7 of 7

Text: Proverbs 16:1-3

Key verse: Proverbs 16:1 "Mortals make elaborate plans, but God has the last word."

A greedy man knew he didn't have much longer to live, so he advised his lawyer to liquidate his assets and put it all in his casket when he died. At the funeral service, however, one of the man's relatives who knew of the man's plans, asked the lawyer why he could see none of the man's wealth in the casket. And the lawyer said, "I put a personal check in his pocket."

When God has not been consulted about our plans, we should not be surprised when things don't work out. Yet, even when we do consult with God about our plans, they may still seem not to be working, anyway. Perhaps it is because people who are supposed to be part of the solution are not listening to God or are not obedient to what he would have them do. Or it may be that God has answered the person's prayer in another way.

I knew of a man who worked all his life so that he could enjoy his retirement. Unfortunately, his plan was not to develop the way he had hoped. He was not much of a practicing Christian so perhaps he had not expressed this plan to God or received his blessing on it. Nevertheless, he contracted cancer and died after only receiving 2 social security checks. Even so, he did have time to make his peace with God and so his life of pleasure is happening in heaven rather than on earth.

This is not to say, however, that we should not plan, because we should. It's just that we need to realize that God is in control and that he works in miraculous, yet inscrutable ways. We need, then, to be open to the refinements that he may have on those plans. But most of all, we must remember that he is good and that he loves us. That way, we don't have to worry about the changes.

REFLECTIONS

Prayer

Prayer is one of the distinctive features of the Christian life. It is nothing less than communication with God- expressing our hopes, fears, requests and thanksgiving. Jesus, the son of God, found it essential to his earthly direction and ministry and he encouraged its regular use among his disciples and followers. Although God knows our thoughts and needs, he encourages us to pray because it both recognizes our dependence on him and our faith that He is able and willing to help us.

In my life, prayer changed as my outlook toward God matured. At first, prayer was just a memorized litany to be said at bedtime or the expected precursor to an evening meal. I turned to God if I was sick or in trouble or wanted something. In that respect, God was no more than a kindly "Grandpa", to be taken down from the shelf when needed and put back when things returned to normal.

But when God became God in my life, prayer became a lifeline- a connection to crucial direction, heartfelt thanks and confession as well as a conduit for my daily thoughts and requests for myself and others. How is it for you?

Lessons on Prayer - Part 1 of 7

Text: Isaiah 40:27,31

Key verse: Isaiah 40:31a "But those who wait on the Lord will renew their strength;"

Each Sunday evening around the dinner table, the dad would ask each family member to pray for one person that week. So, when it was the son's turn, he advised that he pray for his friend, Eddie, because he was so bad at school. The next Sunday night the dad asked his son if he was going to pray for Eddie again. And the son said, "No, I prayed for him last week, and he's still bad."

As funny as it sounds, a lot of people's prayer requests go something like that. If they don't get something from God the first time they ask, that's it. Today's key verse tells us, however, that God should get more than a "once and done". Just because God doesn't give us the answer, we want the first time doesn't mean that he doesn't hear or care. Perhaps it may mean that God wants us to re-evaluate our request or test the maturity of our faith. In any event, we have to admit that God has a better perspective than we do.

An aircraft pilot was following a major highway and observing the traffic below. Yet one particular vehicle caught his attention. The driver of a car was attempting to pass a tractor trailer driving up a long, curvy hill. Yet, each time he would pull out to pass, another vehicle would always be coming. And he thought to himself, "If I could only communicate with that guy, I could tell him when it's safe to pass." This is the point of prayer: God has a better perspective on our situation than we do, and prayer is one way he could help us through.

Lessons on Prayer- Part 2 of 7

Text: 1 Samuel 8:4-7/9;1,2,17

Key verse: 1 Samuel 8:5b "Now make us a king to judge us like all nations."

The little girl was disappointed with her grandmother's Christmas gift: A thimble. But, not wanting her grandmother to feel bad, she wrote her this note: "Dear grandma, thank you for the thimble. It is something that I always wanted-but not much."

It can sometimes work just the opposite. The Israelites could hardly wait to get a king. But when they got him, they were disappointed that having a king wasn't the blessing they thought it would be. Samuel, the prophet, tried to warn them, but they wouldn't listen. Clearly, sometimes you have to be careful of what you ask for, for you just might get it.

The key issue here, however, is that God picked the king. Now Saul looked at the part and was humble enough and the people and Samuel were initially pleased with the pick. But the question remains: did God pick Saul, knowing how he would turn out or did he actually pick the best there was at the time, hoping that Saul would make better choices? This we'll never know.

We just have to keep in mind that God is good and seeks to bless us. He can, if he so desires, let us have our way so that we learn through our mistakes that we should have let God have his way. Or he could withhold our request for something far better. You see, he knows how we learn best- even if we don't. Some lessons just come from maturity and/or through retrospect. And some lessons can only be learned the hard way.

Lessons on Prayer - Part 3 of 7

Text: Romans 8:26-27

Key verse: Romans 8:26c ",..but the Spirit himself makes intercession for us..."

A guy from El Salvador was working toward becoming a naturalized citizen in America, but occasionally had problems picking up on English idioms. When that happened, he often turned to his friend and co-worker, Jeannette, to help him. This time he wanted to know what a c-section was. Having delivered all her 3 children that way, Jeannette explained the procedure. But when her friend looked even more confused, she asked in what context he had been asked about a c-section. He then explained that he had been in the lunchroom during break, reading the newspaper, when another worker asked him for the c section.

No wonder Jeannette was confused. And so, it sometimes is with us in turning to God in prayer when we're not sure what it is we want. That's why today's scripture is so important: the Holy Spirit, that knows our heart and the mind of God, makes intercession for us when we are confused so that God will understand specifically what it is we are asking.

We see this process at work in the disciple Philip's life after Christ's resurrection in Acts 8:24-40. Philip had been literally dropped into a desert area where an Ethiopian government official was reading scripture and needed instruction. Philip could not have known this, but his desire was to "spread the gospel" and so the Holy Spirit interpreted it for him in taking him there.

Such an event is probably difficult, if not impossible, for someone without faith to accept. Unquestionably, God and the Holy Spirit work in mysterious ways. But we who do believe must be faithful in sharing our unusual faith experiences after we earn their trust.

Lessons on Prayer- Part 4 of 7

Text: Matthew 6:5-13

Key verse: Matthew 6:9a "Pray like this…"

A ship was sinking in the middle of a storm, so the captain called his crew together. "Does anyone here know how to pray?", he asked. "I do, sir!", said one of his crew. "Excellent", said the captain, "you pray while the rest of us put on our life jackets. We're one short."

I'm not sure the captain really saw that as a solution to the lack of life jackets, but I am sure that the young man would rather have had a life jacket on while praying than not. Jesus' disciples were not as confident in their prayer life, either so they asked him to show them how to pray.

In essence he told them that prayer was not an information briefing for God or the result of some secret formula. It was an attitude of the heart- an attitude of humility and expectation expressed toward a father who loved them and forgave them as they were forgiving toward others.

Perhaps more importantly, Jesus, himself, showed these disciples how his prayer life gave him peace when he was able to sleep through a storm at sea which threatened to wreck their boat in Mark the fourth chapter. Indeed, when they woke him up, he chastised them for their lack of faith and then he called for the wind and waves to cease, and they obeyed him. This peace through prayer is possible to all who are faithful in its practice in faith. Thus, it matters not the ship we are on, the only hearts that can weather the storms of life are those that have Jesus inside.

Lessons on Prayer - Part 5 of 7

Text: Luke 11: 9-13

Key verse: Luke 11:9 a "…:ask, and it shall be given unto you,…"

A grandmother and her grandson were walking along the beach one sunny day when a big wave came up and swept her grandson under the waves so she could not see him at all. Immediately, she prayed that her grandson be returned to her. And her prayer was answered with the next wave that brought him back, soaked, disheveled and shook up, but otherwise ok. She then looked up to heaven, thanking God, but added, "You know, Lord, he did have a hat on."

In today's lesson, we are advised to ask, seek and knock for the things we need, but we often aren't thankful enough for what we receive. Is that God's fault? Hardly! God is not like some store clerk that must be shown what to do. Indeed, we should never ascribe to God a lesser trait than what we would expect a good man to do. And we must remember that God is good and wants to bless. It's just that he loves us too much to just give us what we ask for because he alone knows what is best for us.

Thus, we are never quite sure where our prayer request sits with God. There is no tracking number to follow the transaction. We just have to have faith that God's decision and timing are perfect regarding our request. Yet, there's one thing more. Although God doesn't need any help in granting our request, he often chooses to allow people to assist. When they are not attentive to God's direction, the answers we seek may be delayed. Again-not God's fault. In fact, we may be the guilty party in someone else's request.

Therefore, let us be open to God's direction, not only in that which pertains to us-but in all things. Let us also continue to ask, seek and knock. Our answer may just be "coming in on the next wave."

Lessons on Prayer - Part 6 of 7

Text and key verse: Philippians 4:6 "Do not be anxious about anything, but in every situation, by prayer and supplication, with thanksgiving, let your requests be made known unto God."

A ship was sinking in the middle of a storm and so the captain called his crew together. "Does anyone here know how to pray?", the captain asked. "I do, sir!", replied one of his crew. "that's great. You pray while the rest of us put on our life jackets. We're one short."

A young child prayed: "Please bless mommy and daddy. But please, Dear God, take care of yourself. If anything happen to you, we're sunk!"

According to the scripture for today, this was an appropriate request. To Jesus, however, prayer was as important as any life jacket- and it should be so for us, as well. I mean, if we could get to the place where we believed this scripture as Jesus did, it would revolutionize our lives. We would not put our faith in anything but God.

This child had her priorities right for a child. As matured Christians, however, our prayers should include our gratitude for what God has already done. Amen?

Many years ago, there was an ocean liner built that people claimed was unsinkable. Its name was the titanic. Because of many people's faith in the work of man's hands, many people died. For the most part, this terrible tragedy could have been avoided. But because it was not, it serves as an excellent example of how we could find ourselves in such a position. From defective materials to a lack of humility to company agreed to a lack of common sense, there were a lot of guilty parties to blame. But it all boils down to the place where we place our faith.

And so, it is with us. If we believe that God is good and loves us, why would we not turn to him first? It is said that prayer changes things. But its most crucial change is in USSO that we are freed to trust God above all.

Lessons on prayer- part 7 of 7

Text: James 5: 13-15

Key verse: James 5:13 "and the prayer of faith will raise the sick;…"

A wealthy businessman was dying in the hospital when his pastor came to see him. The pastor prayed for him and after he had finished, the businessman said this: "Pastor, if God heals me, I will give a million dollars to the church!" The businessman was not immediately better, but started to make good progress and was released from the hospital. In time he felt like new and went back to work, although his church attendance began to suffer. But about 3 months later, the pastor saw him on the street and remarked that God had really done a good job in making him better. Then he reminded the businessman of what he said he'd do if God healed him. And the businessman replied, "Did I say that? That just goes to show you the crazy things people say when they're in pain."

Although the businessman did get his healing, many people do not. And it isn't because they don't have money. This is a mystery of God that we call sovereignty. God will do what God will do. Although he loves us and wants us to prosper, not everybody gets what they pray for. And we cannot obligate God to act on our behalf-as if we could deserve what he has to give.

Even so, today's scripture gives us a prescription to use in praying for the sick. Specifically, it says the prayer of faith will raise the sick. We just need to understand that that does not necessarily mean healing in the same sense that we have. So, in considering what I have shared, some people may say, "What's the use?" This is where faith comes in: we don't know what God will do and so we don't know that God won't heal. We do know that God loves us and wants us to prosper. But most importantly, prayer changes us so we will be enabled to accept whatever answer he gives. So, keep praying-don't say no for God. And don't feel guilty for asking God to heal you before you try to help others. Once you experience God's power over pain in your life, you can more enthusiastically share that perspective with others.

REFLECTIONS

Promises of God

It is important to differentiate between the promises that God makes and the promises that people make to each other because if we assume God's promises are like ours, our faith will be seriously compromised. It's not that people don't keep some of the promises that they make to one another, it's just that, usually, they are not consistent in keeping them.

I know that I have let people down in my life. And, in my life, I have also been the one let down. On several occasions, I have been "unlucky" in love. And I've had several let-downs in my military and secular work life. As a pastor, I've officiated at several weddings where people have promised to love and honor one another and couldn't keep that promise.

I say all this to contrast the promises of God. Although he hasn't always given me what I ask for, he has always, without exception, given me what I needed and listened to any complaints without punishing me for expressing them. And I believe that, if we're truly honest with ourselves, he has done the same for all of us.

Lessons on the Promises of God – Part 1/7

Text: Genesis 9:8-17

Key verse: genesis 9:13a "I have placed my bow in the clouds…"

The governor of a southern state was making a tour of a mental hospital, when he got thrown off by a question posed by a patient doing some painting, "Who are you and what are you doing here?" After regaining his composure, the governor said, "I'm the governor of this great state and I'm here to help in any way I can." "Great," said the patient, "Grab a brush and get busy."

Clearly, this was not what the governor had in mind when he said he was there to help. And so, it is with many of the so-called promises that people make to each other. And it stands in stark contrast to the promises of God-which are sure.

Such is the case in today's scripture lesson: the promise of God never to destroy the earth again through flood. I'm sure that Noah and his family were glad to hear that since they were the only human witnesses to the destruction. Yet, it was even more important for them to know that their children and their children's children would have the same chance they did to live a full, productive life. And, since the promise was not written down, the fact that its confirmation would always be visible after a rain would be proof to future generations that God's promises would be kept.

Of course, not all of God's promises are that specific. He promises, for example, that he will never "leave us nor forsake us." And, although that is true, it does not necessarily mean that we will get what we want when we want it. It just means that we can count on his presence. In the case of New Hope United Methodist church, his presence was what got us through until we were able to obtain our present building- a time period of several years. For the famous hymn writer, Fanny Crosby, his presence didn't mean she would get her sight back, but it did mean that he was with her to help account for her prolific song-writing success.

Lessons on the Promises of God - Part 2/7

Text: Genesis 12:1-5

Key verse: Genesis 12:2a "I will make you into a great nation."

A woman went to visit a fortune-teller. Hoping to receive a favorable report on her future, she was surprised to learn that she was going to become a widow soon as her husband was going to be killed. After taking a few moments to compose herself, she asked, "Will I be convicted?"

When God promised that Abraham was going to be the father of a great nation, I think Abraham wondered how such a thing could happen, in that he was 75 years old. As is often the case, he was thinking in the literal sense. What God meant, that we can appreciate in retrospect, was that Abraham was going to be the faith "father" of the church- of which we are included.

When the congregation of New Hope Ynited Methodist church moved from its former building to its present location, I'm sure that many long-time members were at least a little scared of how it would all work out. But this is where faith comes in. When people make promises to people, we judge the validity of the promise by the person making it. But when God makes a promise, we don't have to assess; we know its validity. Such was the case with Abraham. He knew who was making the promise, so he complied.

This is the expectation of all Christians today. We may not be asked to do any great thing like Noah, Moses or Abraham, but we are expected to be obedient-just as these great "faith" heroes were.

And this is why we can approach death without the trepidation of those who have no idea of what that holds. We had been promised paradise. Why would we expect anything less?

Lessons on the Promises of God – Part 3/7

Text: Isaiah 41:8-13

Key verse: Isaiah 41:10b "Don't be afraid, for I am your God;…"

A man devoted his life to making money and made quite a bit from it-so much so that he made his wife promise, after deducting a certain amount for her needs, to put the rest in his coffin when he died to take with him. After the funeral service was over, she hurried to put a small box in the coffin before it was closed. When her friend asked her what she had done, she told her about the promise. "Well, you didn't do it, did you?", the friend asked. "I certainly did", she replied, "I'm a Christian and I keep my promises." "Then you're crazy, "said the friend. "No, I'm not," the wife replied, "I wrote him a check!"

A continuing theme of this promises section seems to be that while the promises that people make to one another may often be "hit-or-miss", the promises of God are sure and certain. And so, when God promises to always help and protect his chosen people (the Israelites), he can be sure to follow through. Now that we have been adopted into the family of God, those promises apply to us-which should give us a great sense of security and hope for the future.

Yet, for many, that's easier said than done. "How can God say that about me when I have let him down so many times?" People surmise. And that's because we have trouble relating to someone who keeps his promises-whose love is not conditional.

Consider the following true story: a little girl who had polio always asked her mother to wear her locket when she dropped her off for Sunday school. Her mother thought it was because she liked the locket. But, in the girl's eyes (though now a woman), that wasn't it at all. She knew that she wasn't worth coming back for-but the locket was.

This is regrettably the mindset of many people as they relate to God. Why would he love them so? We, then, as Christians, need to help them see themselves in a new light. It's not about them or their unworthiness; it's about the love of God, who keeps his promises.

Lessons on the Promises of God – Part 4/7

Text: Isaiah 45:15,16

Key verse: Isaiah 45:15d "…,I will not forget you."

An elderly couple were taking a trip when they decided to stop at a roadside restaurant. When the wife was eating, she took off her glasses and left them on the table. When they were finished, however, she forgot to pick them up and didn't remember them until they were quite a distance down the road. So, on the way back, the husband complained the whole way. When they finally got there and the wife went in to retrieve her glasses, the husband yelled to her, "While you're in there, you might as well get my hat."

You don't have to be older to forget. In today's lesson, the Israelites seem to have forgotten the many times the Lord had rescued them and alleged that God had forgotten them. But he indicated through the prophet Isaiah, that a new mother would forget her baby sooner than he would forget them. In fact, he said their names were inscribed on the palms of his hands.

The problem with forgetting, then, lies with us. The soap opera show called "The Guiding Light" was, at one time, the longest running drama of all time. It came on radio on January 25th, 1937, and finally ended on September 18th, 2009. I know my mother watched it often. But be that as it may, the story was based on a lady's misfortune of giving birth to a stillborn child and the comfort she derived from listening to on-air sermons. It was the sermons, then, that provided the material for the program. The "guiding light", then, referred to the lamp that the pastor would turn on in his study to let people know he was there and ready to talk to people about their problems. Over the years, the shows' original tenets were forgotten or scrapped, and the show degenerated into the typical stories of exploitation and glorification of sin.

We run the risk of trouble when we similarly forget that God is with us. If we could somehow remember that he is always near, perhaps we would be more inclined to do and say the right things.

Lessons on the Promises of God – Part 5 of 7

Text: 1 Corinthians 11:27-30

Key verse: 1 Corinthians 11:29 "For those who eat and drink without discerning the body of Christ, eat and drink judgment on themselves."

Two little boys who were best friends all their lives pursued professions in the ministry- one a preacher and the other a priest. They lived and worked in the same town and met once a week for coffee at the same diner. One such meeting day, they shook hands after their fellowship and went to their cars. But the preacher friend was a little too much in a hurry to get to a home visit and pulled out in front of his priest friend, causing an accident. After assuring himself that his friend was not hurt, the preacher, who felt he caused the accident, apologized profusely to his friend and openly expressed his hope that the accident had not dampened their friendship. The priest said, "Of course not. Let's drink a toast to our continued relationship," and poured out 2 communion cups of wine, one of which the preacher readily drank. The priest, however, did not, which caused the preacher to ask why. "I'll just wait until the police leave the scene of the accident."

I'm just thankful that our relationship with God isn't likely to be affected by such a minor thing as an accident. However, our relationship has some reciprocal requirements. In today's lesson, we learn that failure to consider the sacrifice of Jesus while taking communion can lead to some serious consequences. That's why we are advised to examine ourselves before partaking of this sacrament. This self-examination means not only how we look at the sacrament itself, but what the sacrament should mean to us regarding any flawed aspects of our relationships with others-that those flaws should be addressed first. Otherwise, we should not be surprised that diseases linger longer than customary, or death happens when the disease or accident did not first appear to be serious.

Lessons on the Promises of God – Part 6 of 7

Text: Isaiah 40:29-31

Key verse: Isaiah 40:31 "But those who trust in the Lord will renew their strength; they will soar on wings like eagles; they will run and not grow weary; they will walk and not be faint."

Two construction workers had just opened their lunch buckets to get their noon meal when one of them complained, "Not meatloaf again! I hate meatloaf!" The other worker, having heard this complaint many times before, suggests, "Why don't you just ask your wife to make you something different?" "Wife? I'm not married, I make my own lunch."

Sometimes the fixed points in our lives prove dysfunctional. For most people, when they become aware of that dysfunction, they change- but not all. If, however, God's word is our fixed point, God, himself, will help us stay on course. Few things in life are that dependable.

On day 6 of the ill-fated Apollo 13 space mission, the astronauts needed to make a critical course correction in order to be in position for re-entry. But this course correction had to be done manually for a brief 39-second interval. To do it correctly, mission commander James Lovell needed a fixed point to focus on. He found it by keeping the earth centered on his field of vision.

This is just as critical for us in terms of living life successfully. Today's key verse reminds us that no matter how "out-of-control" things seem to be, if we can just hang on, God will provide the way. But, more than this, he promises to be all in in his blessing of us.

The question, then, is not "Is God all in" but "are we all in for him?"

Lessons on the Promises of God - Part 7 of 7

Text: Exodus 16

Key verse: Exodus 16:4 "Behold, I will rain "bread from heaven" for you."

The kids had talked mom into getting them a hamster, promising to feed and care for "Danny" faithfully. But in 2 months' time, mom was not surprisingly the sole caretaker of "Danny". So, wanting the kids to learn a lesson, she called them together to tell them she was going to give "Danny" to a new owner. Realizing their error and that mom was not going to back down, they all, one by one, began their expressions of pain: "I'll miss him." "He's been around here for a long time. "Maybe he could have stayed if he ate less and wasn't so messy." Finally, mom said, "Ok, kids, say your last good-byes to "Danny". "Danny?", the kids wailed," we thought you said daddy."

From the book of Exodus, we find that God's people often acted like children in terms of their lack of responsibility or appreciation. It seems like they complained constantly about one thing or another. Even so, God forgave their childish attitudes and provided for their needs. In the 16th chapter, we read about God's provision of manna. Yet, even so, he gave them plenty of opportunities to grow in faith. But again, and again they were disappointed. They did not follow directions on gathering the manna and eating it the same day, nor did they believe that the manna gathered on Saturday would last until Monday.

So, what do we learn from their example? That God's promises are not conditional. They are provided regardless of the recipient's response or gratitude. We also learn that God can provide immediately or over time, depending on the need. Our main problem in that respect is our inability to wait. Yet that is precisely the attitude we need and that God, I believe, is trying to teach. His timing is perfect regardless of our schedule.

REFLECTIONS

Rewards

Everyone knows that actions have consequences. Yet, often times, people "Sow Wild Oats", then, at the same time, pray for crop failure. This is a particularly fatal error as far as our Spiritual life is concerned. As Christians who accept the sacrificial death of Jesus Christ as their only claim to righteousness, we can look forward to a life in heaven after we die. For those who do not, their reward will be much different.

As I think back to my youth, I remember being punished for my "Bad" actions and commended for the "Good'. This helped me to understand the concept of justice. I'm not quite so sure as to what happens with kids today. Sometimes their errors are punished and sometimes forgotten. Sometimes the punishment fits the crime and, other times, it is much more severe- depending on their parents' mood, level of intoxication or how well their day at work went. Often things are purchased to keep them from being "Bad" or to reward them for being "Good". Thus, for many, the concept of justice is flawed and their reaction to it inconsistent.

Lessons on Rewards - Part 1 of 7

Text: Luke 16:19-31

Key verse: Luke 16:28 "…send him to the house of my father where I have 5 brothers to tell them the score and warn them, so they won't end up here in this place of torment."

An atheist had an old tree in his yard. During a storm, however, the tree fell on his neighbor's house, causing much damage. The next day, the atheist called his insurance agent to see if it would pay for the repairs. The insurance agent, who happened to know that his caller was an atheist while he was a Christian, kept his composure although he knew this situation would cause his client considerable anguish. So, he answered," it depends. If the tree fell because it was dead, the insurance won't pay. But if the tree falling was an act of God, then the insurance will pay. So, I ask you: which was it?"

In today's lesson, the rich man was not characterized as an atheist, but he acted like it in terms of not caring for poor Lazarus, who lived by his gate. So, in death, the rich man finds that his circumstances have been reversed and is in torment. In a manner of speaking, he had failed to see that he had a responsibility to people other than himself with the wealth that was entrusted to him.

Thus, one could make the point that his garden required him to tend to the needs of those around him just as Adam was responsible for tending the garden of Eden. And since he had free choice to fulfill his obligations or not, he himself was only receiving his just reward.

Yet, I consider it interesting that the rich man does not dispute his reward but only fears that his brothers will end up as he is if they don't change their ways. That is, God had not apparently "gotten their attention" either. My question, then, is it because the rich man had (as his brothers were also doing) hardened his heart about what Moses and the prophets were saying or because it had not been presented in a more compelling way?

Lessons on Rewards - Part 2 of 7

Text: Luke 23:39-43

Key verse: Luke 23:43 "...today you shall be with me in paradise."

The little girl had been bad and so her punishment was to eat her dinner on a tray table facing the wall while everyone else got to sit at the table. No one paid much attention to her until she said her devotions, which went something like this: "I thank you, Lord, for preparing a table for me in the presence of mine enemies."

Clearly, she did not think she deserved the punishment she received. But in today's lesson, we learn about a guy we know did not receive what he deserved. And, of course, I'm talking about the thief on the cross, whom Jesus saved with almost his dying breath. The trouble we have with this is that it seems so unfair. Why, we reason, should a person lead such a miserable, crime-filled life and get the same reward as a person who had been righteous all his life? Or we wonder how fair it was that a person could live as sinful a life as that and just be able to pull it out at the last possible moment? We think that, unless the person was us.

Some perspective can be of some help here, I believe. First and foremost, we need to understand that God does not want anyone to go to hell. In this particular case, the thief confesses his unworthiness while testifying to Jesus's righteousness- the minimum needed to be saved. Second, I believe this story provides clarification for all those who feel it is too late for them to be saved. No one could have been more unworthy or waited as long as this thief. And the Bible does not mention any other instances like this of last-minute conversions because that is not the preferred way. The Bible unequivocally states that people should not wait or wait until a more convenient time. Finally, how could anyone know what shape they'll be in when they are ready to take their last breath? Maybe they won't be in their right mind to know what they're doing.

So, in effect, it may not seem fair, but neither is our salvation. All have sinned and come short of the glory of God. Thus, in taking the sacrifice of Jesus, we get what we could never deserve.

Lessons on Rewards - Part 3 of 7

Text: John 14:2,3/ Revelation 21:4

Key verse: john 14:3 "and if I go and prepare a place for you, I will come again, and receive you unto myself; that where I am, there you may be also."

An elderly couple passed away and found themselves in heaven, where St. Peter commenced to show them around. He showed them their stately mansion, a beautiful golf course that they could play anytime they wanted and the dining area which carried the best, most impressive variety of food that either of them had ever seen. The husband, then, looked at his wife and said, "If you hadn't made me eat those bran muffins, I could have been here 10 years ago."

Heaven will, no doubt, be the most wonderful place any of us has ever seen. And there will be no pain, crying or any other factor that will hinder our enjoyment of it. Yet, i wonder, if this is true, why does that not cause more people to choose Christ and live for him? Is it because they think that they would be missing too much here by living for him now? Or could it be that we don't respond favorably to distant rewards?

It is not my intention to try to answer those questions. I would just like to suggest that perhaps there may be some other factor-some other incentive- that is more effective in producing consistent Christian behavior. And that factor, I am suggesting, is love. It is love, not reward, that drives their efforts.

When we love someone, there is nothing that we would not do within our ability to please them. And so, when that someone is Jesus, we desire longingly to return our love to him. Our love is directed outwardly-toward the object of their devotion.

Yet, some people's love is directed not to someone but to something. Yet the outcome is still the same. When it is fame, or wealth or power, they spend all available time and talent to achieve that goal. In effect, their love is directed inwardly- to make themselves someone that others will love.

Lessons on Rewards - Part 4 of 7

Text: Acts 16:16-34

Key verse: Acts 16:30 "…,sirs, what must I do to be saved?"

The wealthy old man wondered if his lovely young wife had married him for his money. So, he asked her, "If I lost all my money, would you still love me?" And she replied, "Of course, I'd still love you. Don't be silly! But I sure would miss you."

The Bible says, "for where your treasure is, there will your heart be also." In the case of the young wife, it's easy to see where her heart was. In today's lesson, we find that it is possible, however, for our priorities to change.

In this story, Paul and Silas had cast a demon out of a girl, whose fortune-telling had made her business associates a great deal of money. Now, because the fortune-telling Spirit had gone out of her, they were angry and turned the city and its people against Paul and Silas, resulting in their being beaten and thrown into prison. But God caused there to be an earthquake there, which allowed their bonds to break and the prison doors to spring open.

Now this, in itself, was a great story of God's deliverance, but it is not the whole story. At this point, then, the focus of the story becomes the jail keeper. His focus, at least up to this point, was to keep the prisoners assigned to him locked up until they were called for. So, when he saw that the prison doors were open, he assumed that he had failed and so he prepared to commit suicide. However, realizing this, Paul yelled that he and Silas were still there and that he need not do harm to himself. This changed his focus entirely to an eternal one, as he now, more than anything, wanted to know how he could be saved.

This is the kind of focus that we must encourage because it makes all the difference not only in this life, but the next. A woman was asked by her friend, "Do you ever wake up grumpy on Sunday morning?" And she replied, "No, that's the day I usually let him sleep." It is a mistake to think that just because we have Christ that we are happy all the time. We won't be. But we can have joy that is not affected by external circumstances. This is what the jail keeper found, and it can be and will be ours, as well.

Lessons on Rewards - Part 5 of 7

Text and key verse: 1 Corinthians 2:9 "Eye hath not seen, nor ear heard, neither hath entered into the heart of man, the things that God hath prepared for those who love him."

A little girl was reading about "Jonah and the whale" while taking an airplane trip. The man seated next to her happened to notice what she was reading and asked her, "You don't believe that story, do you?" "Yes, I do because it's in the Bible." "Come on, now", he said, "A man getting swallowed by a fish and living to talk about it? How could you prove that?" "When I get to heaven, I'll ask Jonah about it." "Well, what if he isn't in heaven?" "Then you can ask him."

For many, the idea of heaven is just too good to be true and the idea of hell something intended for only those who have done very bad things. Yet, for those who believe that the Bible is the true word of God, they know that heaven and hell are very real destinations and pray that theirs will be heaven.

Today's scripture lesson gives added proof of that description. Although we have some brief statements about heaven in the Bible, most of what we know comes from people who have had near-death experiences. Yet, even these seem inadequate as the ones experiencing it have found it difficult to put into words. Thus, it seems to me that we will have to be satisfied that a loving God who created us and knows our hearts will provide a place for us that will easily exceed all that we, in our finite minds, can imagine.

Even so, there have been those who have tried to put such thoughts in a way that we can understand and aspire to. An elderly lady, who had been a devoted Christian for many years, had received a terminal diagnosis. And so, thinking of those who would be left behind, she made all her funeral arrangements herself- down to the clothes she would wear. And when she had finished, she had one last request for her pastor-to be put in the casket with a fork in her hand. When he asked why, she explained that going to heaven was sort of like waiting for dessert-that the best is yet to come.

Lessons on Rewards - Part 6 of 7

Text: 2 Timothy 4:7-8

Key verse: 2 Timothy 4:7 "I have fought the good fight, I have finished the race, I have kept the faith."

A New York city businessman moved to the country intending to become a chicken farmer. So, after buying his farm, he went to the local feed and livestock store and ordered 100 baby chicks. "That's a lot of chicks!" said the owner. "Well, I'm serious about chicken farming!" said the businessman. About a week later, the man came back into the same store and ordered 100 more chicks. "You do mean business, don't you?" The owner said. "I do, but I'd do better if I could work out a small problem." "What problem?" "Well, I think I planted that last bunch of chicks too close together."

In this scenario, the businessman did ok with his first decision before quickly getting off track with the rest. It has been said that with every choice we make, we become a little different than we were before. If that is true, it could also be said that with every decision we make, we move a little closer or a little further away from where we want to be as Christians.

In today's lesson, the apostle Paul is referring to a daily growth process, too. As he was facing death, he compares his faith journey to a fight and a race- two actions that entail either a blow–by–blow progression or a stride-by-stride process. I don't think that this was a poorly chosen analogy. In the Christian faith, when we accept Jesus as our savior and Lord, we have just begun. "Keeping the faith" then becomes a day-by-day (and sometimes a moment-by-moment) way of life with many peaks and valleys. Hopefully, we are moving steadily in the right direction.

A man saw that a neighbor of his was struggling with a large appliance at the entrance to his house and so decided to try to help. But after several attempts, they seemed to have come to an impasse. The guy looked at his Neighbor in frustration and said, "It looks like we're never going to get this out." "Get it out?" he said. "I'm trying to get it in!"

Lessons on Rewards - Part 7 of 7

Text and key verse: John 10:10b "I came that they could have life-indeed so they could live life to the fullest."

Billy Bob went to the local diner for breakfast. Now that diner, to drum up a little extra business, was in the habit of giving away small gifts by means of peel-off stickers on their coffee cups. So, when Billy Bob peeled his sticker off, he started jumping up and down, claiming he won a motor homs. The waitress, well aware that the gifts were never that big, went over to see if she could get to the bottom of it. But, no, Billy Bob insisted, he did win, saying, "See, it says it right here-win a bagel."

Obviously, such a prize would bring anybody great joy. But the peace of God and the abundant life spoken of in the Bible does not mean just heaven or some future reward only. But it refers to abundant life even now.it does not usually mean material wealth, although in some cases, it might be part of it. Often it merely manifests itself in an unexpected gift of kindness, just when it is most needed.

A young single mom worked in a bank then came home and fed, cared for and entertained her 3 children until it was time to go to bed. Then she would do it all again the next day. But imagine her surprise when a caring neighbor offered to pick up the kids and care for them so that the young mom could have a break. This is the kind of caring that Christians do for one another-which brings us joy.

Perhaps, though, it would be good for all of us to reconsider our use of time and how at least some of it could be used in the service of others-to make others' lives a little more abundant. After all, part of the abundant life that is described will come from us. A 55-year-old man decided that he would only have maybe a thousand Saturdays left, so to speak. So, he went to 3 toy stores and bought a thousand marbles and put them in a clear bowl on his mantel. Every Saturday, he takes a marble out and throws it away. This reminds him that his time is fleeting and to do whatever good works to others that he can. We need to find a way that works for us as well for if we seek to do good, God will provide the opportunity.

REFLECTIONS

Sacrifice

It is impossible to talk about the "Christian way" without talking about sacrifice. Yet, I think that the idea of sacrifice should not be an unfamiliar one for those either within or without the church. I mean there are plenty of examples of sacrifice all around us. People routinely make sacrifices of time and relationship for the sake of their jobs. People routinely make sacrifices of time and money for friends and relatives. And people routinely make sacrifices of all kinds for their kids. I know my parents made sacrifices. My dad made many sacrifices for his job. My mother made sacrifices for her family. They never had much money, but they never splurged on themselves. And they sacrificed to send my brother Paul and I to college. Over time, I made sacrifices for work and relationships. I made sacrifices to serve my country in the military. I've made sacrifices for my kids. And my situation is probably not much different from anyone else's. Yet, even so, there are many who have had to sacrifice more and longer than I. So, to talk about sacrifices for one's faith is not something that should seem so out of place as the life of Jesus was all about that, and lovingly so.

Lessons on Sacrifice - Part 1 of 7

Text: Matthew 21:1-11

Key verse: Matthew 21:8a "A very large crowd spread their cloaks on the road,…"

During quail season, an Atlanta journalist met an old farmer hunting with an old hunting dog at his side. Twice the old dog ran out ahead with difficulty and pointed. And twice the old farmer shot into the air. When the journalist saw no birds arising, he asked the farmer why he shot. "Shucks," said the farmer, "I knew there weren't any birds in that grass, but Spot's nose ain't what it used to be. We've had some good times, me and him, over the years and it'd be pretty mean of me to call him a liar at this stage of the game."

I guess you might say that the shots were a "sacrifice of praise" from the farmer to his dog for all the hunting they had done together. By the same token, the cloaks the people laid on the ground when Jesus made his triumphant return into Jerusalem was sort of the same thing. They probably had no cloaks to spare but, at that point, their desire to praise him was more important.

And so that brings us to the place where we consider what might be considered such from us. In other words, what do we do or what have we done that will cost (or has cost) us sacrificially in praising God? In some cases, it might mean loss of friends, or loss of respect. But it must mean something to give up whatever it is or was. The point is, Jesus must be first in our life.

A legend is told that a small village in Spain decided to honor a visit by their king by each donating a cup of their best wine for the king to drink. So, the people lined up to pour their cup in. When the king came and tasted it, however, it was almost like water. Everyone withheld their best, thinking that the king would never know the difference.

Well, friends, we have a king who knows the difference-who knows who has given their best or not. And based on what he discovers, it will either be, "well done" or "depart from me." Which would you prefer?

Lessons on Sacrifice - Part 2 of 7

Text: Matthew 2:1-12

Key verse: Matthew 2:2b "…, we saw his star when it rose and have come to worship him."

The Butterball Turkey company had set up a telephone call–in service to help customers with questions about preparing their holiday turkeys. And so, a lady called and asked if a turkey that she had in her freezer for 20 years would still be ok to eat. The expert taking the call advised that it would probably be safe to eat if the freezer had been kept at 0 degrees all that time but added that the taste may have deteriorated some and wouldn't advise eating it. "That's what we thought, so we'll just give it to the church."

Clearly, this was no sacrifice. A sacrifice cannot be a sacrifice unless it costs you something. That's why people often give God what's left instead of what's right. In today's lesson, however, the 3 wise men make a big sacrifice to come and worship the baby Jesus.

This sacrifice had many aspects in terms of time and money spent, being away from their families and friends, risking their safety from robbers and the like along the way and the gifts they brought the Christ child. God permitted them additional aid by warning them in a dream to return a different way than how they came.

Yet, as with many sacrifices, they felt that the reward far outweighed the costs and willingly withstood the trip and its hardships. Their life's work was in studying the stars and had never seen anything like the "Star of Bethlehem."

Two businessmen were taking a tour of Korea after WW2 and remarked about a boy plowing a field without an ox. The missionary guiding the tour explained: that family did have an ox, but when they were asked to help build a church, they sold it. "What a sacrifice! "Exclaimed the tourists. "They didn't see it as such", explained the guide, "They considered themselves grateful that they had an ox to give." Such is the attitude that accompanies sacrificial giving, and such was the attitude of the 3 wise men.

Lessons on Sacrifice - Part 3 of 7

Text and key verse: Malachi 3:10a "bring all the tithes into the storehouse,..."

Two young women were talking. The one says, "I heard you broke your engagement to Joe. What happened?" "I just don't feel the same towards him as I did." "Does that mean that you'll be returning his ring?" "Oh no, "she said, "my feelings toward the ring haven't changed at all!"

When it comes to material goods, some people want to hang on to all they have. But this feeling runs counter to the scripture lesson for today- for in this scripture, everyone is urged to test God's promise to bless by giving the tenth of their goods to the church.

It has been said that in most churches that 20% of the people give 80% of the offering. Unfortunately, that 20% is not often the 20% who are most able to give. The problem is we all want God's best, but too many want to give God what's left instead of what's right. What's right, though, is not stated ambiguously. God says a tenth.

This is not a new problem- this doing for God what they thought best. Jesus criticized the religious leaders of the day because they just wanted to follow rules rather than respond to God out of love. But people today want to make up their own rules. They think if they tithe that it will leave less for them to live on. What this reasoning really reflects, however, is a lack of trust that God will do his part.

What I think needs to happen is for everyone to adopt a team attitude toward the work of the church-to realize that we all have a part to play. Such was the attitude of the New Testament church after the introduction of the Holy Spirit. But the attitudes of the church leaders are crucial in this. People must see that there are no separate rules for them and the leaders. Everyone must get "On the same page." Yet such teamwork takes time to build.

When the Niagara Falls suspension bridge was first built, a kite was used to place a thin line across the expanse. Then that line was used to send a rope across, then a heavier rope, then a cable and finally a cable strong enough to support a bridge. A journey of a thousand miles begins with a single step.

Lessons on Sacrifice - Part 4 of 7

Text and key verse: James 4:4b "Don't you know that friendship with the world makes you an enemy of God?"

The early Roman navy used men to row their ships into battle and so these men had it particularly hard when greater speed was called for. One evening the man who beat cadence for the rowers declared that these rowers were going to be served a sumptuous meal and be allowed to take it easy for a while. But after their rest, the captain wanted to water ski.

Today's scripture talks about being an enemy of God. What I think about in that respect is losing touch with people who are struggling. I think it means withholding help when offering that help is both possible and needed. And I think that it is turning our back to the love of God for us by refusing to be in relationship with God-to reject the gift of grace that is Jesus Christ.

In the parable of the good Samaritan, a priest and a Levite went by without helping. Why the hurry to pass the victim by? An important meeting? The possibility of greater involvement? Or getting one's hands and clothes dirty? I submit that such influences are those presented by the world.

But how should it be? We have the example of the good Samaritan, but we also have real-world examples, as well. A group of salesmen had gone to a regional sales conference in Chicago and were in a hurry to get home to their families. In their haste to get to the bus taking them to the airport, somebody knocked over a table of apples that a blind girl was trying to sell. The apples were knocked every which way, and she couldn't see to pick up them all. All the salesmen but one got on their bus. The one who stayed back, told the others to call his wife and let her know that he would take the next available flight while he helped the girl re-set her table. As he helped, he could not help but notice that some of the apples had been gouged and bruised in the mishap and so he put them in a separate bag and gave her $20 for them. As he began to leave, she called out to him, "Mister, are you Jesus?" Now whose friend, was he?

Lessons on Sacrifice - Part 5 of 7

Text: Luke 23:50-53

Key verse: Luke 23:52b "…, he asked for Jesus' body."

The city editor had just been informed that a wire had fallen across main street in a storm, so he called in his 2 youngest reporters. "No one knows if the wire is live or not, "the editor said. "So, I want one of you to touch it and the other to write the story."

Not an auspicious start to their career, was it? And why would he call in his 2 youngest, if not for the possibility that one might be just foolish enough to take a chance? In any event, bravery is knowing the risks involved and doing it anyway. Such was the case of Joseph of Arimathea, a member of the religious council. In asking for the body of Jesus, he was taking a chance that such an action would alienate him from a group that some people had probably worked their whole lives to be a part of. Yet it was a sacrifice that he was willing to make.

That brings us to a very relevant question as it relates to our faith; what would we be willing to sacrifice for what we believe? For the nominal believer, they might not be able to answer that question because they would not be able to count the cost. But for those of us who have experienced the "more abundant life", this is a question that each of us must be able and willing to answer.

In the movie, "Saving Private Ryan", Captain Miller questions the wisdom of sending out a squad of men to bring back the Ryan family's last son. Yet, he does his duty to the best of his ability. In his last scene in the movie, when he has taken a mortal wound, he tells Ryan to be worth it-to live a life worthy of the sacrifices made on his behalf.

In my mind, Jesus asks us to do the same: to live a life worthy of his sacrifice. What is a worthy life? That depends on our gifts and graces and the opportunities we are given, along with the handicaps we are called on to overcome. So, it remains a question that only we can answer. The only thing I know for sure is we will hear the question again.

Lessons on Sacrifice - Part 6 of 7

Text: Matthew 10:27-28

Key verse: Matthew 10:28a "Do not be afraid of those who kill the body but cannot kill the soul…"

Two men were talking over coffee one day. One said, "I'm concerned about my wife lately as she seems to be talking to herself a lot." "Mine does, too," the other man said, "but she doesn't know it yet. She thinks I'm listening."

Today's lesson is not only about listening but also about telling. Specifically, the lesson tells us to be bold in our personal evangelism-to not be afraid of those who could kill us for doing so. Clearly, it is a "call to arms" for all Christians, as the time for "sitting on the fence" is over. We must reveal our true colors-which could be a great sacrifice for some.

But the sacrifice we make can be the means by which some people can be saved from eternal death in hell. This is what really must be feared-and not just for the people we care about. God doesn't want to lose anybody.

Eva Hart remembers the night of April 15th, 1912. It was the night the Titanic sank. Yet what she remembers most was the cries of drowning people. Although 25 lifeboats had been launched, most of them were only partially filled- the people in them being afraid that too many drowning people would swamp their boat. As a result, most of them rowed a way away while one after another struggling floater froze in the icy water and sank.

In effect, we are safe in the lifeboat that is Jesus and those who are floating around us are those who have not responded to his call. However, our lifeboat will not get swamped-it will not sink, regardless of the ones we can get in. The only difference is that the floaters do not know the danger they are in. They must be warned and given the opportunity to get in. When it is put that way, how can we do anything less?

Lessons on Sacrifice - Part 7 of 7

Text: Luke 9:23-25

Key verse: Luke 9:23 "Whoever wants to be my disciple must deny themselves and take up their cross daily and follow me."

A man's foot got caught in some railroad tracks as he was walking on them one day. Try as he might, he just couldn't dislodge his foot. But it really started to bother him when he heard a train whistle off in the distance. So, he began to pray: "Lord, if you help me, I'll stop drinking." Yet he remained stuck as the train whistle sounded closer. "Lord, if you help me, I'll stop drinking and cussing." Still nothing. So he really got serious: "Lord, you've got to help me now. And if you do, I'll stop drinking, cussing and give all my money to the poor." Then, suddenly, his foot came loose, and he tumbled down from the tracks. "Thanks anyway, Lord, "he said, "I took care of it myself."

No need to make a sacrifice if it isn't on the line, right? In today's scripture, however, Jesus tells us all that we must sacrifice if we really are serious about being a Christian. So, what, then, does that entail?

Self-denial means our putting an end to striving after what the world deems necessary- to find contentment in our daily bread. But it could mean much more than that, if the Lord places that "on our plate." During the Civil War, conscription was not absolute. So, a person could take another person's place if they so desired. Thus, a farmer by the name of Blake got drafted. But his neighbor, by the name of Durham, took his place because Blake had a family, and he did not. Sadly, Durham got killed in the first battle in which he fought.

Taking up one's cross means that we must face the rejection of the world because we are not "of it". In most cases this will happen in stages, but it will happen. The closest thing in our country to that happening transpired with the returning veterans of the Vietnam war. Since it was an unpopular war, many people took their frustrations out on the returning servicemen- calling them names, spitting on them, etc.

Yet, for Christians today, stage 1 has already arrived, and it's best seen in the media depictions of those running for elected office. And it will get worse.

REFLECTIONS

Salvation

My guess is, what with people's focus on worldly matters, that many people don't understand salvation or the need for it today. Simply stated, we all have a sin nature which causes us to live just the way we want instead of the way God wants. Unfortunately, God's standard is perfection so no one can make themselves right with God in and of themselves. That's what the Bible means when it says in Romans 3:23 that all have sinned and come short of the glory of God. Left in that condition, we would go to hell when we die as punishment for our sins. That's what the Bible means when it says in Romans 6;23 that the wage of sin is death. And that's why we need to saved.

The good news is that God loves us too much to leave us in that condition and has provided the only acceptable sacrifice for our sin-his son Jesus Christ. The reason Jesus was acceptable was because he had no sin. When He was crucified, he took on our sins and paid the penalty. When we accept his payment for our sin, we inherit his righteousness and are thus welcomed into heaven when we die just as if we ourselves had never sinned.

Lessons on Salvation - Part 1 of 7

Text: Luke 18:18-23

Key verse: Luke 18:18 "…, good teacher, what must i do to inherit eternal life?"

The Browns were proud of their ancestral heritage and wanted to have a family history compiled. The only problem was with Uncle George, who was executed in the electric chair. So, when they made arrangements with the person doing the work, they expressed their concern with how that part of the family history would be handled. The person said that he was sure he could do it to their satisfaction and so they gave him permission to go ahead. When history came out, they were indeed happy to see that Uncle George was depicted this way; "George Brown occupied a chair of applied electronics at an important government institution and was attached to his position by the strongest of ties. His death, then, came as a great shock to all who knew him."

I guess you might say that he came out much better than his record would indicate. And I would also guess that we would hope for that as well. In today's scripture lesson, known as the story of the rich, young ruler, the young man hoped that his record of works would gain him his desired end. What Jesus says, however, tells us that our priorities must be different than that.

In the story, the young man hoped that his keeping of the law would get him in. Yet even he suspected that that was not enough. And he was right! It is not only keeping the law but keeping our priorities right that counts. And those priorities are made by the attitude of the heart.

The great baseball player, Pete Rose, has done more than most baseball players to get into the Baseball Hall of Fame. Yet he will always be denied entrance because of gambling on the outcome of games. He put himself above the law.

By the same token, rule-following by itself will not get us into the kingdom of heaven. Our hearts must be in the right place. Pete Rose put his own self-interest above the game. The rich young ruler put his love of money above the kingdom of heaven.

Lessons on Salvation - Part 2 of 7

Text: Luke 23:32-43

Key verse: Luke 23:43 "…, today you will be with me in paradise."

A man and his wife were returning to their seats at the theatre when the husband stopped at the end of one of the rows. "Did I step on your toe as we were going out?", he asked the man at the end of the row. "You certainly did!", replied to the man, expecting an apology. The husband then said to his wife, "Hey honey, this is our row!"

Unfortunately, this tends to happen much more frequently these days, with so little consideration given to others. But this was not Jesus' way. He was considerate even up to the very last-asking John to care for his mother, and in today's scripture, where he assures a thief of his salvation.

Obviously, God's sending of Jesus to the cross was the epitome of consideration for us. Without that, we'd have no hope of heaven. And so we see that forgiveness lies at the crux of the concept of salvation. That is, when we recognize that we have sinned and accept Jesus' sacrificial death as our own, we are saying "Please forgive me", and God replies, "You are forgiven!"

There is no better example of forgiveness than God and Jesus, but the world needs to see it in us before they look for its source. Indeed, when they do, they realize that although forgiveness doesn't change the past, it sure enlarges the future. And one person who enlarged the future for us was Thomas Edison. When he and his staff were working on the incandescent light, it took hundreds of hours to make even one bulb. So, one day, after finally making one, Edison gave it to a young errand boy to take up the steps to the testing lab. But the boy tripped going up the steps and the bulb smashed to pieces. Edison didn't yell at the boy as we would expect, but simply stated that it was an accident and got his staff to work on the next one. When it was finished several days later, Edison confidently gave the bulb to the same errand boy to take to the testing lab.

Isn't this the type of forgiveness we seek? And isn't this the kind of consideration that the world needs to have modeled?

Lessons on Salvation - Part 3 of 7

Text: John 4:1-26, 38-42

Key verse: John 4:39 "Many of the Samaritans from that town believed in him because of the woman's testimony,"

A Russian couple was walking down the street when the man said he felt a drop of rain. The woman disagreed, saying it was not rain but snow. The couple went back and forth for a while on this when the man said, "Let's not argue. We'll just ask this communist official coming down the street to settle it for us." So, the man stopped him and asked, "Comrade, which is it, rain or snow?" The official, named Rudolph, said, "It's rain, of course." After he departed, the woman still maintained that she was right, to which the man said, "Rudolph, the red, knows rain, dear."

Often times, it takes a stranger to give us the perspective we need to make a change. Such was the case for the woman at the well, in today's lesson.

But there are other things that we should notice about this interaction. Jesus did not pre-judge this woman because she was a Samaritan or because she was living with a man who was not her husband. She was simply a human being in need of salvation. And because of how he treated her, she went and told others of what she experienced. This is the essence of witnessing-to share good news with others.

Even so, it isn't always our words that influence. It's our actions, as well. Bill was saved at a downtown mission. Prior to this, he was considered a hopeless alcoholic. But when he got saved, he became an entirely different person. There was no job at the mission that he would refuse to do-even if it required cleaning toilets or cleaning up after sick drunkards. This example did not go unnoticed among the downtrodden clientele there. So, one night, after the evangelistic sermon, a homeless guy came forward to repent his sins and be changed. The whole time at the altar, he cried, "Lord, make me like Bill, make me like Bill. "The chaplain there came close and suggested that this man ask God if he could become like Jesus. And the man looked at the chaplain and asked, "Is he like Bill?"

Lessons on Salvation - Part 4 of 7

Text: John 8:1-11

Key verse: John 8:11b "…, neither do I condemn you; go and sin no more."

A woman dies and appears before St. Peter at the pearly gates. She asks how she can get in and he tells her that she has to spell a word. "Which word?", she asks. "Llove", St. Peter replies. She spells it correctly and comes in. About 6 months later, St. Peter asks her to man the gate for a short while as he had some other tasks to do. So, while she's there, her husband from their life on earth appears before her and she asks him how he had made out after her passing. "Quite well, actually", he said. "I married the nurse that took care of you. Then I won the lottery and I sold our little house and bought a mansion in that part of town that you always liked. Then, with the rest of the money, we travelled all over the world. It was on one of those trips that I had the skiing accident that brought me here. But enough about me; how do I get in?" "You have to spell a word." "What word?", he asks. "Czechoslovakia."

You know, some people would be ok with that-with spelling a word to get into heaven. But obviously, that's not a requirement. The requirement is much closer to something she didn't show forgiveness for-the theme of today's scripture lesson.

The religious leaders of Jesus' day thought they had him now. They brought a woman before him who had been caught in the act of adultery. They were hoping to expose him as a hypocrite who didn't support the law of Moses, which called for her to be stoned. Instead, he turns the tables on them, advising that the one of them who was without sin be the one to cast the first stone. Convicted by his words, they all left the scene quietly, without condemning her.

Jesus thus showed the true essence of salvation in his act of mercy. The only requirement, then, was for the woman to accept the gift-which brings us to the dilemma we, as Christians, face today. In Christ's sacrificial death at Calvary, we have the means for obtaining the salvation we so sorely need. But without accepting this gift, the act in and of itself cannot be applied.

Lessons on Salvation - Part 5 of 7

Text: James 4:13-14

Key verse: James 4:14a "How do you know what is going to happen tomorrow?"

A guy hadn't been feeling well and went to see his doctor, who conducted a series of tests. About a week later, the doctor's office called to advise him to come back as soon as possible. When he came in, the doctor sat him down and said, "I have bad news and I have worse news. Which do you want to hear first?" "I guess the bad news", he said. "We've identified that you have a rare health condition and cannot give you more than 24 hours to live." "That's the bad news? That's the bad news?", the gut blustered. "I can never get my affairs in order in that short a time. Yet you say there's worse news? What could be worse than what you just told me?" "Well, I had this information yesterday, and forgot to call you."

In today's scripture, James warns us that we can never be sure what will happen tomorrow. Therefore, in things that are important, we need to take care of them right now. This is especially so in our salvation. Other scripture supports this view as well: 2 Corinthians 6:2 states, "Now is the accepted time; behold, now is the day of salvation".

A sign at a nursery proclaimed, "The best time to plant a tree was 15 years ago". But there was a second sign hanging close to the first, which said, "but the second-best time is today." Again, this is especially true with our salvation: the best time to have accepted Jesus Christ as our savior was years ago. But the second-best time is today.

The problem, of course, is that we all think we have more time. And this is one of Satan's most effective lies. As long as we feel we have more time, we will put off everything we can, as long as we can. But salvation is not one of those things.

Lessons on Salvation - Part 6 of 7

Text: Luke 13:1-9

Key verse: Luke 13:5b "But unless you repent, you too will all perish."

At a monastery perched high on a cliff, one could visit only by means of a rope basket that was raised and lowered by means of monks handling the pulley system. One day, as a visitor was being pulled up, he noticed that the ropes were beginning to fray. So, he asked one of the brothers there how often they changed the ropes. And he replied, "Whenever it breaks."

In today's scripture lesson, Jesus explains that there is little certainty in length of life but great certainty in going to hell without confession of sin. The emphasis, then, he placed was, I believe, in salvation. And that is supported by the pronouncement of Peter in 2 Peter 3:9 that says that God is unwilling that any should perish but that all come to repentance.

Even so, people continue to live their lives as if tomorrow was a certainty. That is, until something occurs close to home that changes that thinking. For the novelist, Dostoevsky, going before a firing squad completely altered his outlook. You see, the czar had had him arrested and sentenced to die as a political prisoner. But the czar often did this to people who did not support him. However, in the case of Dostoevsky, he just wanted to scare him and had blanks issued to the firing squad. But what the czar hoped would destroy Dostoevsky's Spirit, enlivened him-allowing him to look at the gift of life in a whole new way. Dostoevsky now became more thankful and loving, even to people he had previously hated.

Such should be our outlook as well since we too have been saved from eternal death to everlasting life in Jesus Christ. As Christians, then, we need to make this salvation more real to those who don't believe to give them the change in perspective they need.

Lessons on Salvation - Part 7 of 7

Text: Luke 15:3-7

Key verse: Luke 15:4 "Suppose one of you has a hundred sheep and loses one of them. Doesn't he leave the ninety-nine in the open country and go after the lost sheep until he finds it?"

An umpire was stopped for speeding but pleaded with the policeman for leniency as the ticket would cause his insurance to go up. The policeman, however, was relentless, saying that he could take it to court if he didn't like it. A few months later, at a softball game he was umpiring, this same policeman came up to bat. They recognized one another, so the policeman asked how things went with the ticket- to which the umpire said, "You'd better swing at everything!"

My guess is that most people fail to realize how much God wants us to come to salvation and how relentless he is about it. Thus, we have the parable of the lost sheep that the shepherd goes out to find. Yet we too know something about relentlessness. Because of our sinful nature, we often times are relentless in holding on to our sinful ways. It's just that God is much more so about bringing us back.

CS Lewis once wrote, "(his) love is not wearied by our sins or our indifference,", so he is not about to give up like we might be inclined to do. And we see it in the lives of such people as John Newton and Francis Thompson. Each of these men were held in bondage by sin that they, of themselves, were powerless to overcome. Newton was a slave trader and Thompson an addict of drugs and alcohol, yet each found his way back through the relentless wooing of God's love, and each has left a lasting testament of that experience in their works-Newton in "Amazing Grace" and Thompson in "The Hound of Heaven". As God is no respecter of persons, he is perfectly willing to do the same for us.

REFLECTIONS

Satan

Satan or the devil has, for most of my lifetime, been jokingly characterized as a mythical being whose job it was to get us into trouble-as in "the devil made me do it", and the like. Yet for those of us who are not satisfied with this description and are willing to look further, the devil is a very real being. Originally, this being was an archangel in Heaven with many God-given powers. Yet when he decided that he should be like the highest, he was thrown out of Heaven along with the other angels who sided with him. Since then, he has made it his mission to bring God's creation to ruination, or, failing that, to substitute his creation for God's. He continually plays on our sin nature, then condemns us before God. He continually requests that God put his human creatures to the test by causing us pain. Jesus called him a liar and the father of lies, as well as a lion who prowls around, seeking whom he may destroy. He tried to tempt Jesus into serving him, but to no avail. And he does the same with each of us. The Bible teaches, however, that there will come a comeuppance for this creature and his servants-a lake of fire and everlasting punishment.

Lessons on Satan - Part 1 of 7

Text and key verse: Mark 4:15b "When the word is scattered and people hear it, right away Satan comes and steals the word that was planted in them."

A priest who had served the congregation for 25 years was being honored by that church and a leading politician and member of the congregation was asked to make the presentation. However, the politician was late, so the priest told a little story to fill in the time. "When I was first assigned to this parish, I did not know what I was getting into by the sounds of the first confession I heard: the man said that he stole a tv set but lied to get away with it. Then he said he stole money from his parents, embezzled money from his employer, had an affair with his best friend's wife and was doing drugs. Luckily, I found that not everyone was like that." Then, suddenly, the politician burst on the scene with many apologies and began his talk this way: "I'll never forget the first day our priest arrived. As a matter of fact, I had the honor of being the first confession he heard."

Obviously, the politician had had the word stolen from him. Even so, he was not the first or will be the last as this is part of what Satan does. He preys on people who don't have or have never developed any depth to their faith. Indeed, when a person first comes to God, they are in a very vulnerable position. That's why evangelists such as Billy Graham would always emphasize the need for new Christians to get involved with a Bible-believing church.

But throughout history, we can see examples of this word-stealing. It causes people-even whole countries- to forget the source of their blessing. In 1923, Japan suffered a terrible hurricane that caused widespread devastation. But the United States stepped up through the Red Cross and donated some $10 million in food, clothing, volunteers and medical supplies to help meet the need. Japan was grateful and said that they would never forget. Yet, some 18 years later, they launched a devastating attack on Pearl Harbor.

As Christians, we can never afford such lapses of memory. Without the sacrifice of Jesus, we would all be lost.

Lessons on Satan - Part 2 of 7

Text and key verse: Luke 22:31 "And the Lord said, "Simon, Simon, behold, Satan hath desired to have you, to sift you as wheat."

A sentry on guard duty had strict orders to shoot anyone without a special windshield sticker. So, as fate would have it, a big army car pulled into the gate and the sentry asked, "Who goes there?" The chauffeur, a corporal, said, "General Wheeler!" The sentry replied, "That may well be, but my orders are to shoot anyone who tries to drive thru without a special sticker!" From the back seat, the general says, "Drive on!" The sentry though refused to open the gate, preferring instead to walk to the rear window of the car and say this: "General, I'm new at this. Do I shoot you or the driver?"

We can be sure that there will be times, like with Peter in today's lesson or the sentry, when Satan desires to sift us. I remember when my mother sifted flour when I was young, but I never looked at it from the standpoint of the flour. The metal sifter would be drawn over and over again over the flour until it went through the mesh screen- probably not a pleasant thing, if the flour could talk.

I'm not sure what our sifting will look like, but for Peter, I believe it was his impulsiveness. When we look at his part in the gospel accounts, he is usually quick to talk but not always faithful in following through. And because of what his role would become in the church, my guess is that that part needed to be sifred. No doubt, it is the same for us.

In one 11-year-old's life, it went this way: he would go along when his dad went to the neighborhoods surrounding his dad's church to hand out gospel tracks. In any event, on this one Saturday, it was raining, and his dad said he didn't have to go. But he went by himself because he felt led to do so. As usual, there were more lows than highs, and he didn't think that what he did made much difference. That is, until one elderly lady gave her testimony: when the pastor's boy came to my door, I was about to commit suicide as I was depressed after the death of my husband. But when I saw that he was drenched, yet faithful in giving me a trak about God's love, I had to see what that church was about.

Lessons on Satan - Part 3 of 7

Text: 1 Kings 17:7-16

Key verse: 1 Kings 17:12b "I am gathering a few sticks to take home and make a meal foe me and my son- that we may eat it and die."

A woman, while visiting at a friend's farm, encountered a pig with a wooden leg and inquired about it. The farmer answered, "That's our pig, Betsy. She's a real lifesaver." Then he went on to explain that it was Betsy whose oinking saved the family during a fire and their daughter from drowning. "But that doesn't explain why she has a wooden leg." "But it does, "he said. When you have a pig that good, you don't want to eat it all at the same time."

The farmer could appreciate the pig- just not enough to keep from eating it. Similarly, when the devil thinks he has us "over a barrel", he's not satisfied until he finishes the job.

In today's lesson, the widow thinks her life and that of her son is nearly over. But regardless of what God through Elijah does, she still holds on to her worst fears. That is Satan's handiwork, although he, himself, is never mentioned. Even though she sees that her meal and oil is never totally depleted, she refuses to believe that she is experiencing a miracle.

Similarly, when God does the miraculous, many people are perfectly willing to "chalk it up" to luck or some such thing. Or they believe that God is not powerful enough to solve their problem-that he cannot make a difference. This is why Jesus often said, "O ye of little faith."

Thus, it is clear as to our course of action. We must point out to unbelievers when something is the work of God. If they don't believe what their eyes tell them, we must use ours to help them.

A story is told of an old man tossing starfish stranded on the seashore back into the ocean. A young man, watching him work, remarked that however many he tossed back in, it would never make a difference. To which he replied, as he tossed one in, "It made a difference to that one!" Similarly, saving even one from Satan, is important.

Lessons on Satan - Part 4 of 7

Text and key verse: 2 Corinthians 11:14 "and no marvel; for Satan himself is transformed into an angel of light."

A woman bought a dress that her husband thought too extravagant and asked her why she bought it. She replied that "The devil made me do it." He replied, "Why didn't you say, "Get thee behind me, Satan"? Then she said, "I did, but when he got behind me, he said it looks just as good in the back as in the front."

In today's lesson, the apostle Paul is defending himself concerning the false teachers who have infiltrated the Corinthian church that Paul had founded. It would appear that they have condemned Paul and his teaching, substituting false doctrine for true.in representing themselves as apostles, Paul compares them to Satan, who has at times represented himself as an angel of light in order to mislead.

This is an important aspect of Satan's work that we must be careful not to miss. Because someone seems to be wise and good does not always mean that they are that which they appear to be. The Bible refers to them as wolves in sheep's clothing.

After Lee's surrender at Appomattox, Jefferson Davis, the President of the Confederacy, was in grave danger. So, he tried to escape to Florida. But he was captured before getting there, dressed in a woman's overcoat and shawl.

Yet, even so, just the opposite may be the case. A few years ago, a United Methodist pastor dressed up as a homeless man and sat on the church's front steps on a Sunday morning. To prepare for this event, the pastor had not shaved in a week, he wore old, mud-riddled, beer-soaked clothes and wore a broken pair of glasses and a scraggly old wig. As the parishioners approached, they did not recognize their pastor and did not offer to help him in any way. But when he walked up to the front of the church and removed his wig and broken glasses, they were convicted by their neglect of him and their unwillingness to help one of the "least of these". We, therefore, must pray for God's discernment.

Lessons on Satan - Part 5 of 6

Text: Acts 10:28-35

Key verse: Acts 10:28b "But God has shown me that i should not call anyone unpure or unclean."

A United Methodist 3rd grade Sunday School teacher had a pair of twin girls in her class that attended faithfully. They came from a poor family and dressed in rather worn and out-of-date clothes. So, feeling sorry for them, she raised some money and bought them 2 new dresses. The next Sunday, however, the girls did not appear and so the teacher called to find out if they were ok. The mother explained that they were fine but that they looked so nice in their new dresses that she sent them to the Presbyterian church, instead.

Prejudices apparently come in all shapes and sizes. And although we may come by them naturally, there is no reason to hold on to them when evidence is seen to the contrary- no reason, that is, unless the devil has blinded us to the truth.

In today's scripture lesson, Peter has held on to his prejudice against gentiles until God, in a vision, has helped him to see the error of his ways. Freed from his misconception, then, he preaches to the household of Cornelius, gaining new followers to the kingdom of God.

I believe God continues to work against prejudices even now although his methods are completely unpredictable. The question then becomes: are we willing to listen? In the early part of 1962, you probably would be hard-pressed to find a bigger racist than the Governor of Alabama, George Wallace. But in May of 1972, he was shot 5 times, leaving him paralyzed and wheelchair –bound. During his recuperation, he had time to think and came to the conclusion that he had himself caused much pain. And so, one evening as he was being driven home, he had himself wheeled in to Dr. Martin Luther King Jr.'s old church during worship and asked the assembled congregation for their forgiveness. Clearly, God had worked in his life through a terrible tragedy, but it doesn't have to be that way for us- knowing that God is no respecter of persons.

Lessons on Satan - Part 6 of 7

Text: Jonah 3:3-4:1

Key verse: Jonah 4:1 "But to Jonah this seemed very wrong, and he was angry."

After the Sunday service, Mary came up to the pastor with tears running down her cheeks. "Pastor, my husband passed away last night." "Mary, that's terrible!", the pastor replied. "But did he have any final requests?" "Yes, he said, "Mary, please put down that gun!"

Certainly, that's one way to deal with our resentments. But it is not God's way. And we see that in the way Jonah reacts to the compassion of God toward Nineveh. In the story, we know that Jonah has been spared by God from the belly of a great fish so that he can deliver a message of destruction to Nineveh. What he didn't expect, however, was for Ninevah to repent of their sins and God to forgive them. When that happens, Jonah pouts and fails to heed God once again.

He could not get over his resentment. But we must if we hope to give our best service to God. Charlotte Elliot, the writer of the hymn "Just as I am, Without One Plea", had to learn this the hard way. Born an invalid, she greatly resented the constraints that her disability put on her service to God. And this resentment was made greater by her jealousy of her brother, who was actively serving as a clergyman.

Clearly, resentment is a useful tool in the devil's hand, and is made even more damaging when compounded by comparisons with others. But our ability to turn our resentments over to God little-by-little can help us, like Charlotte Elliot, to overcome. In time, she came to see that the hymn she wrote was her service to God and became less upset with her brother. Indeed, later in life, the brother lamented that his lifelong ministry fell short of the impact of his sister's famous hymn. At last, she realized that she could not get better as long as she was bitter.

Lessons on Satan - Part 7 of 7

Text: Luke 12:19-21

Key verse: Psalm 90:12 "So teach us to number our days that we may get a heart of wisdom."

When Danny, the 3-year-old grandson, was visiting his grandparents, grace was said before they ate. Yet Danny wasn't sure what that was about but that it was important to take the time to do. So, when his parents came to pick him up and share a meal together, Danny stopped his dad from eating his sandwich until grandpa could read his plate.

Unfortunately, many people today are too much in a hurry to "read their plates". Yet, when it comes to the things of God, they feel they've got all the time in the world. This is one of Satan's worst lies and is reflected in the text story, "The parable of the rich fool". In this story, a farmer has such a productive harvest that he doesn't know what to do with it all. The problem comes with his solution, which is to build bigger barns to store it all rather than to be considerate of those who had too little.

The lesson for us, then, seems to be that we need to do what we can for others while we can or to accept Jesus as savior while we still have the chance. The reason is because we cannot be sure how much more time we have. Time is, indeed, of the essence. That's why scripture admonishes us that "now is the accepted time; now is our salvation closer to us than ever before."

We cannot be like the guy who had a leak in one of his tires. He noticed while it was in his garage-where his air compressor was available. But he decided that he could get away with filling it later only to have it go flat on a lonely, deserted highway late at night.

The end of the parable reveals God's words to the rich fool: "Thou fool, this night will thy soul be required of thee. Then who will get what you have prepared for yourself?" Let this not be God's words for us!

REFLECTIONS

Sin

Sin is a falling short of God's standard-which is perfection. As none of us will ever be perfect, we have a problem if we want to earn God's approval on our own.

But God took care of our problem by having his perfect son take the punishment that our sin deserved. Thus, in accepting his sacrifice, we meet God's standard.

The devil, however, tries to get us to reject the Lordship and thus the sacrifice of Jesus so that we will, because of our sin nature, try to earn God's approval on our own. Thankfully, though, God has also provided us with the help we need to thwart the devil's plans. This help is the Holy Spirit, which resides within us to give us the power and courage to resist the devil.

Thus, sin does not have to be our undoing. If we confess our sin, God is faithful and just to forgive us our sin and cleanse us from all unrighteousness.

Lessons on Sin - Part 1 of 7

Text: Genesis 3:1-9

Key verse: Genesis 3:4 "You will not certainly die,…"

In an imaginary discussion held between God and Adam, God suggested the perfect companion for Adam. He said she would be intelligent, sensitive, caring and beautiful. And she would be able to sense his needs before he did and meet them. But, he said, that such a creature would cost him an arm and a leg-to which Adam reportedly answered, "What can I get for a rib?" It is important to begin our consideration of sin where it started-in the garden of Eden. The essence of Adam and Eve's original sin was in thinking that they knew better than God did about what was best for them- sort of like Adam's fictitious negotiation over Eve's value. It was unquestionably a yielding to temptation. Yet at its source was a lack of faith and a desire to retain control.

Consider, if you will, the possible end results of such a rigid mindset : In the summer of 1986, two ships collided in the Black Sea off the coast of Russia. Hundreds of passengers died as they were hurled into the icy waters below. News of the disaster was further darkened when an investigation revealed the cause of the accident. It wasn't a technology problem like radar malfunction-or even thick fog. The cause was human stubbornness. Each captain was aware of the other ships' presence nearby. Both could have steered clear, but according to news reports, neither captain wanted to give way to the other. Each was too proud to yield first. By the time they came to their senses, it was too late.

The Bible clearly states that the wage of sin is death. However, the possibility of eternal separation from God in addition to physical death is an even more serious outcome. Thus, because it is possible to realize one's error and not confess it to God before death, we, as Christians, need to gain a sense of urgency re: their dilemma. We must befriend them and gain their confidence so we can be trusted to tell them our faith story. Then, hopefully, they will submit to the Holy Spirit's convicting power and make the decision that will change their final destiny.

Lessons on Sin - Part 2 of 7

Text: Genesis 4:6-9

Key verse: Genesis 4:9c "Am I my brother's keeper?"

A local painter was hired to paint the old church on the hill. He was a good painter but was apt to maximize his profits if he wasn't watched closely. So, he decided to thin the paint he used to save a few dollars. But just before he finished, there was a voice from heaven that boomed, "Repaint! Repaint! And thin no more!"

Not long after the first sin of Adam and Eve, we find that sin was again "Crouching at the door". This time it was for Cain, the son of Adam and Eve. Cain's sacrifice to God had not been accepted while his brother's had, and Cain was angry. Just like the painter, he had not given his best and had been caught. God tried to reason with him-but to no avail as Cain killed Abel.

Sin can sometimes seem worse when it is compared with the righteousness of others. I believe this was the case for Cain, but it did not have to be an excuse. Cain knew what he did wrong and could have easily "fixed it". He just didn't want to do it.

Consider this example: Pastor Hayes were a popular, well-respected pastor in his church, and it seemed to thrive under his leadership. But one day, a rumor was started that intimated that he had an inappropriate relationship with an attractive parishioner. Although it was not true, his effectiveness was damaged, and his wife and son suffered greatly. But the pastor hung in and the rumors died off. However, 8 years later, a former elder confessed that he had started the rumor because he was jealous of the pastor's popularity and scriptural authority. The elder knew it was wrong, but he did it anyway.

So, in effect, we, too, have choices in our behavior. We, too, know right from wrong. But, as Christians, we have to try to be "above reproach" for the sake of our Christian witness. If we depend on God, he will help us and keep us from comparing ourselves with others.

Lessons on Sin - Part 3 of 7

Text and key verse: Exodus 32:9 "I've been watching these people and know how stubborn they are."

A zealous part-time pastor felt that it was his duty to convert all non-believers who rode on his bus. So, when a drunk stumbled onto his bus one day, he pulled off to the side of the road and walked back to where the drunk was sitting and asked him, "Do you know you're headed to hell?" "Oh no, "said the drunk, "Am I on the wrong bus again?"

In today's lesson, God is sick of the stubborn attitude of the Israelites in conforming to his directives. But, at the same time, many well-intentioned Christians can be stubborn in the way they "browbeat" non-believers-turning them off to change. So, it is important for believers and non-believers alike to learn from God's response in this lesson. That is, although God was so fed-up with the Israelites that he was about to destroy them all and start over with just Moses, it was to his credit that he was willing to listen to Moses 'intervention on their part. He was not stubborn.

Yet the real lesson is in why he was not. He loved the people enough to give them another chance. By the same token, if the Christian "browbeaters" acted out of love and the leading of the Holy Spirit rather than a sense of duty, they wouldn't be so inclined to "browbeat".

This point has even wider application, however. Consider the boss's response to the worker who worked 18 hours of overtime to cover for 2 fellow employees who were sick so that he could finish the big report. The next day when he came in, the boss, instead of thanking him for his diligence and loyalty, scolded him for leaving the lights on so long.

Now it is possible to be stubborn about doing the right thing, as long as we are adaptable enough to recognize when we have gone too far. Love for others, then, can serve us as well as it does God. It will help us to stay on the "right" bus.

Lessons on Sin - Part 4 of 7

Text: 2 Samuel 11:1-12:10

Key verse: 2 Samuel 12:7 "You are the man!"

On the last day of his visit to America, the pope was delayed longer than he wanted to be in a meeting and was afraid of missing his flight. So, a limo was called to take him directly to the airport. But when the limo driver learned that it was the pope that he was driving, he drove much slower and more carefully than he ever did, which concerned the pope even more. So, the pope offered to trade places with the limo driver and immediately had the vehicle up to 85 miles per hour. So before long, the limo was pulled over by a cop. But when the cop saw who was driving, he had to call back to the station for clarification. "Chief, I just pulled over a limo for speeding but I'm not sure how to handle it." "What's the problem?" "It's the biggest VIP I've ever stopped." "How big could they be?" "Let's just say the pope is driving him to the airport."

When David was king, he was the biggest human VIP. But that didn't put him above God's laws. And so when Nathan the prophet accused him of adultery and murder, he confessed his guilt but still had to pay the penalty for his sin: the son he had to Uriah's ex-wife, Bathsheba, died.

The nature of God requires justice. But today the price exacted from us has already been paid in the sacrificial death of God's perfect son as long as we confess our sin and turn from it. With out our part, however, our death would be required.

Around 1830, a man by the name of George Wilson was convicted of murder for killing a postal employee. He was sentenced to hang but was pardoned by then President Andrew Jackson. But when Wilson refused the pardon, the Supreme Court had to decide what to do. They decided that without accepting the pardon, Wilson had to die.

There is a lesson for us in this, as well. We have pardon for our sins. But if we don't confess and repent of them, the pardon is revoked.

Lessons on Sin - Part 5 of 7

Text: Luke 18:9-14

Key verse: Luke 18:14b "for all those who exalt themselves will be humbled,…"

A prideful man was walking through the arcade at an old amusement park with his wife when they spotted a coin-operated scale which gave both the person's weight and personality assessment. So, he got on the scale, put a coin in and got a card which gave his weight and this assessment: you are the kind of man that other men look up to and women admire. "Look at this!" he said in giving the card to his wife. "Looks like it got your weight wrong, too," she said.

In today's lesson, the parable of the pharisee and the tax collector, the pharisee thanks God that he is not as sinful as the tax collector, who is at the temple praying next to him. Yet Jesus says that, because of his humility, it was the tax collector who went home justified.

This is a key aspect of our study of the concept of sin: sin is not comparative with God. As Romans 3:23 states, "all have sinned and come short of the kingdom of God." So even 1 sin is too many. Thus, the attitude of the pharisee should have been like that of the tax collector-guilty and condemned.

Unfortunately, too many of us tend to look at sin in comparative terms-as if God graded "on the curve". That's why it is helpful for us to have someone-like the prideful man's wife- to ensure that we have the right perspective.

A man was taking a guided tour of an art museum when he became very interested in a particular picture of the crucifixion of Christ. "Lower!" said the guide to the tourist. "You can't get the artist's artistic intent unless you view the painting on your knees." And so, it is with us: we must approach God in reverence and humility as the price for our sin could never have been paid by our efforts alone.

Lessons on Sin - Part 6 of 7

Text and key verse: Phil. 1:6"…he who began a good work in you will carry it on to completion until the day of Christ Jesus."

A man was driving to work when a truck ran a stop sign, hitting him broadside and knocking him out cold. A passerby pulled him out of the wreck and revived him. But, suddenly, the man in the wreck started to struggle so strongly he had to be sedated. When he came to in the hospital, he was asked why he had struggled so at the scene of the accident. And he said, "I remembered the impact and then nothing until waking up on a cement slab in front of a big, flashing Shell sign but couldn't see the "s"".

Knowing that we have all sinned and come short of the kingdom of God, it would give one a start to think that they had gone to hell. That's why it is so vitally important that we tell the good news of Christ's sacrificial death at Calvary to gain forgiveness of our sin to as many people that we can- so they don't have to live in fear of the unknown.

However, it is also vitally important to know that in spite of how nice we think we are, that without that death, we would all be headed for hell. In other words, we all must come to the conclusion that we are guilty of sin with no way of making ourselves right with God in and of ourselves. It is personal. But so is our salvation.

That said, I know that I will go to heaven in spite of my road rage. It is a sin that is ever before me. But Christ has died for that sin, too. That doesn't mean that I can treat it any less seriously. It only means that it doesn't have to be the death of me as long as i confess it as a sin and try to do better. You see, the Holy Spirit has already given me the insight that my problem is a lack of seeing people on the road as being made in the image of God. Once that realization really hits home, I should begin to make better progress. And the reason I know that is that God has begun a good work in me and will continue it for as long as I live. That, friend, is a promise of God made to all and everyone who believes in him.

Lessons on Sin - Part 7 of 7

Text and key verse; James 2:10 "for whosoever shall keep the whole law and yet offend in just one point, he is guilty of all."

The pastor ended his service by saying that the following week he was going to talk about the sin of lying and that to prepare for this message that everyone should read Mark 17. So, the next week he asked for a show of the hands of those who had done the requested reading, and everyone raised their hand. "Very well,", said the pastor, "since the gospel of Mark only has 16 chapters, this show of hands tells me that the sin of lying will be a very appropriate lesson."

Obviously, no one wanted to seem less religious than their neighbor, so they lied about their Bible reading. But in doing so, they demonstrated the ease by which sin is introduced. They also demonstrated their perception that this small lie was of such a minor nature that they could easily be forgiven. I mean it wasn't like murder or robbery. Yet that's just the point: sin is sin in God's eyes and even the most minor infraction makes us fall short of the kingdom of heaven in our own righteousness.

The fault here is two-fold; that there is a difference between big and little sin and that God judges on a curve. Neither point is correct, which is easily demonstrated by this illustration. An unemployed cleaning lady who lived in St. Louis in 1989 noticed a few bees buzzing around the attic of her home but thought nothing of it. Over the summer, however, more and more bees started to fly in and out of her attic until, unbeknownst to her, her whole attic became a hive. Even so, she did not realize the danger she was in until the ceiling of her second floor caved in under the weight of hundreds of pounds of honey and thousands of angry bees. Although she herself escaped serious injury, her home became unhabitable.

Similarly, when a few minor sins crop up that we think too small to address, we are amazed at how quickly they mount up and how powerful they become when we do finally try to rid ourselves of them. We must not let that happen!

REFLECTIONS

SUFFERING

I cannot say I have a good handle on suffering. I've not had any serious medical or mental condition. I have lost people in my life that I loved, and I've made bad decisions that have caused me and others unnecessary pain- the memory of which still grieves me. In essence, I can say that, unlike some others, that my suffering has not and does not define me. And for that I am most grateful. Perhaps this is because I was not raised that way, or because of the unattractiveness I've seen in others who were or still are defined by their suffering. Conversely, I have encountered and have read about many people who have known suffering who have not let that suffering define them. And so, I believe that to a significant degree suffering, though not avoidable, is not necessarily one's defining aspect. It depends on one's perspective.

Lessons on Suffering - Part 1 of 7

Text: 1 King 19

Key verse: "What are you doing here, Elijah?"

A visitor at a zoo noticed an attendant weeping quietly over in a corner. Concerned about this, they asked another attendant what the problem was. "Oh", said the attendant, "he's crying because of an elephant here that died recently." "He was that attached to it?" "Not really," they replied, "he just has to dig the grave for it."

In today's lesson, Elijah seems to be experiencing deep depression over fear for his life. It was no idle threat as Queen Jezabel had the means and determination to follow through. So, he goes into hiding and asks the Lord to take his life.

The fact that he is a servant of the Lord should not necessarily come as a surprise as depression affects approximately 1 out of 20 people at some point of their life. Yet I believe that God's handling of Elijah bears some attention as God's actions toward Elijah could be relevant in coming up with a plan of treatment.

First, in considering the context of his complaint, God knew that a low point of emotion commonly follows after a high point. In this case, Elijah, with God's help, had defeated the 450 prophets of Baal in a contest to show God's superiority over Baal and put them to death.

Second, God sent an angel to advise Elijah to rest and have something to eat. Again, God knew that many people experience some signs of depression because of a poor diet and lack of sleep.

Third, instead of letting Elijah sit and mope, God gave him a job to do. He knew that activity begets motivation.

Finally, God gave Elijah information that he didn't have before. We, too, often fret over things that have no basis in fact.

Even so, I don't believe God expects us to be mental health experts. We can, however, pray for wisdom and discernment that starts the process of healing and wholeness.

Lessons on Suffering - Part 2 of 7

Text and key verse: Job 1:12 "Very well, then, everything he has in your power, but on the man, himself do not lay a finger."

A woman came to a Methodist minister to conduct a funeral service for her dog. The minister advised her that he didn't do these but that the Baptists might. She told him that she would call the Baptist minister but wanted to check with him on something first. "Do you think that a $10,000 donation to his church would be a sufficient fee for his services?" To that the Methodist minister replied, "Why didn't you say that your dog was a Methodist?"

Apparently, there was a price for whatever service was needed. In this case, the limit was met or exceeded. But in the case of suffering, God clearly sets the limit. Knowing this should ease the pain we experience at least to some extent.

In today's lesson, Satan accuses God of protecting Job from harm so that his Godliness never had to be really tested. So, God allows Satan to test Job but sets the limit as to how far Satan can go.

This brings up a more fundamental question: why does God test us at all? I can only surmise that he tests us to find out what he's working with. If he can't trust us with some difficulties or pain, how can he trust us when souls are on the line? Work is just too important.

Consider the story of Oswald Smith. He wanted to be a missionary more than anything else, but his frail health kept him from being accepted. He could have responded by getting out of the Lord's work as the Lord didn't give him what he wanted. But instead, he said, "If I can't go myself, I'll send someone else." So, he founded the People's Church of Toronto, which established itself as one of the leading missionaries –sending churches in North America.

The other possible part of the reasoning behind God's testing is so that we might be blessed. That is, if he can trust us with the responsibility, then he wants us to share in the reward and that truly reflects his nature-the nature of love.

Lessons on Suffering - Part 3 of 7

Text and key verse; Luke 9:23 "If anyone would come after me, let him deny himself and take up his cross daily and follow me."

Two ladies were waiting at a bus stop, when one turned to the other and noticed what a beautiful diamond ring she was wearing. "Thank you," replied the other, "It is known as the Klopman diamond, but it comes with an awful cross to bear." "What's that?", the lady asked. "Mr. Klopman".

These days, the phrase bearing one's cross is used to mean anything from a small inconvenience to something truly aggravating. But the saying as it was originally meant had to do with a denial of self. Some would even take that to mean a sort of death to self.

Thus, within the context of Jesus' words, we find that he meant that in being one of his followers that our lives were no longer our own but God's. Indeed, when we see how this played out in the lives of the disciples, it required the ultimate sacrifice.

In some countries today, that is still the cost of discipleship. Although that is not the case here, there are still certain tell-tale signs that show we are other-directed. It starts with the Spiritual disciplines like prayer and Bible-reading and reflection. It continues with how we spend our time and the people we associate with as well as how we spend our money. For lack of a better definition, it is being "sold-out" to God.

Evangelist Billy Sunday was a modern-day example of this. He was a good professional baseball player in the late 1800's. But when he got converted, he denounced drinking, swearing and gambling-which was a big turnaround for ballplayers at that time. But then, in time, he became one of the most popular evangelists of the early 1900's.

Of course, there have been many more such turnarounds. The point is, however, that their lives reflected a 180-degree change from the pursuit of selfish desires to God-ordained ones-regardless of personal cost.

Lessons on Suffering - Part 4 of 7

Text: Luke 8 :26-39

Key verse: Luke 8:30 "What is your name? "And he said, "Legion" …"

A man went in to see a psychiatrist, claiming that he had 2 problems. "Ok", said the psychiatrist, "What are they?" "My first problem is that I think that I'm a Pepsi vending machine". So, the doctor went through his usual procedures to try to get to the bottom of the problem but had no success. So, out of frustration, he took out 3 quarters from his pocket and forced them down the man's throat. He then said, "Ok, give me a Pepsi." "That's the other problem, doctor, I can't because I'm out of order."

Probably some of the most difficult cases where there is suffering comes with people who have mental disorders. Because there are no obvious physical problems, the patient has less sympathy from whatever support system is in place. That doesn't mean that the suffering is any less or the pain caused to loved ones is any less severe.

In today's lesson, we encounter a man with a severe mental disorder. We hear that he has supernatural strength that no one can bind him. In fact, the times that has been attempted with chains, he has broken them apart. He cuts himself with sharp stones and wears no clothes. There is no diagnosis given other than that he is demon-possessed. It's interesting to note, I think, that there is little said today about demon-possession- quite possibly because the cure would have to be Spiritual in nature-which the scientific world tends to discredit. In any event, Jesus casts out this man's demons and he is completely cured. In fact, he wants to follow Jesus.

A couple of things stand out for me from this lesson. First and foremost, Jesus can heal anything-even the most maddening mental condition. Second, I was initially surprised that Jesus did not permit this cured man to follow him. Upon further reflection, however, it seemed apparent that the people of the formerly crazy guy's town needed the man's continuing testimony in order to come to faith-that, in time, they would see this healing as a good thing.

Lessons on Suffering - Part 5 of 7

Text: Luke 23:42-43/ John 19:25-27

Key verse: John 19:26b "Woman, behold your son."

An old man lay dying on his bed at home. Yet from the kitchen he smelled something wonderful-it was his favorite chocolate chip cookies. "What a wonderful wife i have, that in my last few hours here on earth, she is showing me her love by making the thing I love to eat the most!" So, marshalling all the strength he still had, he forced himself out of bed and slowly, painfully down the steps toward the source of that wonderful aroma. Finally, he looked at the tray of his beloved cookies and reached out his hand to enjoy just once more this favorite treat when-wham! -he felt the sting of a spatula slapping his hand. "No! -those are for the funeral!"

It's easy to take the man's side in this but his wife is not the only one to withhold something for later when the real blessing could have been appreciated sooner. I guess you might say, at times like this, prioritizing the most important things can get put on the backburner. Be that as it may, Jesus could not be accused of this. In today's lesson, Jesus attends to his mother's and the thief's last needs as he hangs on the cross.

At first glance, it would appear that these 2 people's needs would be at the opposite ends of the spectrum. The need of his mother for a source of care in her widowhood seems so much more important than some thief who he does not know and who has shown himself to be a sinner clearly deserving of judgment. Yet, upon further consideration, his need is more immediate. In a short period of time, this thief was to stand before God himself in his own righteousness, which is sadly lacking.

Thus, in his actions, Jesus shows us what's most important when our time is short-our relationships. And so, knowing this, he provides both direction as well as confidence in our suffering. We know what we must attend to as well as when our need is greatest.

Lessons on Suffering- part 6 of 7

Text: Acts 5:12-42

Key verses: Acts 5:38b, 39 "Let them go. For if their activity is of human origin, it will fail. But if it is of God, you will not be able to stop these men..."

A man's car stalled in heavy traffic just as the light turned green. All his efforts to start his car failed, so, as you can imagine, there began a loud chorus of honking horns. So, the guy gets out of his car and goes back to the car behind him and says, "I'm sorry but my car has stalled, and I can't get it to start. But if you'd like to try, I'll go back to your car and honk your horn for you."

Certainly, there are things other than illness and broken relationships that cause us pain and suffering, but a peaceful attitude can help make our suffering a little easier. In today's scripture, the Jewish Rabbi, Gamaliel, uses a cool head to defuse a dangerous situation when those around him wanted blood. This peacemaking gift is a gift worth having in today's world as well.

Consider this illustration: a girl came home from school upset about some interaction she had at school and asked her dad, who was a cook, for his advice. He took her into the kitchen and took out 3 saucepans and filled each with boiling water. When the pans began to boil, he added a single ingredient to each pan. In one he put in carrots. In another, he put eggs. And in the third he put coffee beans. After letting each boil awhile, he turned off the heat, drained the pans and showed his daughter the outcomes of each of the ingredients. "When trouble comes", said he, "some people get soft like these carrots, allowing people to walk all over them. Others act like these eggs and get hard. They don't want to hear what anybody says and have a hard time getting along with anyone. But others act like these coffee beans, and change the atmosphere around them, leaving a pleasant aroma with all who encounter them.

Which do you think Jesus was? And what would he hope for from us?

Lessons on Suffering - Part 7 of 7

Text and key verse: Hebrews 12:11 "No discipline seems pleasant at the time, but painful."

A preacher was really getting into his sermon as he said, "Brothers and sisters, in order for this church to run, we must first learn how to stand!" And the church responded, "Let it stand, Pastor! "The pastor then said, "in order for this church to run, it must then learn how to walk!" And the church responded, "Let it walk, Pastor!" Then the pastor said, "and in order for this church to run, it must then learn to give sacrificially!" And the church responded, "Let it crawl, Pastor!"

There is a price to pay for learning to live Godly lives. Giving sacrificially is part of that-but not all. We as Christians must become like professional athletes in terms of our preparation. And there are many who would like that to God's using a planer on us rather than a sander. Another less harsh description we hear a lot today is "tough love".

A few years ago, allied troops captured a young American fighting for the Taliban in Afghanistan. This caused quite a stir in the Us media as many wondered how such a thing could happen. Upon further examination, though, it was found that this young man was raised by parents who did not say no. They did not say no when their son decided to drop out of school and become a Muslim. They did not say no when he asked them to pay his way to Yemen or when his closest friends included savage gunman. In effect, their son got started on the wrong path because his parents didn't give him what the Taliban did- standards and discipline.

Similarly, when discipline is missing from our daily devotions, the results show just as readily. When the gospel first caught hold in Africa, many early converts built their own private prayer huts. These huts were only big enough for one person and their use was evident in how the path to that hut became worn down. Whenever someone became negligent in their prayer discipline, a person holding them accountable would say, "Friend, the grass grows on your path!" Thank God for such friends or parents who hold us accountable!

REFLECTIONS

Temptation

There's an old story told about a young American Indian who seeks counsel from his grandfather, a wise old Chief. As they sit around a campfire one evening, the young brave says, "Grandfather, there seems to be a war going on within me. It's like a bear and a wolf fighting. The bear, who wants to do good, is constantly opposed by a wolf, who wants to do bad. My question, then, is who will win?" The Grandfather thought about this question for a few moments, then said, "The one you feed will be the one who wins."

And so, it is with us. We Christians have a Holy Spirit who lives within and consistently implores us to do good. But we also have an inbred sin nature which wants us to do just the opposite. These 2 natures compete for our attention, the struggle between them we refer to as temptation. The apostle Paul refers to this struggle in Romans 7:15, when he says he does the things he does not want to do. But Paul also refers to the fact that God will not allow us to be tempted above that which we are able to withstand in 1st Corinthians 10:13. Thus it would appear that with help, we can overcome.

Lessons on Temptation - Part 1 of 7

Text and key verse: Luke 9:26 "If you are ashamed of me and my teaching, then the son of man will be ashamed of you when he comes in his glory and in the glory of the father and of his holy angels."

A student attending a college chapel service said, "Oh no" when he read who would be giving the message that day. An older lady seated next to him then asked what the matter was. "It's the preacher. I have him for one of my classes and he's the most boring teacher I have." "Do you know who I am?", said the woman. "No", said the young man. "Well, I'm that preacher's wife!" "Do you know who I am?", said the young man. "No", she replied. "Hallelujah!", exclaimed the young man.

This student was happy that he wouldn't be identified with his words about that day's speaker. Yet, many Christians don't act as if they want to be identified with their open acceptance of the gospel message. And, according to the latest survey on people professing Christianity, the way things are going, by 2042, Christians may be in the minority. This certainly bodes poorly for the Christians who come after us.

In the early days of the church, people who were baptized were identified as Christians and were often ostracized and persecuted because of it. Yet as long as they didn't get baptized, they weren't. I wonder, then, if it were still that way today, how many would make that decision?

Today, there is not that kind of pressure. Yet, as I said, many people are still hesitant to identify themselves as Christians-particularly in the fields of politics or motion pictures.

Friends, the easy way out is not the way of Christ. And when we remember what he did for us at Calvary and the shame he endured to gain us forgiveness of our sins, is it not our reasonable service to proudly claim him as our Lord and savior?

Lessons on Temptation - Part 2 of 7

Text: 2 Samuel 1:17-27

Key verse:2 Samuel 1:27 "How the mighty have fallen!"

Three burly guys on motorcycles come into the little roadside diner where a little truck driver is eating his lunch. They take his food and laugh in his face, trying to provoke an argument. But the little guy didn't say anything and got up, paid his bill and went out. The three guys, proud of their little confrontation, shared their glee with the waitress: "He wasn't much of a man, was he?", they said. "Not much of a driver, either apparently. Look, he just drove over your three motorcycles!"

As much as this outcome might please us, God holds us Christians to a much higher standard. And we see this standard in the actions of David toward Saul-both when Saul was alive and when he had been killed. At no time did David forget that Saul was God's anointed king of Israel, despite how badly Saul had treated him. In fact, David leads the nation of Israel in their mourning over Saul.

We see similar actions in the life of Abraham Lincoln in his treatment of his rival, Stephen A. Douglas, and in Douglas's response to Lincoln after the election of 1860. You see, Douglas was by far the better public speaker, and he wanted this nomination very badly. So, he put Lincoln down in every way that he could. But after the election, he put their differences aside and worked tirelessly to unite both Democrats and Republicans behind Lincoln. He toured the south, trying to talk to state leaders, urging them not to secede from the union. As a result, he and Lincoln became the best of friends. Douglas died not long after, but it is thought that Douglas might have become Lincoln's running mate in the election of 1864 if he had lived.

To me, this has to be the influence of God. As we pray that God will love our enemies through us, the feelings of animosity vanish as he allows us to get rid of those we hate by making them our friends.

Lessons on Temptation - Part 3 of 7

Text: Matthew 4:1-11

Key verse: Matthew 4:7 "Thou shalt not tempt the Lord thy God."

Two wealthy brothers had been troublemakers in town for decades- treating their employees and their wives terribly, being publicly drunk on many occasions and abusive to their children. And so, when one of the brothers died, the town and most of its inhabitants thought that it was a cause for celebration. But the other brother came to the town minister and asked him to give a eulogy that referred to his brother as a saint. The pastor said that, in good conscience, he could not lie about the brother that way. "Well pastor, I'm prepared to give $100,000 to your church if you do this." So, the pastor agreed to give the eulogy and he did it this way: "Brothers and sisters, you all know what a deceitful scoundrel the deceased was, but compared to his brother, he was a saint."

It would appear that today everyone has a price. For some it's money and for others it's fame or power. But temptation can be overcome and Jesus in this lesson shows us how. At the end of a 40-day fast, he is tired, hungry and at the beginning of a ministry whose goal is to save the world. My guess is that at this point, he feels anything but a world beater, especially since he has emptied himself of his divinity so he could relate to our weakness. Yet, Jesus realizes that his father is strongest at the point of our weakness, and it is his dependence on God and his word that gets him through Satan's best efforts.

Later on, the apostle Paul realized this as well. Indeed, it is the realization of our powerlessness that is the secret of our strength. It is just too bad that people at the height of their success are also the most vulnerable. Consider, if you will, the great German aviator, Manfred Von Righthofen, the Red Baron. At the time of his death, he was far and away the greatest combat pilot of his time, with some 80 air victories. But one day, he chased another plane too close to the ground and was killed by a shot fired at him from the ground. Apparently, his past success made him careless to the point when he should have been more watchful. Clearly, pride goethe before a fall.

Lessons on Temptation - Part 4 of 7

Text: Matthew 14:22-33

Key verse: Matthew 14;31b "...why did you doubt?"

At one point in the book, "Alice in Wonderland", Alice asks the Cheshire Cat which direction to go. And the cat says, "Where do you want to go?" Alice says she doesn't know. Then the cat replies, "Then it really doesn't matter, does it?"

Unfortunately, this often describes our walk of faith. I mean, we know where we want to end up, but too often do not pay attention to the little decisions along the way. In today's lesson where Jesus walks on the water, Peter asks that he too walk on water. But when Peter loses his focus, he begins to sink.

In analyzing this Bible story, we often focus on Peter's lack of faith. Yet he alone was willing to get out of the boat. Thus, I believe that the true point of our emphasis should be on his inability to stay focused-which shortfall we too often share.

Indeed, we become a little like the big cats we see in the lion tamer's cage. When the lion tamer holds a chair out in front of him, they don't know which chair leg to focus on and become totally manageable creatures.

To be the growing Christians we need to be, we must do a better job in focusing our eyes on the prize. We'll never know the joy and fulfillment that's possible until we really get hungry and thirsty after righteousness, until we ask enough, seek enough and knock enough to get the full measure of what God has for each of us.

Lessons on Temptation - Part 5 of 7

Text: Matthew 19:16-30

Key verse: Matthew 19:26b "…, but with God, all things are possible."

A man took a liking to hollandaise sauce and began to put it on just about everything. Unfortunately, the hollandaise sauce was deteriorating his dentures. So, when he went to see his dentist, the dentist gave him this ultimatum: either cut back on the hollandaise sauce or get a new set of dentures out of something more expensive, like chrome. The man wouldn't cut back on the hollandaise so told his dentist to start on the new dentures. "But just one question, Doc: why chrome?" And the dentist replied, "For there's no plate like chrome for the hollandaise."

Indeed, there are sometimes difficult choices to make when we get carried away with the things we like. Such was the case with the story of the rich young ruler. Apparently feeling as if he was missing something in his Christian walk, this young guy approaches Jesus to try and get an answer. When Jesus perceived that it was the young man's love of money, the young man went away quite sorrowful, for he loved his money too much to give it up and follow Jesus.

Of course, we may not be aware when our love of something gets that bad until something worse happens. A young man with wealthy parents calls home to say he's coming back from his tour of duty. What he doesn't tell them is that he has become terribly disfigured by his injuries. He tells them instead that he wants to bring a buddy home like that to stay. His mother, very much used to a busy social life, advises him not to do that as it would "cramp their style." So that same night, his parents get a call from the police, advising them that their son has committed suicide.

Certainly, you don't have to be a rich socialite to appreciate the heartbreak of receiving such a call. Nor do you have to be a soldier with significant, life-altering injuries, to understand the rejection he felt. The point is without Jesus, it doesn't matter what we have because without him we are lost.

Lessons on Temptation - Part 6 of 7

Text: John 6:5-13

Key verse: John 6:9 "Here is a boy with 5 small barley loaves and 2 small fish, but how far will they go among so many?"

Rodney Dangerfield, the comedian, based his acting on the idea that he could never get any respect. For example, he told of going to his psychiatrist and being told that he was crazy. When he asked for a second opinion, the doctor said he was ugly, too.

In today's lesson, the feeding of the 5,000, the disciples needed to be shown that even when what we have seems insufficient or lacking respect, that Jesus can take our little and make a lot. And Jesus does this by taking a small boy's offering of 5 loaves of bread and 2 fish and feeding a great multitude-and not only that but having enough left over to fill 12 baskets.

John D. Rockefeller could relate. He had become a millionaire by the age of 23 and a billionaire by the age of 50. Yet his entire life had been directed solely to the pursuit of wealth. However, when his health began to fail, his vast wealth could find him no relief. Finally, a dream he had where he learned what he could not take with him he could not take with him turned him around. He directed his accountants to redirect his vast wealth into a foundation to support hospitals, research and mission work. When he did this, his health began to improve, and his foundation helped fund cures for a number of diseases.

Of course he had a lot to give. We are not so blessed, for the most part. Thus, we are tempted to think that what we have can never make a difference. Yet the idea is still the same. Whether we have a little or a lot, God can take what we have to give and make a great blessing to others.

I can relate. I remember thinking back to when our young children were baptized, how unprepared for parenthood I felt. The awesomeness of the task seemed insurmountable. Yet when I gave what meager talents that I had in raising those kids to God, he used what I had to do a better job. And he can do the same for you!

Lessons on Temptation - Part 7 of 7

Text: Philippians 4:6-7

Key verse: Philippians 4:6a "Do not be anxious over anything…"

A man was telling his friend that he had a mountain of credit card debt, that he had lost his job, had his car repossessed and that his house was in foreclosure. Yet he was not worried. "How do you manage that?" his friend asked. "I hired a professional worrier, who does all my worrying for me." "That's great," said the friend, "How much does he charge?" "$50,000 a year." "Well, how are you going to afford that?" his friend asked. "That's his worry!"

We do have a great temptation to worry or be anxious, but God's word has a cure. It's just too bad that so few of us use it. That does not mean, however, that all worry is bad. If a little worry causes us to address our problems, then it can be useful. But when worry paralyzes us and keeps us from taking steps to improve our lot, that's not so good.

A story is told that a certain mental hospital's criteria for discharge involves a little test where a person is put in a room with an overflowing sink and a mop. If the person first turns off the spigot before mopping, they are considered ready for discharge. But if they don't turn off the spigot but keep mopping away, they are not. I believe this story has some relevance for us as Christians. When we worry, the problem becomes the priority, not God. But when we make God the priority, God promises to help us fix the problem.

Yet that is not the only benefit. God, in this verse, tells us that he will give us peace while addressing our problem. That's why it's called a peace that passes our understanding.

REFLECTIONS

The 10 Commandments

In a family of boys, there was a tendency toward aggressive interaction-whether it was in play or in settling differences. But that's where our mother's influence was the greatest. She did not allow that. So, by her influence, we were rewarded for being peaceful. It was her expectation, and we all desired her approval. In like manner, our heavenly father, I believe, desired his special creation to abide in peaceful co-existence. For those who desired his approval, his influence was enough.

But sin separated us from God-so much so that we no longer sought or even desired his approval. God could have allowed us to go our sinful way. But He loved us too much to do that. So, he made the 10 commandments to clearly express what he intended. Thus, it becomes for us a yardstick to hold up to ourselves to monitor how we're doing.

Yet it also serves to direct us to realize that, on our own, we can never hope to measure up-that we require help. And so, he had to provide the means by which we could do this in order to eliminate the separating effects of sin.

Lessons on the 10 Commandments – Part 1 of 7

Text and key verse: Exodus 20:8 "Remember the sabbath day by keeping it holy."

A preacher rode by a parishioner/farmer harvesting his crop on Sunday, and stopped to say, "Hey brother, don't you know that God made the world in 6 days and rested on the sabbath?" "Yes, I know all about that", the farmer said. "But he got finished and i didn't."

The Bible also says that God made the sabbath for man and not man for the sabbath. So how do we interpret this seeming contradiction for greater understanding? As I was growing up there were Blue laws that prohibited certain activities from happening. Now it would appear that anything goes. People routinely work on Sundays. Stores are open on Sundays. Kid's sporting events often are scheduled on Sundays. What has changed?

Perhaps a better question might be: what has not changed? I believe people still need time away from work to reconnect with their families, to rest and to "recharge their batteries". For most people, seven days at work is still not sufficient to get everything done. And the human body still is not designed for "all work and no play".

No, I believe it is our perspective on what's important that has changed. Pleasing God isn't and making money is. Today we tend to be defined by the things we own or the positions we've held. We act as though there isn't a price to pay for that decision. But there is.

Unfortunately, that realization often comes too late. Successful men never reflect on their deathbeds of not making more money or owning more houses. Most likely they reflect on the relationships in their life that could have been better and aren't. Then in heaven they will lament their inattention to the relationship to their savior that they should have had but didn't.

How much better it would have been for that successful businessman to have reflected like Chick-fil-a owner, Cathy Truett, that if he couldn't do enough business 6 days a week and be profitable, then it mustn't been God's will for him to be in that business. You see, when God's first, he takes care of what's really important.

Lessons on the 10 Commandments – Part 2 of 7

Text; Exodus 20:2-17

Key verse: Isaiah 1:11 "I am sick of your sacrifices", …

A man thought he had solved the problem of forgetting the important dates in his and his wife's marriage. You see, he went to a local flower shop and set up an account where flowers would be sent out at each of these occasions, signed, "Your loving husband". And it worked pretty well until one day, many important occasions later, he remarked, "Nice flowers, honey. Where'd you get them?"

At that point, she realized that his love for her had been replaced by a sense of duty. Similarly, we must be careful that we do not do the same thing in our loving relationship with God.

You get a sense of this in today's key verse. In that context, the Israelites were just "going through the motions" in expressing their love for God. In effect, it was as if it wasn't love at all. That's why I believe God responded as he did.

In the 10 commandments, we could fall into the same trap. Certainly, Jesus saw this in the actions of the religious leaders of his day. It was the reason he found fault with them so often. It wasn't given to us as some sort of checklist or some new year's resolutions of which our failure was considered as no big deal.

Friends, our love for God must be held to a much higher standard! When Adolf Eichmann, one of the Holocaust's most evil masterminds was brought to trial, people were surprised that he did not appear to be the personification of evil as they believed him to be. In fact, he looked, to all the world, like one of them.

The point is in accepting ok or not too bad in terms of our love for God, we appear exactly as anyone who doesn't love God at all. If we say we love God and mean it, one proof of that would seem to be our relishing the opportunity in keeping the 10 commandments.

Lessons on the 10 Commandments – Part 3of 7

Text: 1 Samuel 15:20-38

Key verse: 1 Samuel 15:22a "Obedience is better than sacrifice."

A man walked up to a coffee vending machine and put his money in. No cup appeared but the machine went into action, nevertheless, sending in order coffee, cream and sugar. After the proper amounts went down the drain, the machine clicked off. "Now that's real automation," said the man. "It even drinks it for you."

Unfortunately, we often approach worship and our whole God experience the same way. We come to church, take a seat, say a prayer, sing a song, hear a sermon and be on our way. Nothing has changed. We have done our duty and so we've satisfied our requirement to God for another week. You could say that we even approach the 10 commandments the same way: don't lie, steal, kill, commit adultery, etc. And we will be ok. Yet the question remains: Where's the love?

In today's lesson, Saul takes the command of God and interprets it as he chooses and thus loses out on the blessing of God for his kingdom. In effect, he disobeyed God by not following all of what he was told to do. If he had been anxious to serve God from his heart, his hands would have followed.

So, once again, when our motive in serving God is not love, we fall short. When our motives are wrong, our focus is in filling the pews, not the person. Until those changes, the church won't become the hands and feet of Christ on earth as it was intended to be.

In Saul's case, you can see this in his reaction to Samuel's confrontation with his sin. I know i'm wrong, but just don't let me lose face among the elders of israel. For the modern-day Saul, the desire is to maintain a resemblance to outward righteousness, while not addressing the larger sin within. Worship as it should be entails a meeting with the God who seeks to communicate with us and reside within us. When we get that, there is a divine energy released that is not just a Sunday thing, but a 24/7 thing, that is reflected in our love for others, our devotion to family and our work. That's the difference that love makes.

Lessons on the 10 Commandments – Part 4 of 7

Text: Deuteronomy 8

Key verse: Exodus 20:3 "Thou shalt have no other Gods before me."

An elementary teacher was telling a story to her class that made the point of advising them of the dangers in not dressing warmly enough in cold weather. In her story she told of a little boy who went sled-riding without his hat, mittens, boots and snowsuit. As a result, he caught pneumonia and died. After her story, little Johnny raised his hand and said, "Teacher, may I ask 2 questions? "Yes, Johnny," she replied. "Who has his sled now and may I have it?"

Nothing tends to get our attention faster than the possibility of getting a windfall-even if it comes at someone else's expense. This was the situation in today's lesson, where the israelites were just about to enter the Promise Land. Moses, in knowing his people so well, was afraid that in taking over the land that they would forget the God who gave it to them.

Unfortunately, it would appear that we have not learned that lesson yet as the things we own so often come back to us. This was never God's intent as we see in the very first commandment. In a way, our materialism leads us to Spiritual leprosy- we become de-sensitized by God's provision and, as a result, do not feel the pain of our growing separation from God.

Clearly, the aspect of our behavior that is lacking is our gratitude. In taking God's blessings for granted, we forget that we do not actually own anything but are merely temporary stewards of what God allows to use. We miss the point that God has not raised our standard of living as much as he has raised our standard of giving. You see, friends, it is our standard of giving that determines the abundance of life.

Lessons on the 10 Commandments – Part 5of7

Text and key verse: Exodus 20:12 "Honor thy father and thy mother…"

Three boys in a schoolyard were bragging up their dads. The first boy said, "My dad scribbles a few words on a piece of paper, calls it a poem, and gets $100 for it." "That's nothing!" Said the second boy, "My dad scribbles a few words on a piece of paper, calls it a song and gets a $1,000 for it." "I've got you both beat!" Said the third boy. "My dad scribbles a few words on a piece of paper, calls it a sermon and it takes four people to take up all the money."

We all smile when a son thinks his dad is special, for the isn't the reality for many sons. Indeed, there are many instances today where dads have completely abdicated their responsibilities as father and have left the mother to try to fill both roles. These situations rarely turn out well. As a matter of fact, in mother-only homes, most are below the poverty line, most sons become sexually active sooner and are more likely to be delinquent, and most adult sons drop–out sooner, divorce earlier and make less money than those households with two parents.

So, it makes sense to think about just what role the father plays in the household. And children tend to get clues from their dads as to how to handle adversity, anger, disappointment and success. In short, if a father does not go to church, no matter how faithful his wife's devotions, only one child in 50 will become a regular worshipper. If a father does go regularly, regardless of the practice of the mother, between two-thirds and three-quarters of their children will become churchgoers (regular and irregular).

The Bible tells us to honor our dads, as hard as it may be at times; so, we must try. But when we see them through God's eyes, it becomes doable and honorable.

Lessons on the 10 Commandments – Part 6 of 7

Text: Exodus 20:3-17

Key verse: 1 Corinthians 13:2b "…if I have faith that can move mountains but don't have love, I am nothing."

The meadow next to the museum's parking lot was used by a local farmer to graze his cows. But when some visitors got out of their car to visit the museum, they thought it would be a good place to let their dog have a run. The thing they didn't bargain for, however, was that this meadow was surrounded by an electric fence. When the dog saw the cows, it wanted to chase them. But after a jolt from the electric fence, it changed its mind completely and went off down the road, howling. It took almost an hour to get the dog back in the car and so seeing the farmer standing nearby, the dog's owner thought he'd yell at the farmer for not putting up a sign about the electric fence. When the dog's owner finished his appeal, the farmer said, "If I knew your dog could read, i would have put one up."

The dog owner was suggesting that the farmer's sin was one of omission. But what he was really saying was that the farmer was showing a lack of love. In considering the ten commandments, then, it is important to first realize that love was the basis of them, and that love is the necessary pre-condition for properly keeping them.

When Jesus was asked what the most important commandment was, he didn't specifically pick any of what we know them to be. He said we must love God first and foremost and our neighbor as ourselves. So, what he was saying in effect was that love was the key. And love was the key omission from his day's religious leaders. It was and still is the main thing.

Many years ago, the city of Pittsburgh built a brand-new post office building. At the grand opening, the governor made a speech, a band played, and the people cheered. But when the first man went into that building to mail a letter, the mail drop was missing. It was a small thing but a most important omission. By the same token, when we try and follow the 10 commandments without love, we make a big omission. We miss the main thing.

Lessons on the 10 Commandments – Part 7of7

Text: Mark 14;26,32-42

Key verse: Luke 1:38a "Behold the handmaid of the Lord…"

A woman who was interviewing for the position of maid was asked if she served company. She replied that she did-both ways. "What do you mean- "both ways"?" asked the interviewer. "So, they'll come back or stay away," she replied.

When you think about it, this is the choice we often make in our service to others. But this is not a lesson that Jesus taught.in today's lesson from the Garden of Gethsemane, we see 2 examples of service-one by Jesus' disciples and one by Jesus, himself- both of which we will consider.

In this story, Jesus asks his inner circle of disciples-Peter, James and John- to watch and pray. But they are tired and fall asleep. They, in effect, dropped the ball at a critical time for their master. Now I'm not saying that they had no reason to be tired. What I am saying is that their failure reflects the distance they still had to go as God's willing servants.

If we are honest with ourselves, we may be able to see some of their failures in us. Sometimes our service is mitigated by our own personal wants and desires. When that is the case, it shows particularly to the ones we seek to serve. Jesus himself tells a story about an ungodly judge who helped a lady out because he was worn out by her persistence-not because of his mercy or goodness.

Jesus' example, conversely, reflects what our service should look like. In the Garden, Jesus fully realizes what he is about to face and pleads with God for some option. When one is not presented, he willingly submits to his father's will. It wasn't what was best for him but what was ultimately best for sinful mankind.

The closest we get to this is in the service we give to our family. When one of our kids wants to take something out of the oven, we advise them to use a potholder, so they won't get burned. We know what getting burned feels like and want to save them from that. That's the purpose of his rules.

REFLECTIONS

Thanksgiving

Thanksgiving has always been one of my favorite holidays. And I suppose my family's celebration of it would resonate with many families-lots of food, family, football games, shopping and a general looking forward to Christmas. Yet the being thankful part is a more recent phenomenon. When I was younger, I took a lot of things for granted. It wasn't until I had experienced some losses that I really learned something of being thankful- the key loss being when my mother passed away. Thomas Wolfe once wrote that you can't go home again. Now I'm not sure in what context he wrote that, but for me, it means I can never experience that same Thanksgiving joy that I once got from being with my birth family in the old family homestead. That doesn't mean that Thanksgiving can never be fun or enjoyable. It is but in a different way. And I can never replace that feeling again.

Lessons on Thanksgiving – Part 1 of 7

Text and key verse: 1 Timothy 3:5 "If anyone does not know how to manage his own family, how can he take care of God's chuurch?"

Grandma was awakened by her little 7-year-old grandson, who brought her coffee in bed. In trying the coffee, she found it to be probably the worst cup of coffee she had ever had. But she managed to finish it, though she was surprised by the 3 little plastic army men in the bottom of her cup. "What are these army men doing in my cup?" she asked. "Grandma, don't you know? The best part of waking up is soldiers in your cup."

No doubt we all have cute little family stories we keep as treasured momentos of family times together. And so, when we stop to "count our (Thanksgiving) blessings", family would probably be near the top on most people's lists. In today's text, the apostle Paul recognizes that one's relationship to family can be instrumental in their relationship to the church. I believe that we can learn much about church dynamics by understanding how our own family works.

Being the youngest of a large family, I missed some of those dynamics. My older brothers advised that, particularly, our father had become much mellower by the time I came along. I do know that my sister "butted heads" with my dad on a number of occasions but didn't know why and so I asked them about it. They told me that mom and dad had a pre-arranged plan as to how interpersonal matters were handled. So, in effect, when they discussed those matters, my dad would handle what things he thought he should, leaving the rest to my mother to handle. There was no "wait 'til your father comes home". Toward that end, my dad handled matters re: dating and school, which worked fine for me but not so well for my sister, who wanted to be more independent than the rest of us.

For my part, i can now see how their Christian influence helped me to see the world (and my place in God's church) as a place where fairness and compassion and a stong work ethic are instrumental to positive interaction.

Lessons on Thanksgiving – Part 2 of 7

Text and key verse: 2 Timothy 4:7 "I have fought the good fight, I have finished the race, I have kept the faith."

A man was riding on a stagecoach in the old west, traveling to Dodge City. All of a sudden, a rider on a horse pulled up to one side of the stage and a riderless horse pulled up to the other side. The rider opened the stagecoach door, got down off his horse and onto the stage, ran across the stage, opened the other door, and jumped on the other horse. As he was about to pull away, the man in the stage called out to him, "Mister, what was that all about?" "Oh," he said, "it's just a stage I'm going through."

We may also go through many "stages" in our Christian walk, but we need never to forget to be thankful for the journey for there are many things to appreciate along the way. But that depends on how we look at things. A blind boy sat on the steps of a building with a hat at his feet and a sign that said, "I'm blind. Please help." When a man came by and saw that there weren't too many coins in the boy's hat, he changed the sign and put it back where it was and said he would be back. Later that day the man did come back and saw that the contributions changed greatly. The blind boy thanked the man and asked what he had written. The man said, "not much different than what you wrote-just that Today is a beautiful day and I can't see it." The sign had aroused people's thankfulness for their own sight.

But secondly, we need to be careful not to assume we know all there is to something-to be open to learning. A young man had a dream of coming to America and so saved all his earnings until he had the money to purchase a ticket on an ocean liner. When the time came for him to go, he packed his meager belongings and enough crackers and peanut butter to last several days and got on board. After a few days at sea, he attracted the attention of the ship's steward, who suspected that the boy was a stowaway because he always slept on deck and never ate in the dining room. But when the boy showed the steward his ticket, the steward apologized and informed the boy that not only was his room included but also the meals in the dining room. Just like this boy, we can always learn.

Lessons on Thanksgiving – Part 3 of 7

Text:luke 12:16-21

Key verse: luke 12 :20 ..."this night will your soul be required of thee. Then who will get the things you have prepared for yourself?"

A young guy found himself with a couple of hours to himself one afternoon, so decided to play 9 holes of golf. Just before teeing off, however, an old guy came up and asked if he would mind his playing along. The young guy replied that he wouldn't mind and so they played pretty evenly for the next 8 holes. But on the 9th hole, the young guy hit his ball behind a tree. As he was lining up his shot the old guy said, "When I was your age, I hit a shot like that over the tree." Taking the challenge, the young guy swung mightily but only hit it ¾ of the way up the tree. Then the old guy said, "But when I was your age, that tree was only 3 feet tall."

That's why you have to be careful with whom you play. Even so, golf can be a lot of fun and certainly something to be thankful for. But it is possible to get too much of a good thing. At Thanksgiving, we can also get too much of a good thing when it comes to facing the feast that is prepared before us.

That doesn't make us bad people for over-indulging, however, unless it becomes a pattern of behavior. In today's scripture lesson, a farmer with an over-abundant harvest thinks only of himself in hoarding his blessing and suffers eternal consequences. We, as Christians, must be willing to share when we have more than we need. The farmer let his worldly goods become his God. We are held to a much higher and others-centered standard.

So, in effect, we are expected to let our actions reflect our thankfulness. That doesn't mean we can't enjoy the blessings God showers on us. It just means that we need to keep the needs of others in mind as much as our own and be ready to do something about them.

Lessons on Thanksgiving – Part 4 of 7

Text: Luke 17:11-19

Key verse: Luke 17: 17 "Were not all ten cleansed? Where are the other nine?"

In a Peanuts cartoon, Charlie Brown is bringing out Snoopy's dinner on Thanksgiving. But it is just the usual dog food. The cartoon then shows Snoopy thinking this thought: All the rest of the world is having turkey today and all I get is dog food. How fair is that? The the cartoon shows Snoopy's thoughts a little later: Well, I guess it could be worse. I could be a turkey.

Although we are supposed to be thankful on thanksgiving, many are not. And perhaps it has always been so. In today's scripture lesson, we find that jesus has healed ten lepers, but that only one has returned to give thanks. We wonder (do we not?) what is wrong with people?

What's wrong, I believe, is nothing that could not be said for anyone who has not had thankfulness modeled for them. It is a learned behavior that should be taught at home first, but certainly at church. But it can be learned at school, at work or in the neighborhood. We just can never assume that it has been.

A businessman went in to work a couple of hours earlier than usual as he had some things he wanted to accomplish before the crowd came in. So, when he got there, no one was there except for old Tom, the custodian, emptying ashtrays, dusting the furniture, and just tidying up. So, the businessman took a minute, went up to Tom and said, "tom, as I look around this place, I can't help but thinkwhat an asset you have been to our company all these years. You are an important member of this organization and I want to let you knowthat I appreciate you and all you have done." Old Tom said, "Thank you, boss," and went out. But a few minutes later, Tom came back-this time with a tear on his cheek. "Boss," Tom began," I just want to tell you something. I have worked here for the last 17 years and today was the first day anyone ever told me they appreciated anything I did. I just want you to know I appreciated what you told me this morning more than any of the paychecks I ever received."

Then he turned and went back to work. Do you see how important thankfulness is?

Lessons on Thanksgiving – Part 5 of 7

Text and key verse; Colossians 4:2 "Devote yourselves to prayer, being watchful and thankful."

The Butterball Turkey company established a turkey preparation "hotline" several years ago to help people with the problems that would come up on Thanksgiving. The most memorable call received in 1993 was from a woman whose Chihuahua had jumped into their turkey's cavity and had gotten stuck.

In today's scripture lesson, we are advised to be both watchful and thankful. But in this case, we can see what is possible when we're not.

Even so, Paul, although he hadn't started this particular church, was writing to it because of reports of false teachers coming in and trying to get the followers there to adopt some other teachings into what they had originally been taught-thus weakening their faith.

In today's society, this same false teaching can be a concern for us as we are continually being "bombarded" with adopting worldly standards for Spiritual ones. Jesus clearly admonishes us that we cannot serve both God and mammon, or wealth.

A father, recognizing his son's worldly tendencies, gave his son a Bible as part of his graduation gift-hoping that the Bible would serve as a help and guide. What the son didn't realize was that the father had also included the keys to the sports car that his son had hinted he wanted. So, the son, not realizing that the keys were in the Bible, stormed out of the house, leaving the Bible behind-never to return. Although the son became successful on his own and had a nice family and many possessions, he later felt guilty and decided to come back and reconcile with his father. But before he could do so, he received a letter that his father had passed and left him a sizable inheritance. When he got back to his boyhood family residence, he found the Bible that his dad had given him and saw that his father had underlined certain verses that he thought would be helpful to his son. Then the son saw that a set of keys were attached to the Bible with the dealer's name and the words "paid in full". Thanklessness ruined their connection.

Lessons on Thanksgiving – Part 6 of 7

Text and key verse: 1 Thessalonians 5:18 "Give thanks in all circumstances; for this is God's will for you in Christ Jesus."

Two men were walking through a field one day when they were charged by a bull. But as they ran for the nearest fence, it became apparent to them both that they were not going to make it. So, the one man says to the other, "Say a prayer for us, john. We're not going to make it." "I can't," said the other. "I've never prayed a prayer in public before." "Well, you'd better say something fast for we're in for it." "Ok", John said, "I'll pray the only prayer i know-o Lord, for what we are about to receive, make us truly grateful."

Today's scripture advises that we give thanks in all circumstances, but this one might be stretching it.the primary reason for our thankfulness is that God specializes in bringing good out of bad, even if we can't appreciate it at the time. Nevertheless, this thankfulness is a discipline that must be honed over time and experiences.

A great example of this is the backgroung behind the doxology that most of us sing each week. Bishop thomas ken was born in england 17 years before the pilgrims came to america and came to know a lot about adversity- having lived through both the great fire of london (that destroyed 4/5 of the city) and the bubonic plague. So, in writing these words of praise, he surely had those adversities in mind.

Yet we mustn't think that such examples of thankfulness are in past history. The famous humorist, Erma Bombeck, wrote of a little 8-year-old girl battling cancer of the nervous system who was asked what she wanted for her birthday. Now no doubt that her parents would have "moved heaven and earth" to meet her wishes. Nevertheless, the little girl had to think long and hard before replying "I don't know. I have 2 sticker books and a cabbage patch doll. I have everything."

My hope for you this thanksgiving is that you only have good things to be thankful for. Even so, it is important to remember, that when tragedy strikes, God will help us trace the rainbow through the rain.

Lessons on Thanksgiving – Part 7 of 7

Text and key verse; Philippians 4:6 "Do not be anxious about anything, but in every situation, by prayer and petition with thanksgiving, present your requests to God."

A guy was recovering from a very severe heart attack and was advised by his doctor to not experience any excitement for a couple of months. But when his wife found out that they had won the lottery with a prize of $4 million, she was afraid to tell her husband. So, she called her pastor, hoping that he could come up with some solution. So, the pastor came over and said that he needed to ask her husband for some advice. Since they had a good relationship, the husband said he'd be glad to help. The pastor started by telling the man that he had a theorhetical question about stewardship. "What should a guy do if they came into a large sum of money-like $4 million?" "That's easy", he said," he should give half to the church". Then the pastor took a heart attack.

In today's lesson, Paul advises the church at Philippi to not worry but pray with thanksgiving. After all, he reasoned, it had worked for him. Although he did not specifically share in this letter the things he had gone through in his second letter to the church at Corinth, I'm sure at one time or another, he must have mentionned the beatings, the stoning, and the shipwrecks he had endured.

In sharing his experiences, Paul was advising that there is nothing like hardship to bring one closer to God-a lesson that has been both affirmed and re-affirmed throughout history. Certainly, such was the case among our first settlers at Plymouth.

After arriving at Plymouth in 1620, the Pilgrims' number had been reduced to 47 from 120 during that first terrible winter. But just 3 years later, the colony's governor had proclaimed a thanksgiving for the bounty that God had provided. They remembered what they had gone through and who ultimately got them through. And so should we.

REFLECTIONS

Thought Life

Thoughts are not the same as attitudes, a section that appears earlier. The difference between the two is that attitudes can develop from thoughts that are repeated over a period of time and have been reinforced from one source or another. As a thought can be either positive or negative, it follows that attitudes can also be. Therefore, as we identify a thought as being negative or counterproductive, we must try to gain more information about the thing causing that thought and determine its basis in truth. If it can be determined to be false, we must try to amend that thought and ones like it and banish them before they can become an attitude. This is extremely important for us as Christians, so we do not appear to be wrongly unloving to those that God loves. You see, thoughts can be amended before they become attitudes. And some thoughts need to be.

Lessons on Thought Life - Part 1 of 7

Text: Nehemiah 4

Key verse: Nehemiah 4:16a "From that day on, half of my men did the work, while the other half were equipped with spears, shields, bows and armor."

A man looked up from his hospital bed and said to his wife, "You've always been there with me when I've had trouble: in my bad investment, in my car accident and when I got fired. So, when I think about these events and your presence, I can't help but think that you're just bad luck."

Not a very nice statement of support, is it? And it certainly betrays the team Spirit that a good marriage should exemplify. Indeed, what this husband's attitude reflects is a collection of poor thoughts that had never been challenged by reality.

In today's lesson, the Jews returning from exile to rebuild the walls around Jerusalem could never have succeeded without the thought that everyone needed to work together. Nevertheless, these thoughts of teamwork had to be repeated and confirmed in order to become a solid attitude.

We in the church also need to think about our work as a team effort. As we are a collection of different gifts and graces, it stands to reason that we could not have near the impact on an individual basis that we can when we work together. Indeed, to overcome the Adversary who "prowls about, seeking whom he may devour", we must pool our efforts. We need to become more than the sum of our parts.

Consider this illustration: at a horse-pull in Canada, one horse pulled 9,000 pounds while another horse pulled 8,000. You would think, then, that combining their efforts would yield 17,000 pounds of pull. But in actuality, when these two horses pulled together, they were able to pull 30,000 pounds.

Such can be the effect of teamwork in the church. Indeed, it must be for the church to have its maximum power.

Lessons on Thought Life - Part 2 of 7

Text and key verse: Colossians 4;6 "Let your conversation always be full of grace, seasoned with salt, so that you may know how to answer everyone."

A man was just about to get into bed when his wife reminded him to turn out the light in the shed. But when he looked out the window towards the shed, he not only saw that the light was on but that there seemed to be someone in the shed taking things. He then called the police who were reluctant to send anyone right away since all the squad cars were busy and the thieves were not in his house. They told him to lock the house and wait until a squad car got there. "Ok", the guy said, waited 30 seconds and called the police back. "You don't need to come now", said the guy, "I just went out to the shed and shot the thieves." In a couple of minutes, 3 squad cars, a swat team and an ambulance arrived and caught the burglars red-handed. One of the policemen came up to the house and said to the man who called, "I thought you said you shot them all." To which the guy replied, "I thought you said all the squad cars were busy."

In this instance, the guy responded as he did because the police seemed to think that his problem was not an emergency. And indeed, some people's emergencies are really not emergencies. But if you don't know for sure, can you afford to take the risk of not responding as if it were? So, in this instance the guy's thought about police indifference led to a false report that got them to take action. Yet the guy must have held the attitude that the police were not likely to take action unless there was a threat to life. So, it wasn't the thought but the attitude that led to the guy's misleading report.

Considering today's scripture, then, and our learning from it, we must challenge our thoughts before they become attitudes unless the thought can be proven to be correct.

Lessons on Thought Life - Part 3 of 7

Text and key verse; 1 King 19:18 "And incidentally, there are 7,000 in Israel who have neither bowed down to Baal or kissed him."

A guy who could not swim went deep-sea fishing with a friend and hooked a huge fish on his first try. But he became so excited that he lost his footing and fell overboard. His friend immediately reached for him and grabbed the first thing he could-his friend's hair. But since the guy wore a toupee, it came off in his friend's hand. "Help, save me!", the guy yelled again. So, the friend reached again, and this time got hold of his arm. But since this was a prosthetic limb, it came off. "Help, save me! " he cried again. This time the friend reached and grabbed hold of a leg. But since this, too, was a prosthetic leg, it came off in his hand. "Help, save me!", the guy cried again. "Well, how can I help you when you won't stick together?"

Oftentimes, our perspective changes when trouble arises. Such was the case when elijah was warned that queen jezabel was coming after him. He told the Lord that everything was falling apart and that he was the only one left that followed the Lord. He had taken his eyes off the Lord and focused on the threat. This can happen to us if we're not careful. So, it's instructive to see how the Lord addressed elijah's concerns: he corrected Elijah's misinformation and gave him a new assignment.

After the terrorist attack of 9/11, our enemies thought they had us beat and demoralized. But instead, we prayed and God corrected our misinformation so that we again realized that he, not our enemies, was in control. Then he helped us find the strength to get to work and rebuild –thus taking our eyes off the problem and on him.

Clearly, our perspective on our ability to pull ourselves out of trouble can easily change. It is at those times when we need to rely on God, seek his face and let him redirect our thoughts and actions.

Lessons on Thought Life - Part 4 of 7

Text and key verse: "Summing it all up, friends, I'd say you'll do best by filling your minds and meditating on things true, noble, reputable, authentic, compelling, gracious- the best, not the worst; the beautiful, not the ugly; things to praise, not to curse."

A young bride was terrified about walking down the aisle and standing before a church full of people on her wedding day. So, the pastor counseled her to break it down into 3 manageable steps- the aisle, the altar and finally her groom. He told her that she should just focus on putting one foot in front of the other and not to look at anyone to the left or to the right. Next he advised her to focus on the altar, where she had stood before to be baptized ,to join the church and to read scripture. Finally, he told her to focus on the man she loved and the opportunity to start their life together. Upon further reflection she said that, broken down that way, that she thought that she could do it. And do it she did, although along the aisle people laughed to themselves as the heard her go by, saying, "Aisle, altar him; aisle, altar, him."

When one squeezes a tube of toothpaste, they shouldn't be surprised to see toothpaste come out. It's what's in there. By the same token, when we speak we should not be surprised to hear what we have in our minds because that's what's in there. So it only stands to reason that we ought to fill our minds with the most positive things we can so we will not be embarrassed or cause undue hurt.

The downside of that is that we live in a world that is decidedly unchristian. Thus, we have to exercise some discernment in what we allow in there. When dogs are trained to hunt, they must learn to disregard the smell of fish that are dragged across their path. These fish have come to be known as red herrings. Similarly, we, as Christians, must learn to recognize that which represents red herrings to us, so we won't get distracted.

Lessons on Thought Life - Part 5 of 7

Text: Matthew 20:1-16

Key verse: Matthew 20: 16 "So the last shall be first, and the first shall be last."

The little girl was becoming restless in church with the length of the sermon. So, she leaned over to her mother and whispered, "if we give him the money now, will he let us go?"

The little girl did not feel that it was fair to have to sit so long in church. And this concept of fairness is a very prevalent one not just for church issues but in all facets of life.yet the essential question for us has to do with whether the concept is a preference or a conviction. If it is a preference, it is subject to change. If it is a conviction, it is not.

In today's lesson, a man has hired workers for his field throughout the day and paid them all the same. The ones hired first complained that ti was not fair that they get paid the same because they worked longer under warmer conditions.

At first glance, it would appear that these workers have a legitimate gripe. However, when one considers the larger context of God's giving us what we deserve or that of salvation, our views and thoughts change. That is, do we really want what we deserve from God, considering our sinful condition? Or do we not want the same benefits for the converted sinner who comes late rather than not at all?

That is not to say, however, that nothing should be a conviction. In the musical, "fiddler on the roof", Tevye is a dairy farmer who live sin pre-communist russia with his wife and 5 daughters in a time of great cultural change. His concept about pre-arranged marriages is being questionned and he reasons with himself about the pros and cons of each match and gives in in two cases in favor of the love between them. But when his daughter wants to marry a gentile, he reasons that there is no "other hand".

In matters of faith, indeed, there should be conviction, as hard as it might be to hold to them. It's where the "rubber meets the road".

Lessons on Thought Life - Part 6 of 7

Text: Luke 13:6-9

Key verse: Luke 13:9 "If it bears fruit next year, fine! If not, then cut it down."

Two little old ladies were going down the road in a car when the passenger, Mildred, got the distinct impression that her friend, Mary, had driven through a stop sign. But as she was not sure, she prepared herself to pay attention to the next one just to be sure Mary didn't do it again. But when the next one was coming up, Mary didn't slow down but drove right through. "Mary", Mildred cried, "You just drove through two stop signs!" "Oh", Mary replied, "Am I driving?"

Safety dictates that all drivers be given signs to obey to keep others safe. But, of course, that means that we have to actually obey them! In a larger sense, God gives us signs to follow as well. Some of these are internal, like those our bodies tell us. Others are the result of parental training, like manners and being thoughtful of others. But God has also given us signs in his word, and they usually begin like thou shalt not or beware. However, I believe God looks for signs from us as well, such as in today's key verse.

In other words, God is looking for fruit from us. In one sense that means that we produce more Christians-that we help others choose Christ. But it also means that we exhibit the change that Christ has made in our lives byhow we act-particularly towards others. This is what the fruit of the Spirit is about: love, peace, joy, longsuffering, kindness, goodness, faithfulness, gentleness and self-control.

The point here, though, seems to be that if God does not see that kind of fruit in us, that he will one day have no use for us. That should give us some sense of urgency-much like a "check engine" light on our car's dashboard. And to emphasize this need, he has provided his Holy Spirit to nudge us to do something about it. Of course, some people neglect these nudges just like their "check engine" light and hope that it goes away. But if we neglect this warning (just like the check engine light), we will find that we have no place in heaven-the earthly equivalent of being broken down along the side of a lonely road on a cold, wintry night-forever!

Lessons on Thought Life - Part 7 of 7

Text: John 15:1-8

Key verse; John 15:5 "I am the vine; you are the branches."

A despondent woman was walking down the beach one day when she noticed a bottle in the sand, uncorked it and was surprised to have a genie appear to her. He said "You have released me from my bondage and so I can now grant you 3 wishes. However, I must warn you that whatever you wish for will be received double by your mate." "That hardly seems fair", she explained, "as he left me for another woman." "Even so", said the genie, "It is the way it must be." So, she wished for a million dollars and got that and for a beautiful diamond necklace and got that. Yet it bothered her more that, by this time, her ex had received twice what she had received. So, she said to the genie, "for my last wish, I ask that you scare me ½ half to death."

Friends, one of the great concepts in life is that we are all connected. Yet we must decide what form that connection will take. Clearly, God has decided what form he would like there to be although most people try to live as unconnected as they can from one another-this in spite of the fact that there are today more ways to connect than ever. The essence of what this verse is saying, however, is that there is no life without the connection, regardless of how people act. So part of our job as Christians should be that we help people see the connection and draw life from it.

When Lawrence of Arabia visited Paris after World War 1, the thing that impressed the Arabs was the faucets. They could not believe that all one had to do to get water was to turn on the faucet. So, when it was time to leave, they tried to take the faucets with them. They didn't understand that the faucets gave water because of their connection to a pipeline and water supply.

And so, it is with us. We must understand that the life-giving water of God's provision is in our connection to him.

REFLECTIONS

Valentine's Day

When people talk of Valentine's Day, they generally talk about love and the way they think it should be- not necessarily the way they have experienced it. Indeed, for many, love is the way it is often portrayed in movies-hot and desperate. But based on the real-life lives and loves of actors and actresses alike, they don't seem to be sure what it really looks like, either.

I've been blessed in my life to have experienced many shades of love-from parents, siblings, friends, girlfriends, wives, children and grandchildren. I have been blessed with the love of God sent in many different ways and people. Even so, I am not able to say one type was better than another as each blessed me in a different way. I do not consider myself an expert in this area in any way. I have made many mistakes in how I perceived love and how I expressed it. But I do know what it is not and so, in the lessons which are to follow, I will try to shed light on what I have learned in light of my walk of faith.

Lessons on Valentine's Day - Part 1 of 7

Text and key verse: Isaiah 49:16 "Look, I have inscribed your name on the palms of my hands…"

The wife of a couple who had been married for many years was lamenting that she and her husband no longer sat as close together in the car as they once had. The husband then replied, "Well, I haven't moved!"

Although that statement was true enough, the husband had not done his part to keep their relationship exciting and new, either. And that is where the element of doubt can sometimes creep in. Do you still love me?

The element of doubt can also creep in with our relationship with God when our prayers seemingly go unanswered. Does God still love us? In today's scripture lesson, the Israelites doubted God's love because of their long period of time in exile in Babylon. So, the prophet Isaiah had to remind them that God's silence did not reflect his lack of love. Indeed, God said through Isaiah that their names were written on God's palms, so how could he forget them?

My guess is that they desired some action on God's part to prove it. They failed to realize that God "ain't moved", but they had. So, God turned their request back on them to prove by their actions that they still loved him. This question is still relevant today. How can we prove our love for God by our actions?

The short answer is by giving him the things that we require from those who love us: our time, our talent and our treasure. We cannot hope to fool God with just words.

When I was growing up, one of our family staples was watching "Gunsmoke" on tv. Although the show was a western set in a long-ago time, it seemed very real to us. But if we were to visit the set of "Gunsmoke", we could see that all the buildings of Dodge City were just facades. There was no substance to them. In like manner, when our words are not backed up by our very real actions, God sees right through them and is not pleased.

Lessons on Valentine's Day - Part 2 of 7

Text and key verse; Acts 10:34 "I now realize how true it is that God does not show favoritism but accepts from every nation the one who fears him and does what is right."

Four-year –old Jason was visiting his grandparents. One day he brought a peach to his grandpa and said something his Pap didn't catch, giving the peach to him. Pap assumed that his wife had given a snack to him and ate the peach. Little Jason meanwhile was close to tears when he said, "I didn't ask you to eat the peach, Pap. I just wanted you to get the worm out for me." Good communication requires a clear message and a receptive listener. When either of these factors are missing there will be pain.

This is especially true between those in a loving relationship. As we are supposed to be in a loving relationship with God, the advice applies as well. In today's scripture, God has tried to get a message through to Peter but because he was not receptive, he didn't get it at first. He didn't realize that God wanted the good news of the gospel to be communicated to Gentiles.

The love we have for God, then, must be passed on to other people-some of whom do not speak the same language. A story is told of a missionary to China in his first language class. The teacher, upon entering the classroom, said nothing but simply walked up and down the classroom rows and then walked out. When she came back in, she asked the class if they had noticed anything peculiar about her. No one said anything at first but then one student noticed that she had on a particularly attractive perfume. The teacher responded that the perfume was indeed her distinguishing feature and explained it this way; "You will not be able to tell anyone the gospel at first until you learn the language. So, until then they must smell the fragrance of Jesus on you by the quality of your life."

What is true with God is also true in love. We must communicate with our life that we hope to communicate with our words.

Lessons on Valentine's Day- part 3 of 7

Text and key verse: ephesians 5:25 Husbands, love your wives. Just as Christ loved the church and gave himself up for her."

A husband and his wife had been happily married to one another for many years and felt they knew what commitment was all about. So, when their daughter brought home a rough- looking biker guy, they were concerned. Yet they also didn't want to be too judgmental, either. So, after he brought her home from the date, the mom approached her with a number of questions, which the girl answered with obvious stars in her eyes. "I just wanted to make sure he was nice, honey", the mom explained. "Well, of course he's nice", replied to the daughter, "Why else would he be doing so much community service?"

Understandably, mom and dad wanted what was best, just as the apostle Paul wanted for the church at Ephesus. He knew that the church was made up of relationships-the most important of which was that between husband and wife.

In a marriage, things don't always go as planned. Sometimes the roles one has are changed due to sickness or accident. When that happens, the husband or wife must assume both roles for as long as necessary. This is what they promised on their wedding day.

When I was in the National Guard, we often conducted what we called an "after-action review". In this exercise, we would take apart the training we had done and look for what we had done right, what we had done wrong and make suggestions as to how we might make things better. I believe that this is also necessary in our marriages as well as our Christian walk. Paul felt that Christ's relationship with the church and that which exists between husband and wife were similar in terms of the work that had to be put in and the commitment required.

Lessons on Valentine's Day - Part 4 of 7

Text and key verse: isaiah 11:6d "…, and a little child will lead them."

A young boy received a harmonica as a gift from his uncle. When that uncle next saw the boy, he asked him how the harmonica was playing was going. The boy replied that the playing wasn't going but that the harmonica was the best gift he ever got. "How so?', asked the uncle. "Well, mom gives me a dollar a day not to play it during the dayand my dad give me $5 a week not to play it at night."

It would appear that the little guy was quite the operator. Perhaps that was part of the reason his parents were so endeared to him. But what they might not have considered was how he had helped strengthen their relationship.

Perhaps that sounds weird talking about children and Valentine's Day, but it seems to me that love is where you find it. And if a child is where we find it, perhaps that love will lead us further. In today's scripture, a child is talked about in the context of wild animals peacefully co-existing together. Is it so strange, then, to talk about kids as a means of enhancing the parent's love?

There has been quite a bit of research done on the effect of divorce on children and it would appear that if couples can stay together, the kids are much better off. This may not be possible in all cases, but it does provide an important reason for people to stay together. Yet the Spiritual part of this cannot be overemphasized. It was never God's intent for people to get divorced so I believe that, in staying in connection to him, he will help us "pick up the pieces" and find love again.

Lessons on Valentine's Day - Part 5 of 7

Text and key verse: Proverbs 2:3b "and lift up your voice for understanding."

In the days before no-fault divorce, a judge was interviewing a woman to find out about her side of the situation. He asked, "what are your relations like? "The woman answered, "I have an aunt and uncle in town and my husband has his parents here, also." 'Do you have a grudge?" "No, we have a carport." "Does your husband beat you up?" "Yes, he usually gets up before I do." Finally, out of frustration, the judge asks, "Lady, do you want a divorce?" "No", she replied "It's my husband who wants one. He claims he can't communicate with me!"

I think we can all agree that communication is essential in a relationship.but words without action don't mean very much. The same can be said about our relationship with God. God wants to see our words play out in terms of loving our neighbors as well as him.

A lady was riding a bus from Flagstaff, Arizona to Albuquerque, New Mexico on a cold night in february. When the bus made a stop along the way, a young indian boy got on and quickly fell asleep. In fact, he slept so soundly he missed his stop. When he realized hus error, he asked the bus driver if he could get off and walk back to his destination. The bus driver said no because it was too far, and the weather was too cold. The young guy was now upset since he didn't have the money for a bus ride back from Albuquerque. However, the woman sitting next to him offerred to pay his fare back once they arrived in Albuquerque and would make sure he got on the right bus. After riding along in quiet for about 10 minutes, the boy asked if she was a christian.

On valentine's day, kids like to give little candies with a message. So, if we want to give a loving message to Jesus, let us do it with our actions.

Lessons on Valentine's Day- part 6 of 7

Text and key verse: exodus 20:12a "Honor your father and mother."

A Mother was tucking her small son into bed during a storm. But just before she turned out the light the little boy asked, "Mommy, will you sleep with me tonight?' Mommy answered, "not tonight, honey, I have to sleep with daddy.' After a long silence the little boy said, "the big sissy."

Parenthood is not easy, especially when one is trying to keep everyone happy. And so, I think they are deserving of Valentine's consideration-fathers as well as mothers.

Sir Nicholas Winton was a British stockbroker who engineered the exportation of 699 mostly Jewish children from Czechoslavakia and P oland at the beginning of WW2 out of his concern for what hitler might do. Not only did he arrange for their passage but found them homes in Britain, probably saving their lives-all this before becoming a father himself.

A pastor of a small country church had a particularly devoted family by the name of Davison and so decided to ask one of the Davison men how they had come to be such a Christ-honoring family. What they shared was probably not what the pastor expected to hear as the boys were a rowdy bunch who really sowed their wild oats every Saturday night. That is until one night when they returned home to find their mother out in the family garden on her knees praying for her boys. She advised that she continue to do this as long as they continued their wild ways. So, convicted of the effect their actions had on their mother, the boys all became Christians.

Of course, biological parenthood does not automatically make one a true parent in the Christian sense of the word. It is the importance of their individually practiced life of faith that makes up for the sometimes-dramatic changes we see in their children. Thanks be to God for this type of Godly example.

Lessons on Valentine's Day - Part 7 of 7

Text and key verse: matthew 5:44 " But I say love your enemies. Pray for those who persecute you."

A woman and her friend went to the police station to make a missing person report. She said that her husband was 6' 2", had dark wavy hair, an athletic build, was about 185 pounds, was soft-spoken, well-mannered and usually sharply dressed. The officer took down the description then left the room temporarily. The woman who accompanied her friend to the station said, "That description doesn't fit your husband at all: he's short, fat, bald, and sloppy." "Yeah", the lady responded, "but who wants him back?"

As we consider who we want to send Valentines to, we certainly know who we don't want to send them to. However, Christ would have us send them to our enemies, so, as Christians, we need to try to figure out how to do this.

One way is to look at examples from the Bible. In 1 samuel 24, David is being hunted down as a criminal by the king although David had done nothing deserving of that kind of treatment. So, when David gets a chance to get revenge, he refuses to lift his hand against the Lord's anointed.

Another way is to look at historical examples where such behavior is displayed. President Abraham Lincoln picked Edwin Stanton as his Secretary of War not because Stanton liked Lincoln (because he didn't!) But because he was the person best suited for the job. In the process, Lincoln gained a trusted admirer from an avowed enemy.

Lincoln thus was able to destroy his enemy by making him his friend. I think Jesus would be pleased when we do this. Lord, give us the courage to try!

REFLECTIONS

Veteran's Day

Veteran's Day and Memorial Day are not the same thing. Veteran's Day is for those who were blessed enough to make it back home and return to the lives that Memorial Day heroes did not. Veterans have, probably more so than most, a keen sense of appreciating the fact that liberty costs us something. Because of that, they don't take our way of life for granted. And for many, their service did cost them something- perhaps a physical, mental or emotional impairment, the loss of a job or work opportunity, the pain of separation from loved ones or perhaps the ending of a loving relationship as absence does not always make the heart grow fonder. However, on the positive side, military friendships have often added immeasurably to one's quality of life as fun and hardships experienced together has made for bonds not possible in any other way. Even so, I believe it is right and proper to give those who have served a special day to appreciate their willingness to sacrifice for something greater than themselves. They have earned the right to be remembered.

Lessons on Veteran's Day - Part 1 of 7

Text and key verse: Genesis 9:16 "Whenever the rainbow appears in the clouds, I will see it and remember the everlasting covenant between God and all living creatures of every kind on the earth."

A man running for elected office made a campaign stop in a nursing home, hoping to pick up some needed votes. When one elderly woman didn't seem to pick up on his purpose for being there, he asked, "Do you know who I am?" And she replied, "I don't but if you go up to the nurse at the desk, she'll gladly tell you."

For the veteran, Veteran's Day is essential for helping them to make sense of life and their part in it. A wise person once said that the consideration of what has been given, what has been done with it and what will be passed on to the next generation are part of a continuum that links one soul to another. Those things provide the context to their puzzling that out.

Yet our remembering their service is important for the rest of us as well. For without their sacrifice, our quality of life would certainly be much different and much less than we now experience. In the movie "Saving Private Ryan", Private Ryan is told "make sure your life is worth it"- worth the sacrifice that was made to save it. That is the responsibility we all have as a result of the sacrifice of our veterans.

In today's scripture lesson, God has provided the means of his remembering the covenant he made with the earth's living never to flood the earth again. We, then, need to find the means to help us remember what our veterans have done. What that might be could be very different for one person than for another. Yet it needs to be at least as effective a reminder as the rainbow is for God and the cross for, we Christians.

Lessons on Veteran's Day - Part 2 of 7

Text and key verse: Isaiah 49:16a "See, I have engraved you on the palms of my hand…"

Two older guys were talking, and the one said to the other, "Hey Bill, do you remember how bad my memory used to be?" And bill answered, "I sure do!" "Well, those days are over. My wife and I went to a great seminar on helping our memory and now I have a great memory." "I'm happy for you", Bill said, "But do you remember the name of the seminar?"" Just a minute, what's the name of that flower that guys send to their wives and girlfriends that has thorns on it?" "You mean a rose?" "That's it!" "Hey, Rose, what's the name of that seminar we went to?"

Although we often talk about the need for people to remember our veterans on Veteran's Day, it is also important to remind our veterans that God has not and will not forget them. Today's scripture is proof of that.

However, in the heat of battle, sometimes an element of doubt sets in-particularly if some of the veteran's friends have been shot or killed. An Army paratrooper who served in Vietnam recalled coming back into camp after a mission where several of his fellow soldiers were shot or killed, feeling devastated. But the thing he remembered that helped get him through was "Taps" that was played at night. In his words,"it seemed that, if only for a few moments, there was someone up there sending us renewed hope in those 24 simple notes."

For those of us that have had no such experiences, there is also the need to remember that God remembers. Today's scripture is also for us. And although we hear no "Taps", God gives other hints of his care if we are alert to them. I remember during a difficult time when my wife and I were providing care for her elderly aunt and were worried about how we could resolve the issue, that God sent a white heron to dwell outside the place we were staying as if to say "hang in there". The issue became resolved shortly after that visit, when the heron moved on.

Lessons on Veteran's Day - Part 3 of 7

Text: Judges 6:14 and 15 "Go in the strength you have and save Israel out of Midian's hand. Am I not sending you?" "Pardon me, my Lord, but how can I save Israel? My clan is the weakest in Manasseh and I am the least in my family."

A juggler got stopped by the police as he was traveling to his next performance. When the policeman saw all the bayonets in his back seat, he asked the juggler about them. "I use them in my act." "Oh yeah?", asked the policeman. "Let's see you juggle them." So, the juggler got out of his car and demonstrated his ability. Another driver slowed down to look, then remarked to his friend, "Wow, I'm glad I stopped drinking. Look at the tests they're giving now!"

The test that this driver was referring to be a sobriety test. But the veteran today must often face the test of battle. Now some see this test as some kind of romantic, exciting adventure. But those who have been through it will tell you that it is one of the scariest experiences one can have. When I was in advanced infantry training in Fort Polk, Louisiana, we were often trained by Vietnam veterans. They described their experiences as sheer terror and advised us to tell our congressmen to get us out.

When considering the Old Testament, there were many battles fought. And my guess is that none of them were pleasant. Yet when we consider the battle strategy used under the Lord's direction, it was nothing like what would be used today. In today's scripture lesson, God choses a very unlikely person to lead Israel's troops. Gideon is a farmer and certainly nothing close to being a warrior. Gideon has to be brought along slowly, putting God to the test. Then God removes all but 300 of Gideon's men to fight the much larger Midian army. Yet God caused Gideon and Israel to be victorious.

Even so, the New Testament gives a much different perspective on war and fighting. Jesus displayed the attitude of mercy towards our enemies and peace as our goal. Perhaps that is a much harder test.

Lessons on Veteran's Day - Part 4 of 7

Textand key verse: Hebrews 13:15 "Through Jesus we should always bring God the sacrifice of praise, that is, words that acknowledge him."

An older couple was having trouble remembering thingsso they mutually decided to begin writing things down. So, one night the wife asked her husband if he wanted a bedtime snack. He said that he wanted a chocolate sundae with a cherry on top. As she left for the kitchen, he asked if she was going to write that down. She said no because she was going right out to the kitchen to make it and would not forget. After a while, she brought him his snack: hash browns, eggs, bacon and a glass of orange juice. He looked at his snack and said, "I told you that you should have written it down. You forgot the toast!"

Although many older people do have trouble remembering things, many people of all ages seem to forget the sacrifices of our veterans. Even so, I believe they are at least entitled to the sacrifice of praise. This concept comes to us from the book of Hebrews where the writer talks about how God should also receive the sacrifice of praise for his sacrifice of his son.yet to give such praise is not what I consider to be a sacrifice in the way we usually think of one. It is the least we can do.

What we get confused about sometimes is when the service we receive is a part of someone's job. A lady was given a loaner car by the dealer while her car was being fixed. As she was driving by a grocery store, however, an older lady she didn't know flagged her down. When she stopped to see what the old woman wanted, the old woman opened the back door and proceeded to load her groceries in. Not being in a hurry, though, and being willing to do a good deed, the driver drove the old lady to her home. Upon arrival, the old woman asked for help in getting the groceries in, which the driver did-with nothing more than a nod of appreciation in return. On the ride back home, the driver figured it out- the car had "free courtesy" on its doors- a kindness misconstued as a job. Our veterans deserve better.

Lessons on Veteran's Day - Part 5 of 7

Text and key verse: Proverbs 18:24 "One who has unreliable friends soon comes to ruin, but there is a friend who sticks closer than a brother."

Charlie Brown asks his friend Linus this question: "What would you do if you felt that no one liked you?" And Linus replied: "Well, Charlie Brown, I'd take a long hard look at myself and ask myself if I was doing something that turned other people off, or if I could improve on something." And Charlie Brown replied, "I hate that answer."

I guess he should not have asked that question if he really didn't want to hear the answer. But, on the other hand, it is good to have a friend who will tell you the truth.

In my 29 years in the military, I had friends of both kinds- the kind who would tell me what I wanted to hear and those who would tell me what I didn't want to hear. Even so, the military tends to cause one to appreciate one's friends- to help them get through- and perhaps to be a better friend oneself.

Nowhere is this more firmly implanted than in Ranger school-a grueling 9-week course that tests the limits of one's mind and body. The first task assigned in that training, though, is to find a friend-someone to go through the course with you.

I believe that there is or should be a correlation with that idea to our walk of faith-that we need to have someone to hold us accountable as well as someone they are accountable to. Although we are all different in terms of our dedication and abilities, we all need someone that will push us to stay on the course or to get back on track. The Bible is full of those kinds of mentoring relationships. In the New Testament we have Barnabas with Paul and Paul with Timothy- examples of mutual encouragement and Godly instruction.

Yet the best example of "A friend that sticks closer than a brother" is Jesus. In spite of his rightful place as Lord and master, he considered his disciples as friends. He listened to them and taught them and answered their questions and calmed their fears-which he still does with us!

Lessons on Veteran's Day - Part 6 of 7

Text and key verse: Matthew 6:15 "But if you do not forgive others their sins, your father will not forgive your sins."

In the days when butchers made house calls, the mother gave specific instructions to her son as to what to say when he is arrived-telling him to call for her. But her son forgot who it was that he had been given instructions for, so when the minister came calling, he yelled, "Mom, that guy's here!" Because she was still not ready to come down, she yelled to her son so that her visitor could hear:" I can't come down now. So, give him the money out of my purse and tell him we didn't like his tongue last time, so we're going to switch."

I would have liked to have seen the minister's face after that message. Even so, I also wonder how long it would take him to forgive? You see, according to scripture, this is what is expected. I just wonder, however, if war might be an extenuating circumstance?

After WW2, Corrie Ten Boom came face-to-face with one of her jailers from Ravensbruck concentration camp who asked for her forgiveness. She did not want to give it, remembering how her own sister had died there. But realizing that it was required, she prayed for strength and admitted to God her lack of desire to shake her former tormentor's hand. But when she did, a power she had never felt before came through her arm and into her heart that enabled her to say, "I forgive you, brother, with all of my heart!" She readily admitted that this could not have been her doing, but the Holy Spirits.

Another instance of God's perspective on forgiveness came after the Civil War. During the first Memorial Day celebration in Washington, D.C., a group of women petitioned the War Department for permission to place flowers on the graves of the deceased soldiers. After considerable haggling, the War Department gave permission-but only for the graves of Union soldiers. So, the ladies did their work carefully to follow the War Department's directive. But after the ceremony was over, a large wind came up and blew most of the flowers to the Confederate side of the Arlington Cemetery. After that, there was no discrimination.

Lessons on Veteran's Day - Part 7 of 7

Text and key verse: James 1:22 "But be sure you live out the message and not merely listen to it and so deceive yourselves."

Many years ago, a woman who appeared to have died was being carried to her burial plot when a pallbearer tripped over a rock and spilled the body to the ground-which revived her and enabled her to live another 7 years-yet not years of marital bliss as far as her husband was concerned. So when she actually died, the husband accompanied the pallbearers the next time and made sure that none of them again tripped.

He wanted to assure that history did not repeat itself. As far as war is concerned, our hope is the same. But on a more personal note, our military veterans hope that their sacrifice has helped make a difference toward lasting peace. Similarly, the universal hope of most people, regardless of military service, is that their life has made a positive difference. Yet that doesn't happen by accident.

Herbert Wirth was a door-to-door salesman who sold dishcloths and other household goods. He made a decent living but kept pretty much to himself-except for the small acts of kindness that he would do for his neighbors and others he had befriended. When Herbert died, the funeral director advised the pastor to prepare for a small funeral as Herbert had no family. So, when over a thousand people came to his graveside service, the pastor and funeral director were dumbfounded until they heard the words and stories of the people that Herbert had helped over the years. He was not a great man but just one who simply lived out the message of love of God and man.

You know there are many people who assume that to be remembered, you had to perform some astounding feat. And although there have been many veterans who did just that, the wars that our country has won have been the result of average men and women who merely did their jobs and carried out their routine duties on an everyday basis.

Our acceptance into heaven will surely be based on the same thing-to daily live out the message of salvation assured only by the sacrifice of Jesus and our reflection of his love of God and our fellow man.

REFLECTIONS

Work/Works

When we talk of work or works, we are actually talking about 2 separate things-both of which are important. Thus, we must be clear about which we are talking about. I'd like to talk about both. In my life, the work I have done has given me the life experiences from which my faith has been shaped. Even the short periods of time spent as a sporting good salesman, factory worker or furniture deliverer are not without some redemptive value, although probably not to the extent of my years in public welfare social work, the National guard or Christian ministry.

On the other hand, my works have followed me all my life-both good and bad. They represent my faith (or lack of it) in action. Although some of my work took place while I was vocationally-employed, they must be evaluated beyond what I was required to do as part of my job.

Ultimately, whether on the job or not, one's faith cannot be separated from one's work. They both are part of the whole. It is my hope that my faith has been clearly displayed in both.

Lessons on Work/Works - Part 1 of 7

Text and key Verse: Judges 6:15 "Pardon me, my Lord," Gideon replied, "But how can I save Israel? My clan is the weakest in Manasseh and i am the least in my family?"

At a day care center, three children were all trying to make themselves seem important. "I take horseback riding lessons," said one. "I take gymnastics", said another. "Oh yeah?", said the third. "I take antibiotics".

It is a natural thing for kids of any age to make themselves seem important. It's just part of a universal desire to think that our lives make a difference. Yet, for most, reality sets in and we tend to evaluate our lives much differently. Such was the case of gideon. After Israel had turned from the Lord, God allowed another nation to run roughshod over them-this time the Midians. When an angel of the Lord called Gideon to save Israel, he was hiding in a winepress, threshing wheat. He clearly saw nothing in himself to take on such a challenge. But God saw things differently and finally encouraged Gideon to successfully fulfill his mission.

He still does today. Alice Murray worked at a textile factory and was discouraged by the abuse she regularly took as the only Christian there. She confided to her pastor that she felt like quitting. Then he asked her "Where do businesses usually put the lights?" She wondered about the appropriateness of such a question, then responded "I guess where it is the darkest." "That's right", he responded. "That's why you've been placed in the position you're in-to shine God's light in the darkness to show the way to him." She took that advice and eventually led nine women in that factory to God.

The things that we think disqualify ourselves for ministry are often the very things that God is looking for. We must not let our brokenness get wasted in misery but let God redeem that misery in his service.

Lessons on Work/Works - Part 2 of 7

Text and key verse: James 1:22 "Do not deceive yourselves by just listening to his word; put it into practice."

The insects were playing with the animals in a game of football and things were going all the animals' way. That is until the second half when the centipede got in. He made tackles all over the field-stopping the lion, the bear and the cheetah on successive plays for no gain. When the animals saw what a player the centipede was, they asked him why he had not played in the first half. He replied," That's easy- I was still tying my shoes!"

Today's section focuses on the need for action in our Christian walk. Often times we tend to let our good intentions stay merely that. We need to follow through for the sake of the Kingdom. 2 Corinthians 6:2 tells us "Now is the accepted time; now is our salvation closer than it has ever been before." Clearly people are going out into eternity without a savior when we have the good news that will save them.

On April 28, 1999, shock-rock singer Marilyn Manson was scheduled to be in concert in Iowa City, Iowa. As this was only 8 days after the Columbine shootings and because Manson's music was a significant part of the Columbine shooters' interests, there appeared to be a great potential for adverse happenings. In fact, the police were making efforts to be ready for battles between Christian groups and Manson groups. Instead, Christians showed up in force to pray for and show love to the Manson concert goers. Pizzas, soda, cookies, and turkey and cheese sandwiches were purchased and distributed to those standing in line. Other groups offered to pray for Manson concert goers' prayer requests. Money was solicited so that concert goers parking would be paid for. When the Manson concert goers asked why they were doing this, the good news of the gospel was shared with 3 people accepting Christ right in line. Manson himself must have picked up on the "Christian vibe" because he only performed an hour before storming off the stage. Finally, a Manson web site opined that "Maybe these Christians aren't half bad." Not bad for Christian love in action, is it?

Lessons on Work/Works - Part 3 of 7

Text and key verse: 1 Corinthians 12:10 "Each person is given something to do that shows who God is: everyone gets in on it. Everyone benefits."

The church treasurer got tired of trying to make the meager church income stretch to meet all requirements and gave up their position, hoping someone else could do better. The owner of the local grain elevator volunteered to take that position, but with one stipulation: that the church would not require a report from him for one full year. The church agreed and so were anxious to see what the end-of-year report was like. When the report was made the people were astounded to find out that church indebtedness was completely eliminated, that there were no outstanding bills and that a cash reserve of $7,000 had been created. When asked to explain, the new treasurer said;"as most of you have your grain weighed at my elevator, I simply withheld 10% of your money and paid it to the church. You never missed it! It's amazing what we can do for the Lord by actually giving our 10%, which is his anyway."

How we handle our money is a work we all share. It falls into the same category as our time and talents-particularly in terms of how we use them to bless others. One of the Bible's most famous examples is the loaves and fishes donated by a young boy to feed the 5,000. In this case it wasn't the gift itself that made the difference but the willingness to give it and what the Lord can do with it.

The Bible makes a compelling analogy to this through how the body operates most efficiently. We can also understand it through the analogy to a successful sports team. But we can also see how it doesn't work by considering the childhood story called "The Little Red Hen". In this story the little red hen goes through all the tasks necessary for a loaf of bread to be made. At each of these steps the hen asks, "Who will help me?". But alas, each animal is too busy to help. Finally, when the bread is ready to eat, the hen asks who will help eat and now all are ready. At that point the hen declines their help because none could help along the way. This is also an enlightening illustration as to how the church should not work.

Lessons on Work/Works - Part 4 of 7

Text and key verse: 1 John 3:18 "Dear Children, let us not love with words or speech, but with actions and in truth."

The father telephoned home and the son answered, "Hi, Son, what are you doing?" "Nothing much, Dad. I'm just sitting on the couch watching tv." "Where's your mother?" "She's out painting the house." "Well, why aren't you out helping her?" "I would, Dad, but grandma's using the other brush."

A lack of activity, caused by laziness or procrastination, can be a hindrance if not a complete "turn-off" to our Christian witness and it can be applicable to both work and works. It is a common human failing, sometimes referred to as the "hamlet syndrome". A few hundred years ago, William Shakespeare wrote a play about a gifted young prince who finds out that his father was murdered by his uncle. But although Hamlet vows revenge, he spends the rest of the play thinking about what he must do but never does it.

This analogy can be made to the things we want to do for the Lord-our works. The second chapter of James in the Bible talks about this as well when we encounter a brother or sister in need without doing what we can to address that physical need. James goes on to suggest then that faith without work is dead. Certainly, this is the lament of many would-be Christians who have refused to commit to Christ because of the many" Christians" who talk a good game but fail to deliver.

Obviously, one's failure to find and keep a job is also a problem as it becomes a drain on resources better used elsewhere. As a former welfare employee, I am well aware of society's stigma attached to those who are chronically unemployed. The Bible also adds its condemnation when it says in 2 Thessalonians 3:10 that anyone who doesn't want to work should not eat.

Clearly there are no options here. As Christians we cannot sit our way to success. Only hens can do that. Let us not, then, "chicken out" on our responsibility to work and do work.

Lessons on Work/Works - Part 5 of 7

Text: James 2:14-18

Key verse: James 2:17 "In the same way, faith is dead when it does not result in faithful action."

A peasant was being recruited to join the communist party and was sent to the party secretary to answer some questions: "If you have 2 cats, will you give one away?" "Yes". "If you have 2 tractors, will you give one away?" "Yes". "If you have 2 houses, will you give one away?" "Yes". "If you have 2 cows, will you give one away/" "No, certainly not." "And why?" "I have 2 cows."

Today's lesson tells us that faith without work is dead. Yet not all good works are reflective of faith. Those works that God considers good are works that take us in a direction we don't naturally want to go- that sacrifice our desires for the needs of others.

The African boy listened carefully as the missionary teacher explained why Christians give gifts to each other on Christmas day. She explained that they give gifts to express their joy over their being given the gift of the Christ child and to show their love for one another. When Christmas day came, the little boy presented the missionary teacher a beautiful seashell. The teacher was amazed at the shell's great beauty and asked the boy where he had got it. "Oh, this shell can only be obtained in a certain bay many miles away." The teacher then replied, "You shouldn't have walked so far to get me this gift, although I appreciate it greatly." The boy just smiled and replied, "Long walk part of gift."

Just before Jesus ascended into heaven to return to his father, he had a talk with his disciple, Peter. "Feed my sheep", Jesus repeated three times. In doing so, Jesus left no doubt as to Peter's work in the time to follow. This feeding of course meant more than a mere food program for Jesus' followers. It meant helping Christians to thrive and grow in God's word and grace as well as helping to meet their non-Spiritual needs as well, despite the inconvenience. And Jesus' words come down to us today. So, in meeting our fellow Christian's needs, we too can say "Inconvenience part of Gift".

Lessons on Work/Works - Part 6 of 7

Text: Galatians 6:7-10

Key verse: Galatians 6:9 "Let us not become weary in doing good, for at the proper time we will reap a harvest if we do not give up."

A man hired his new son-in-law to build him a house, explaining that this house was to be an anniversary present for his wife. Now the son-in-law didn't care for his mother-in-law as she never thought he was good enough to marry her daughter, so he decided to build the house using the cheapest materials possible while charging them for the best. When the home was completed, he handed the keys to his father-in-law, who handed them back, saying that the house was actually their wedding present.

Of course, if he had followed today's Bible admonition to not be weary in doing good, he would have been rewarded. Yet we often get discouraged in doing good when we think it is not appreciated. That's when we need to remember for whom we are doing good-and that is Christ. WHEN WE REMEMBER THIS, it doesn't matter what, if any, affirmation we receive.

This lesson has a secular application, as well. When George Schultz was Secretary of State, he often tested our ambassadors to see if they could find their country on the globe he had in his office. Invariably they would point to the country to which they were assigned. At that point, he would say, in effect, that their country was the United States. That they were in the foreign country to represent us and care for our interests.

I think the same analogy could be made for our families. I had a Christian mentor who shared that his father would always address his boys before they went out for the weekend. He would say, "Remember that you are Kramer's. That means something good and is the result of the dedication to good that our family has worked hard to maintain."

The same can be said for our reputation as Christians. We should never be tempted to bring condemnation on the cause that has been so richly preserved.

Lessons on Work/Works - Part 7 of 7

Text: Romans 3:9-27

Key verse: Romans 3:20 "Therefore no one will be declared righteous in God's sight by the works of the law; rather, through the law we become conscious of our sin."

The wife took her hard-of-hearing husband to the doctor's as he seemed so weak and run-down. The doctor ran some tests and explained to her privately that he had determined that he was suffering from a rare case of anemia. But the doctor had a hopeful prognosis if the wife would faithfully perform the following tasks over the next several months: great meals with his favorite dishes for three meals a day, and special attention to his every whim and want as far as that was possible. When the wife came out of the doctor's office, she had a very sad look on her face. The husband noted this and responded," It's bad news, isn't it? Tell me what he said." "He said You're going to die!"

She apparently felt that he wasn't worth the effort. Yet for most people, they would do almost anything to earn their way into the kingdom of heaven. Unfortunately, it doesn't work that way. Heaven cannot be earned; it is a gift of grace.

Thus, the well-meaning good deeds that people do in hopes that they will be considered good enough are done in vain. During the Great Depression, the Irish government put many irish peasants to work building roads. And as long as the fellows felt that this was important work, they worked hard and well and happily. But soon it occurred to them that the roads they made led to nowhere, they lost heart and passion in what they were doing, and the work suffered.

That's why it is so important that people are made to understand how grace works. It isn't what they do but what Christ has done that gains them heaven. God determined that we were worth the effort and sent his only son to die as the only acceptable sacrifice for our sins.

The good work we do, then, is done with a different attitude: we do them out of gratitude for what was done for us.

www.ingramcontent.com/pod-product-compliance
Lightning Source LLC
Chambersburg PA
CBHW061549120626
46550CB00004B/1421